Self-Knowledge for Humans

Human beings are not model epistemic citizens. Our reasoning can be careless and uncritical, and our beliefs, desires, and other attitudes aren't always as they ought rationally to be. Our beliefs can be eccentric, our desires irrational, and our hopes hopelessly unrealistic. Our attitudes are influenced by a wide range of non-epistemic or non-rational factors, including our character, our emotions, and powerful unconscious biases. Yet we are rarely conscious of such influences. Self-ignorance is not something to which human beings are immune.

In this book Quassim Cassam develops an account of self-knowledge which tries to do justice to these and other respects in which humans aren't model epistemic citizens. He rejects rationalist and other mainstream philosophical accounts of self-knowledge on the grounds that, in more than one sense, they aren't accounts of self-knowledge for humans. Instead he defends the view that inferences from behavioural and psychological evidence are a basic source of human self-knowledge. On this account, self-knowledge is a genuine cognitive achievement and self-ignorance is almost always on the cards.

As well as explaining knowledge of our own states of mind, Cassam also accounts for what he calls 'substantial' self-knowledge, including knowledge of our values, emotions, and character. He criticizes philosophical accounts of self-knowledge for neglecting substantial self-knowledge, and concludes with a discussion of the value of self-knowledge.

This book tries to do for philosophy what behavioural economics tries to do for economics. Just as behavioural economics is the economics of *homo sapiens*, as distinct from the economics of an ideally rational *homo economicus*, so Cassam argues that philosophy should focus on the human predicament rather than on the reasoning and self-knowledge of an idealized *homo philosophicus*.

Self-Knowledge for Humans

Quassim Cassam

OXFORD
UNIVERSITY PRESS

OXFORD

UNIVERSITY PRESS

Great Clarendon Street, Oxford, OX2 6DP,
United Kingdom

Oxford University Press is a department of the University of Oxford.
It furthers the University's objective of excellence in research, scholarship,
and education by publishing worldwide. Oxford is a registered trade mark of
Oxford University Press in the UK and in certain other countries

Published in the United States of America by Oxford University Press
198 Madison Avenue, New York, NY 10016, United States of America

British Library Cataloguing in Publication Data
Data available

Library of Congress Cataloging in Publication Data
Data available

ISBN 978-0-19-965757-5 (Hbk.)
ISBN 978-0-19-877668-0 (Pbk.)

For Deborah

Preface

One of the downsides of writing about self-knowledge is having to explain yourself to the philosophically uninitiated. Flights and dinner parties are usually where this happens, and the problem you face isn't the usual one. It's not that self-knowledge strikes people as being too boring or weird or recherché to be worthy of philosophical attention. Far from it. Self-knowledge as a philosophical topic sounds, as one tires of being told, fascinating. Indeed, it's just the sort of subject which non-philosophers expect philosophers to be interested in.

The disappointment sets in when the time comes to try to explain what philosophers these days mean by 'self-knowledge'. You might try saying this: self-knowledge, as many philosophers nowadays understand it, is first and foremost knowledge of one's own states of mind, that is, knowledge of such things as one's own beliefs, desires, and sensations. In the interests of clarity, you might add that the states of mind that are at issue here needn't be particularly deep or elusive or important. Suppose you believe that you are wearing socks and know that this is what you believe. What philosophers of self-knowledge typically focus on is this kind of seemingly trivial or easy self-knowledge. Of course they don't claim that this is all there is to self-knowledge. There is also knowledge of your deepest desires, hopes, and fears, knowledge of your character, emotions, abilities, and values, and knowledge of what makes you happy. These are examples of what you might call *substantial* self-knowledge, but you have to admit that substantial self-knowledge, for all its undoubted human interest, isn't where the philosophical action is. What philosophers find interesting isn't how you can know your own character or abilities but much more mundane examples of self-knowledge such as your knowledge that you believe you are wearing socks or that you want to have ice cream for pudding.

This is usually news to non-philosophers. They imagine philosophy tries to answer the Big Questions, and 'How do you know that you believe you are wearing socks?' doesn't sound like a Big Question. They don't get why you would be more interested in trivial than in substantial self-knowledge, and are surprised that you would want to describe knowledge of your more mundane beliefs as 'self-knowledge'. So what? The usual move at this point is to argue that what is philosophically interesting can't be decided by what non-philosophers think is interesting, and that a big part of what makes knowledge of one's more mundane states of mind philosophically interesting is that it is *epistemologically* special or distinctive. It's unlike substantial self-knowledge or ordinary worldly knowledge since it isn't based on evidence. To know that you are wearing socks you need evidence that you are wearing socks (you can feel them on your feet) but to know that you *believe* you are wearing socks you don't need evidence that you believe you are wearing socks. To know that you have a particular character trait, say fastidiousness, you need behavioural evidence from which you can infer that you are fastidious. In contrast, you don't normally infer your own beliefs from behavioural or, for that matter, any other evidence. But if knowledge of your own mundane beliefs and desires is, in this sense, immediate, then it would be natural to ask how such epistemologically immediate self-knowledge is possible. This is the question which many philosophers of self-knowledge are trying to answer. They don't worry about how substantial self-knowledge is possible, because it isn't special.

I don't buy this, and that is partly why I decided to write this book. For a start, even if substantial self-knowledge isn't epistemologically distinctive, that doesn't make it unworthy of philosophical attention. There is more to philosophy than epistemology. In any case, the story I've been telling exaggerates the epistemological distinctiveness of trivial or mundane self-knowledge. I claim that this kind of self-knowledge *is* normally based on evidence and *is* inferential. This is currently a deeply unpopular view among philosophers and one of my aims here is to defend it. In addition, there is also very little to be said in favour of the assumption that inferences from behavioural evidence are the sole or even the primary basis on which one knows such things as one's own character and values. As I hope to show, the different varieties of substantial self-knowledge are much more epistemologically interesting than is commonly supposed, and this means that there are sound philosophical reasons for taking this kind of self-knowledge seriously.

Anyway, it's not just about philosophical interest or importance of self-knowledge. There is also its human importance. The self-knowledge which most reflective human beings tend to regard as important is substantial self-knowledge, and they expect philosophy to have something to say about its nature, scope, and value. I don't think that this is an unreasonable expectation. Philosophy needs to pay some attention to forms of self-knowledge that seem humanly important, and this means engaging with substantial self-knowledge. As it happens, I believe that the value of all forms of self-knowledge is something that people often over-estimate, but philosophy had better have something to say about the value of self-knowledge, as well as about why the kinds of self-knowledge which many of us value are so hard to get. The other side of substantial self-knowledge is self-ignorance, and this is another neglected topic about which I have tried to say something.

The desire to engage with humanly important varieties of self-knowledge is one of the factors which led me to write this book, but not the only factor. Another factor is the difficulty I have in recognizing real human beings in philosophical descriptions of how self-knowledge is acquired. The philosophical account of self-knowledge which I have the most problems with and which is in many ways the target of this book is what has come to be called Rationalism about self-knowledge. In its simplest form, Rationalism says that you can know whether you do believe a given proposition P by reflecting on whether you ought rationally to believe that P. You assume that normally what you believe is what you ought rationally to believe, and this assumption is what enables you to know that you believe that P by knowing that you ought rationally to believe that P. The same goes for your desires, hopes, fears, and other attitudes. In each case, knowing what your attitude ought rationally to be puts you in a position to know what your attitude is.

This strikes me as a strange idea, not least because it is often much easier to know that you have a given attitude than to know whether you ought rationally to have it. In such cases Rationalism substitutes a much harder question for a much easier one. For example, it might be obvious to me that I would rather spend the morning relaxing rather than writing, but very far from obvious whether this is how I ought rationally to want to spend the morning. In any case, the assumption that our attitudes are normally as they ought rationally to be seems a bit optimistic if it is real human beings we are talking about. Just as behavioural economists distinguish between *homo sapiens* and *homo economicus*, the idealized rational agent of so much economic theorizing, so I think it's helpful to distinguish real humans as we know them from *homo philosophicus*, the idealized subject of so much philosophical theorizing.

Homo philosophicus is a model epistemic citizen. His attitudes are as they ought rationally to be, his beliefs are properly based on the evidence available to him, and when he encounters good reasons to change any of his current attitudes he changes them. As I see it, Rationalism is an account of self-knowledge for *homo philosophicus* rather than for humans. *Homo philosophicus* can know his beliefs by reflecting on what the reasons require him to believe, but for human beings matters are far less straightforward. Human beings are far from being model epistemic citizens and the extent to which our attitudes are out of line with our reasons makes it hard for us to know what our attitudes are by reflecting on what they ought rationally to be. What we should be looking for is an account of self-knowledge for humans as they actually are, and Rationalism about self-knowledge isn't it. What I'm after is an alternative to Rationalism which doesn't underestimate our cognitive failings and limitations.

I call the respects in which humans are unlike *homo philosophicus* the Disparity, and my account of the Disparity draws heavily on the work of behavioural
economists and social psychologists, including Daniel Kahneman, Richard Nisbett, Lee Ross, and Timothy Wilson. Kahneman's book *Thinking, Fast and Slow*
has been an especially significant influence on my thinking. It has recently
become fashionable for behavioural economists to regard the Disparity as prov-
ing that humans are irrational. However, Kahneman refrains from drawing this
conclusion and so do I. I think it's unhelpful to think in these terms, and that not
being *homo philosophicus* doesn't make human beings irrational. Acknowledging
the Disparity isn't about convicting us of irrationality but of trying to be realistic
in what we say about how we reason and come to know ourselves.

I wrote this book during a year of research leave funded by the Mind Associ-
ation. It's a huge honour to have been elected to a Mind Senior Research
Fellowship, and I'd like to take this opportunity to thank Mind for its support.
Thanks also to Peter Momtchiloff at OUP and to his two readers, Lucy O'Brien
and David Finkelstein. Lucy kindly read the chapters as I was writing them, and
discussions with her in the early stages of the project helped me to clarify my
thinking. I had the terrible idea of calling the book *Reality Check: Self-Knowledge
for Humans*, and she persuaded me to stick to *Self-Knowledge for Humans*. I also
wrote Chapter 12 in response to a question she raised. David's comments on the
whole draft were also incredibly helpful, and I made a number of changes in
response to them. I also need to thank John Campbell for a superb set of
comments, to which I haven't really been able to do justice, and Naomi Eilan
for her valuable input and encouragement. Wayne Waxman also sent me many
useful comments and questions. Discussions with Deborah Ghate helped me to
come up with an account of the value of self-knowledge in the final chapter, and
I was also helped by conversations over lunch with Bill Brewer.

I've given talks and lectures based on ideas from the following chapters in
many places, including: Barcelona, Bonn, Chicago, Copenhagen, Edinburgh,
Fribourg, London, Luxembourg, Porto, Reading, St Andrews, Stirling, Stuttgart,
Sussex, and Zurich. Thanks to the audiences on those occasions for showing up
and asking difficult questions. I presented a draft of the book to an MA class at
Warwick in 2013. The quality of discussion and student presentations was
excellent, and I got a lot out of it. I won't attempt to name the students who
came but I'm grateful to all of them.

The style of this book is conversational, and I've made a conscious effort to say
things in writing more or less as I would say them if I were speaking. I've
also tried to do justice to what makes self-knowledge such an interesting
topic, and to address at least some of the questions about self-knowledge which

non-philosophers ask. Writing a boring book on a boring topic is one thing but writing a boring book on an interesting topic is inexcusable. I have the sense that I've only scratched the surface of some of the issues I discuss here, and I would like to say much more in future about the value of self-knowledge. The Disparity is another topic about which there is more to be said. For moment, however, the pages that follow will have to do.

Contents

1

Homo Philosophicus

Suppose you have carefully examined the evidence for the view that the recession will be over before the next general election. You find the evidence convincing so you form the belief that the recession will be over before the next general election. You then reflect that if the recession will be over before the next general election the present government will be re-elected. So you conclude that the present government will be re-elected. In arriving at this conclusion you form a belief about the government's election prospects. You believe that the government will be re-elected because that is what you think the evidence points to.

If I ask you whether you believe that the present government will be re-elected you have no trouble answering my question. You know you believe the government will be re-elected. And if I ask you why you believe that the government will be re-elected you have an answer: your reason for believing it will be re-elected is that the recession will be over before the election. So you know *what* you believe and you know *why* you believe it. You have (a form of) self-knowledge.[1]

It turns out that I have new and more accurate data about the prospects for economic recovery. My new data, which I share with you, suggest that the recession will go on beyond the next election. You study the new data carefully and realize that you are no longer justified in believing that the recession will be over before the next election. As a result, you no longer believe that the recession will be over before the next election. Since that belief was your only reason for believing that the government will be re-elected you abandon your belief that the government will be re-elected. Pending further evidence about the economy, or evidence that the present government's re-election doesn't depend on economic recovery, you are now agnostic about the outcome of the next election.

---

[1] When I say that you have a form of self-knowledge what I mean is that you have a form of what many philosophers call 'self-knowledge'. In my experience, non-philosophers are quite surprised by the suggestion that, other than in special or unusual cases, knowing what you believe amounts to anything that deserves this title.

In the unlikely event that this is how you think, not just in the present case, but all the time, then congratulations: you are *homo philosophicus*, a model epistemic citizen.[2] If you are *homo philosophicus* then at least the following things are true of you:

1. Your reasoning is what Tyler Burge calls 'critical reasoning', which means it is 'guided by an appreciation, use, and assessment of reasons and reasoning as such' (1998: 246). You always evaluate your reasons and reasoning, and when you carry out a proof you always check the steps and make sure the inference is valid.

2. Your beliefs and other so-called 'propositional attitudes'—your desires, fears, hopes, intentions and so on—are as they ought rationally to be. You believe what you rationally ought to believe, you want what you rationally ought to want, you fear what you have good reason to fear, and so on. When you had good reason to believe that the present government will be re-elected that is what you did believe. As soon as you realized that you no longer had good reason to believe the government will be re-elected you stopped believing it. Your beliefs and other attitudes are responsive to reasons, to changes in what you have reason to believe, and that is why they are as they rationally ought to be. They are not the product of non-rational processes of belief-formation such as wishful thinking. Even if you are a supporter of the government you believe it will be re-elected because that is what the evidence points to and not because you want it to be re-elected.

3. Your beliefs and other propositional attitudes are known to you. You know what you believe, desire, fear, and so on, and you know why you have the particular attitudes you have. You know why you believe the government will be re-elected, why you want it to be re-elected, and why at some point you fear that it won't be re-elected. Self-ignorance is not something you suffer from, and you don't make mistakes about your attitudes. Your self-knowledge is exhaustive and infallible.

If you are *homo philosophicus* how do you know your own propositional attitudes? For example, how do you know that you believe that the government will be re-elected? One possibility is that you know this by using what I'm going to call the Transparency Method, or TM for short. It's worth spending a little time on this because there are philosophers who think that ordinary humans also

---

[2] *Homo philosophicus* is the philosophical cousin of *homo economicus*. There is more about *homo economicus* in Chapter 5.

use TM to acquire knowledge of their beliefs and other attitudes, and that the resulting knowledge is a fundamental form of self-knowledge. Whether or not that is plausible, it's easy to see that using TM would enable *homo philosophicus* to discover what he believes; TM is tailor made for *homo philosophicus*.

What exactly is the Transparency Method? Perhaps the most influential account of TM is to be found in Richard Moran's *Authority and Estrangement*.[3] Moran bases his account on a famous passage from Gareth Evans' book *The Varieties of Reference*, so let me start my account of TM by quoting Evans:

> If someone asks me "Do you think there is going to be a third world war?", I must attend in answering him to precisely the same outward phenomena as I would attend to if I were answering the question "Will there be a third world war?" I get myself into a position to answer the question whether I believe that P by putting into operation whatever procedure I have for answering the question whether P (...) If the judging subject applies this procedure, then necessarily he will gain knowledge of one of his own mental states; even the most determined sceptic cannot find here a gap in which to insert his knife. (1982: 225)[4]

The question 'Do I believe that P?' is an inward-directed question. The question 'Is it the case that P?' is an outward-directed question.[5] What Evans in saying is that I can answer the inward-directed question *by* answering the outward-directed question. As Moran puts it, the question whether I believe that P is in this sense *transparent* to the question whether P is true.[6] How can that be? Evans doesn't say but Moran does: I can legitimately answer the question whether P by considering the reasons in favour of P as long as I am entitled to assume that what I believe regarding P is 'determined by the conclusion of my reflection on those reasons' (2003: 405).[7] For example, suppose that reflection on the reasons in

---

[3] Other proponents of 'transparency approaches' to self-knowledge include Alex Byrne and Jordi Fernández. See, for example, Byrne 2011 and Fernández 2013. I'm not planning to discuss Byrne or Fernández, whose approaches are different from Moran's.

[4] As Moran notes, something like the phenomenon which Evans describes in this passage had already been described by Roy Edgley back in 1969. It was Edgley's idea to describe this phenomenon as the 'transparency' of one's own present thinking. See Edgley 1969: 90 and Moran 2001: 61 for further discussion.

[5] This use of 'inward-directed' and 'outward-directed' is borrowed from Moran 2004: 457.

[6] According to Moran, 'Transparency' stands for the claim that 'a person answers the question whether he *believes* that P in the same way he would address himself to the question whether P itself' (2004: 457).

[7] Here is another passage along the same lines: 'if the person were entitled to assume, or even in some way obligated to assume, that his considerations for or against believing P (the outward-directed question) actually determined in this case what his belief concerning P actually is (the inward-directed question), then he would be entitled to answer the question concerning his believing P or not by consideration of the reasons in favour of P' (Moran 2004: 457). The emphasis on reasons helps to explain why Moran is often described as a 'rationalist' about self-knowledge. It's helpful to think of Moran as answering a 'how-possible' question: given that the inward-directed and outward-directed questions have different subject-matters, how is it possible to answer the former by answering the latter? I have much more to say about how-possible questions in general in Cassam 2007.

favour of the proposition that there will be a third world war leads me to judge that this proposition is true. If I judge that there will be a third world war, and I have the concept of belief together with the concept *I*, then I can also conclude that I *believe* that there will be a third world war; I can't coherently think 'There will be a third world war but I don't believe there will be a third world war'.

So far so good, but how does TM account for self-knowledge of attitudes other than belief? I can't answer the question whether I desire that P by answering the question whether P; even if I conclude that there will be a third world war I obviously can't conclude on this basis that I want there to be a third world war. Fear is another problem for TM: I can't answer the question 'Do I fear that P?' by answering the question 'Is it the case that P?' In this case, the inward-directed question is manifestly not transparent to the outward-directed question. So it looks as though TM will have to be modified if the object of the exercise is to account for knowledge of what one wants and fears. But modified how? Here is David Finkelstein's helpful recasting of TM:

> The question of whether I believe that P is, for me, transparent to the question of what I ought rationally to believe—i.e. to the question of whether the reasons require me to believe that P. I can answer the former question by answering the latter. (2012: 103)

On this account, which is the one I'm going to adopt, the key to TM is the appeal to reasons. If I'm asked whether I believe there will be a third world war I can answer this question by answering the question: 'Do the reasons require me to believe that there will be a third world war?' What is good about Finkelstein's proposal is that it extends TM to attitudes other than belief. I can answer the question whether I want X by answering the question whether I ought rationally to want X. Similarly, I can answer the question whether I fear X by answering the question whether I ought rationally to fear X. As long as my attitudes are determined by my reasons, and I am also entitled to assume that they are so determined, I can determine what my attitudes are by determining what they rationally ought to be.

The same goes for you. Suppose that each of the following is true:

(i) What you believe is what you ought rationally to believe, what you want is what you rationally ought to want, what you fear is what you rationally ought to fear, and so on.

(ii) You know or justifiably believe that what you want is what you rationally ought to want, what you fear is what you rationally ought to fear, and so on.

If what you believe is what you ought rationally to believe, and you know that this is so, then you can determine whether you believe that P by determining whether you ought rationally to believe that P. If what you fear is what you ought rationally to fear, and you know that this is so, then you can determine whether you fear that P by determining whether you rationally ought to fear that P.

It's all very well saying that you can use the Transparency Method to determine your own attitudes if (i) and (ii) are true of you but this raises an obvious question: *are* they true of you? This obvious question has an equally obvious answer, at least on the assumption that you are *homo philosophicus*. Part of what it is for you to be *homo philosophicus* is for your attitudes to be as they rationally ought to be, and this is what (i) says. I've also stipulated that, as *homo philosophicus*, you don't suffer from self-ignorance. Not knowing that your attitudes are as they ought rationally to be would be a form of self-ignorance, so we can also take it that (ii) is true. And if (i) and (ii) are both true then there is nothing to stop you using TM to establish what you believe, desire, fear, etc. Indeed, what TM gives you is not just a way of knowing *what* your attitudes are but also a way of knowing *why* they are as they are. For example, if reflection on the reasons in favour of P leads you to conclude then P is true, then you are not only in a position to know *that* you believe that P but also *why* you believe that P: you believe that P because the reasons require you to believe that P.[8] This, then, is the sense in which TM is tailor made for *homo philosophicus*: TM only works on the basis of quite specific assumptions about how your attitudes are determined by your reasons, and these assumptions are guaranteed to be correct if you are *homo philosophicus*.

Of course, just because it is *possible* for you to know your own attitudes by using TM it doesn't follow that this is how you do in fact come to know your own attitudes. One reason for being careful about assuming that TM is what *homo philosophicus* relies on is this: TM describes a notably indirect route to self-knowledge but many philosophers have the intuition that knowledge of your own beliefs and other attitudes is normally direct or immediate.[9] You normally know what you believe without any conscious reasoning or inference, which means that your self-knowledge is psychologically immediate. There is also the intuition that

---

[8] As Matthew Boyle puts it, 'successful deliberation normally gives us knowledge of what we believe and why we believe it' (2011a: 8).

[9] Moran is someone who makes much of the immediacy of ordinary self-knowledge, which makes it all the more surprising that he also regards TM as a basic source of self-knowledge. It's true that when you acquire self-knowledge by using TM you aren't inferring your state of mind from *behavioural* evidence. Sometimes it seems that this is all it takes for self-knowledge to be 'immediate' in Moran's sense. However, there are also passages in which Moran implies that immediate self-knowledge mustn't be based on 'inference of any kind' (2001: 91). It's on this reading of 'immediate' that there is a problem with saying that TM is a pathway to immediate self-knowledge. The self-knowledge you get by using TM looks, and is, inferential.

your knowledge of your own attitudes is epistemically immediate, that is, not dependent on your having justification for believing other, supporting propositions.[10] But the self-knowledge you acquire by employing TM doesn't seem immediate in either sense. It looks as though you have to reason your way from your judgement that you ought rationally to believe that P to the conclusion that you believe that P. In addition, your justification for believing that you believe that P depends on your being justified in believing that what you believe is what you ought rationally to believe. If this is right, then the self-knowledge which TM gives you turns out to be inferential, psychologically and epistemically, rather than immediate.

Another concern about TM is this: suppose that you have moderately strong evidence that P but that you are aware that there is also evidence that goes the other way. The truth or falsity of P is a question about which reasonable people can differ but you come down on the side of P. It's surely not right in a case like this to say that the reasons *require* you to believe that P.[11] Nor would it be correct to say that it is irrational to believe that P on the basis of less than conclusive grounds. Even if you are *homo philosophicus* you might end up believing that P even though you recognize that the reasons don't require you to believe that P. In that case, answering the question 'Do the reasons require me to believe that P?' won't be a very sensible way of answering the question 'Do I believe that P?' It's not hard to imagine that the answer to the first of these questions is *no* whereas the answer to the second question is *yes*.

This points to a deeper concern about the very idea of what your attitudes 'rationally ought to be'. The concern is that it can be very much clearer whether you *do* believe or hope or fear that P than whether you *ought rationally* to believe or hope or fear that P. Suppose you believe that the recession will be over before the next election and that if the recession is over before the next election the government will be re-elected. Should you believe that the government will be re-elected? Maybe, but suppose you also know that the government is far behind in the opinion polls. In that case, far from concluding that the government will be re-elected, the rational response might be to question the conditional 'if the recession is over before the next election the government will be re-elected'. Or suppose that you buy a lottery ticket with tiny odds of winning. You hope that it

---

[10] There is more on the distinction between different conceptions of immediacy in Pryor 2005.

[11] As David Finkelstein points out, there are actually many attitudes that are neither prohibited nor required by deliberative reflection. Examples include disdain, adoration, jealousy, regret, revulsion, and hatred. What these and other attitudes have in common is that 'even though we sometimes deliberate about their appropriateness, they are rarely thought to be *required* by practical reasons' (2003: 163).

is a winning ticket but what are we to make of the idea that you ought rationally to hope that it is a winning ticket? If a close friend has cancer and you fear you will get cancer, is your attitude as it ought rationally to be? In such cases, the question 'Do I believe/hope/desire/fear that P?' might be much easier to answer than the question 'Ought I to believe/hope/desire/fear that P?' This makes TM look a little strange. Usually when we are faced with a hard question we try to answer it by finding a related question that is easier; Daniel Kahneman calls this 'substitution'.[12] But TM gets things back to front; it represents *homo philosophicus* as answering an easy question by answering a harder question. This assumes, of course, that questions like 'Do I believe that P' and 'Do I fear that P?' are normally easy to answer, but isn't that in fact the case?

These are all perfectly good questions about TM, but none of them amounts to a knockdown objection to the idea that if you are *homo philosophicus* you know, or can know, your own attitudes by employing TM. On the issue of whether TM only gives you indirect self-knowledge you might bite the bullet and say that it's the assumption that self-knowledge is normally immediate, rather than the assumption that we get it by using TM, that needs to be questioned. Maybe, as *homo philosophicus*, you have perfect insight into what you ought rationally to believe, want, and so on, and using TM wouldn't mean that you are substituting a harder for an easier question. In the case in which you have evidence both for and against P you ought to be agnostic about P and so will be agnostic about P. In any case, it's not clear whether, as Finkelstein's version of TM assumes, 'you ought rationally to believe that P' is equivalent to 'the reasons require you to believe that P'.

Whatever the merits of these attempts to rehabilitate TM—and I will have more to say about the pros and cons of TM later in this book—there is one issue they don't address: I have represented TM as tailor made for *homo philosophicus* on the basis that *homo philosophicus* is a model epistemic citizen who can, at least in principle, determine what his attitudes are by determining what they rationally ought to be. As I have just indicated, there may be all sorts of practical difficulties with this proposal, but at least it's possible to see in outline how TM might be a viable source of self-knowledge for a being like *homo philosophicus*. However, it will not have escaped your notice that *homo philosophicus* is not *homo sapiens*. Humans are not model epistemic citizens and it's far from obvious that their attitudes are as they ought rationally to be. In that case, how can we determine what our attitudes are by determining what they rationally ought to be? It's not, or not just, that there are practical difficulties that stand in the way of humans

---

[12] Kahneman 2011: 97–9. I'll have a lot more to say about Kahneman as I go along.

acquiring self-knowledge by employing TM. It's more that the idea that TM is a pathway to self-knowledge for humans seems flawed in principle.

Here is a homely illustration of the problem: suppose that you are frightened of spiders. In particular, you are afraid of the spider sitting in your bathtub right now but also you know that it is quite harmless and that there is no reason to be scared of it. Knowing that you have no reason to be scared doesn't alter the fact that you are scared. Your attitude is, in this sense, *recalcitrant*. What is more, you know that you are frightened, but you can't come to know this by asking yourself whether you have any reason to be frightened of the spider. Of course, if you were *homo philosophicus* there would be no mismatch between what your attitude is and what it rationally ought to be, but I take it that you are not *homo philosophicus*. Even if your fear of spiders is an alien force which affects your life rather than an attitude that is under your rational control, this doesn't alter the fact that you are afraid of spiders and know that you are afraid of them. This is a piece of self-knowledge which TM can't account for.

In case you think that fear is unusual, here is a different example which makes much the same point: you believe the government will be re-elected on the basis that the recession will be over before the next election. Later, I present you with convincing evidence that the recession will continue beyond this next election but you continue to believe the government will be re-elected. The psychologists Richard Nisbett and Lee Ross call this phenomenon 'belief-perseverance after evidential discrediting' (1980: 175). Intuitively, you ought to abandon your initial belief about the government's election prospects but the belief persists. You know what you believe, but not by asking whether you ought rationally to have the belief that the government will be re-elected. The problem is that your belief in this case is not as it rationally ought to be.

One response to such examples would be to argue that they aren't a problem for TM because in cases of belief-perseverance you still believe what you ought rationally to believe *by your own lights*. Maybe you continue to believe the government will be re-elected because you have forgotten that your sole reason for believing this was your belief that the recession will end before the election.[13] That is why you don't automatically revise your belief about the government's election prospects when presented with new evidence about the length of the recession. Relative to your grasp of your grounds for believing that the government will be re-elected it's not obviously irrational for you to hang on to this

---

[13] This is how Gilbert Harman explains belief-perseverance. There is more on Harman in Chapter 2.

belief, and you can still come to know that you have it by asking what you ought rationally to believe.

This attempt to reconcile TM with the phenomenon of belief-perseverance is a form of what might be called *compatibilism*. The question being addressed is the following *sources question*:

(SQ) What are the sources of self-knowledge for humans?

The compatibilist wants to argue that despite the disparity between *homo philosophicus* and *homo sapiens* TM is still a viable source of self-knowledge for the latter; we can still come to know our own attitudes by using the Transparency Method. Compatibilism may be motivated in part by the suspicion that the disparities between *homo philosophicus* and *homo sapiens* are less extensive than I have suggested. It might be suggested, for example, that our attitudes must *by and large* be as they ought to be, and that this allows TM to function as a reliable, though not infallible, guide to our attitudes. If you are *homo philosophicus* and you use TM to determine what you believe you can't go wrong. If you are human and you use TM to determine what you believe you can go wrong but this doesn't mean that TM doesn't give you self-knowledge. For TM to be a source of self-knowledge it only has to be reliable, not infallible.

I will discuss compatibilism, as well as the true extent of the disparity between *homo philosophicus* and *homo sapiens*, in later chapters. However, I'd like to conclude this chapter by asking the following question: why all the fuss about TM? One reason might be that a number of philosophers distinguish between 'Rationalist' and 'Empiricist' approaches to self-knowledge, and that TM is often associated with Rationalism.[14] Indeed, a basic tenet of Rationalism is that knowledge of our own attitudes acquired by using TM is a fundamental form of self-knowledge. So if you are interested in assessing the merits of Rationalism then you ought to be interested in TM. However, this only serves to raise a more basic question: why all the fuss about knowledge of our own attitudes? Indeed, while the range of attitudes is extensive, and includes such attitudes as fearing that P, desiring that P, intending that P, and hoping that P, the usual focus of philosophical attention is knowledge of what you believe. The only other self-knowledge that has attracted as much philosophical attention is knowledge of one's own sensations, and it's a good question why philosophical accounts of self-knowledge have been so narrowly focused.

---

[14] Often but not always. Alex Byrne has a non-rationalist take on transparency in Byrne 2011 and elsewhere. See Zimmerman 2008 and Gertler 2011a for more on the distinction between 'rationalist' and 'empiricist' accounts of self-knowledge.

Even when it comes to knowledge of what you believe, it's striking how bland the usual philosophical examples of this form of self-knowledge tend to be. Apart from Evans' case of knowing whether you believe there will be a third world war, another much discussed example is knowing whether you believe that it is raining.[15] Even if TM can account for this knowledge, the plain fact is that even moderately reflective humans tend not to be terribly exercised by the question 'How do you know that you believe that it is raining?', any more than they are exercised by the question 'How do you know you are in pain?' Intuitively, knowing that you believe it is raining is a relatively trivial and boring piece of self-knowledge. Clearly, even boring self-knowledge needs explaining, and of course it might turn out on reflection that there is value to knowing that you believe that it is raining. Nevertheless, it's worth contrasting the kinds of self-knowledge which have tended to be of interest to philosophers of self-knowledge with the kinds of self-knowledge that tend to be of interest to reflective humans.[16]

Here are some examples:

Am I a racist?[17]
How well am I coping with being a new parent?
Why do I think my boss doesn't like me?
Do I really love her or is it a passing infatuation?
Am I any good at handling conflict in my personal and professional life?
Would a change of career make me happy?

To know the answers to these questions would be to have forms of self-knowledge which no one could reasonably describe as boring or trivial. Knowledge of one's values, emotions, abilities, and of what makes one happy are all examples of what might be called *substantial* self-knowledge. It's easier to see the value of substantial self-knowledge than the value of knowing that you believe it's raining. For most humans, substantial self-knowledge is hard to acquire, and there is little temptation to suppose that it can be acquired by using TM. That is not a criticism of TM, just a comment about its limitations. Once we think about the sheer variety of our self-knowledge it seems obvious that it has a great many different sources. These sources might include TM but there is no excuse for obsessing about TM if the aim is to explain the self-knowledge that is of greatest interest to humans.

---

[15] This is one of Moran's examples.

[16] The distinction I am drawing here is like Eric Schwitzgebel's distinction between 'fairly trivial attitudes' and 'the attitudes I care about most' (2012: 191).

[17] I should say in fairness that not all philosophers have neglected such examples. See Schwitzgebel 2010.

Thinking about substantial self-knowledge will help to concentrate our minds on two other important but neglected questions about self-knowledge. One is the *value question*:

(VQ) What is the value of self-knowledge?

The other is the *obstacles question*:

(OQ) What are the obstacles to self-knowledge?

The value question is worth asking because while it might seem obvious that substantial self-knowledge is valuable it's not obvious what makes it valuable. The obstacles question arises because we need to understand what (sometimes) prevents us from gaining self-knowledge, whether substantial or otherwise. If the obstacles are insuperable the result is self-ignorance, and we should also consider the possibility that some self-ignorance might not be a bad thing.

Having distinguished between *homo philosophicus* and *homo sapiens*, introduced the contrast between trivial and substantial self-knowledge, and identified three basic questions about self-knowledge (sources, value, and obstacles) I'm now in a position to give my plan for this book. In Chapter 2, I will outline some of the respects in which *homo sapiens* might be thought to differ from *homo philosophicus*, and explain why the actual extent of the disparity between them (I will refer to this as 'the Disparity') is philosophically controversial. Substantial self-knowledge, and its relation to knowledge of our own attitudes, will be the topic of Chapter 3. This will be followed, in Chapter 4, by a discussion of why so many philosophers of self-knowledge have concentrated on the epistemology of relatively trivial self-knowledge. My hypothesis is that philosophical accounts of self-knowledge tend to be driven by narrow epistemological concerns rather than by what matters to humans, and that that is why the philosophy of self-knowledge seems so far removed from the questions about self-knowledge that ordinary humans find most interesting. If you start out with the idea that only epistemically privileged, that is, infallible, incorrigible or direct self-knowledge is philosophically interesting then you will end up ignoring large swathes of substantial self-knowledge because a lot of substantive self-knowledge doesn't appear to be epistemically privileged. But why think that the considerations of epistemic privilege should set the agenda for the philosophy of self-knowledge? In Chapter 5, I will compare the radical reorientation of the philosophy of self-knowledge I am recommending with the reorientation of economics proposed by so-called 'behavioural' economists who criticize neo-classical economics on the grounds that it is the economics of the mythical species *homo economicus* rather than the economics of real human beings. The challenge for philosophers and economists is to relate their theories to the way we (humans) are, and theories that fail to do this are in urgent need of a reality check.

The next three chapters, 6–8, delve more deeply into the extent and significance of the Disparity, with a focus on what might be described as damage limitation exercises on behalf of rationalism. Specifically, Chapter 6 discusses claims that there couldn't be a significant Disparity because it wouldn't be possible for us humans to have propositional attitudes at all unless our attitudes are by and large rational. Chapter 7 is about attempts to downplay the significance of the Disparity for rationalism on the grounds that the latter is primarily concerned with how we are *supposed* to think and reason rather than with how we do *in fact* think and reason. Chapter 8 is about whether the Disparity shows that humans are irrational. My overall conclusion in these chapters is that there is no getting away from the Disparity but that we should also refrain from saying that man is an irrational animal; not being *homo philosophicus* does not make *homo sapiens* irrational.

The next block of chapters, 9–13, addresses the Sources Question. In Chapter 9, I spend more time on TM. In Chapter 10, I discuss the idea that we acquire self-knowledge by 'inner perception' or by exercising what is sometimes called 'inner sense'. In Chapters 11 and 12, I finally give my own 'inferentialist' response to the Sources Question. Inferentialism is the view that we know our own minds by inference from behavioural or other evidence. This is a deeply unpopular view among philosophers of self-knowledge but I want to suggest that the poor reputation of inferentialism is undeserved. The focus of Chapters 11 and 12 is inferentialism in relation to knowledge of our own attitudes and feelings. In Chapter 13, I tell an inferentialist story about three varieties of substantial self-knowledge, namely, knowledge of our characters, our values, and our emotions.

The last two chapters tackle the Obstacles Question and the Value Question respectively. Anyone who takes seriously the idea that there are obstacles to self-knowledge is almost certainly going to have to think about the sources and extent of self-ignorance. Self-ignorance is the topic of Chapter 14. The value of self-knowledge is the topic of Chapter 15. We are all familiar with the idea that self-knowledge matters and is worth having but what is much less clear is *why* it is worth having. What's so good about self-knowledge? My suggestion will be that although some self-knowledge is indeed valuable, its value is largely practical. It doesn't have the deeper value or significance which many philosophers and indeed non-philosophers think it has. I call my account of the value of self-knowledge a 'low road' account.

My basic thought in this book is really very simple: we go wrong in philosophy when we forget that questions about self-knowledge, as about many other central topics in philosophy, aren't or shouldn't be of merely academic (in the pejorative sense) interest. What we should be after is an account of self-knowledge for humans and not an account of self-knowledge for *homo philosophicus*. By an account of self-knowledge for humans, I mean an account that explains how self-knowledge of different kinds is possible for creatures with our distinctively human cognitive limitations and foibles, as well as an account which tries to do justice to what it is about self-knowledge that is valuable and important. Coming up with at least the outlines of such an account is the mission of this book.

2

The Disparity

I commented in the previous chapter that it won't have escaped your notice that *homo philosophicus* is not *homo sapiens*. If you really are *homo philosophicus* then you are a model epistemic citizen. Your reasoning is critical, your attitudes are as they rationally ought to be, whatever that turns out to mean, and your self-knowledge is infallible and exhaustive; you are immune to self-ignorance. If you belong to the species *homo sapiens*, then the chances are that you are not a model epistemic citizen. When I talk about the Disparity, I am referring to the various respects in which normal humans differ from *homo philosophicus*. Given that *homo philosophicus* is a mythical species, it might seem a little odd to spend time describing the differences between *homo sapiens* and *homo philosophicus* but it makes sense to do this if, as I contend, many philosophical accounts of the human mind and human self-knowledge implicitly assume that humans think and reason in ways that are similar to the ways that I've characterized *homo philosophicus* as thinking and reasoning.

Key aspects of the Disparity include:

1. The extent to which our reasoning isn't critical.
2. The extent to which we are biased to believe.
3. The extent to which our beliefs and other attitudes survive evidential discrediting.
4. The extent to which our attitudes are recalcitrant.
5. The extent to which we are self-ignorant.

In this chapter, I want to say something about each of these characteristics of *homo sapiens*. Taken together these characteristics suggest that there is an extensive Disparity between *homo sapiens* and *homo philosophicus*. Whether the Disparity can really be as extensive as it appears is a question I will come back to in Chapter 6. The consequences of the Disparity for TM will be the focus of Chapter 9. All I want to do in this chapter is outline some of the respects in which we fall short of the ideal of *homo philosophicus*.

Let's start with the issue of whether, and to what extent, human reasoning is 'critical' in Tyler Burge's sense. Critical reasoning is reasoning that is guided by an appreciation, use, and assessment of reasons and reasoning as such. To be a critical reasoner 'one must be able to, and sometimes actually, use one's knowledge of reasons to make, criticize, change, confirm *commitments* regarding propositions—to engage explicitly in reason-induced changes of mind' (1998: 248). Burge is careful not to suggest that all our reasoning is critical; all he says is that 'critical reasoning does occur among us' (1998: 250). He contrasts critical reasoning with blind reasoning, and claims that much of our reasoning is blind. Animals and small children also reason blindly, that is, without appreciating reasons as reasons. When we reason blindly we change our attitudes without having much sense of what we are doing.

Now consider the following example, which I will refer to as BAT AND BALL: a bat and ball cost $1.10. The bat costs one dollar more than the ball. How much does the ball cost?[1] The intuitive but wrong answer is 10 cents. The right answer is 5 cents. How is it that so many people get this and other similarly simple problems wrong? Kahneman argues in his book *Thinking, Fast and Slow* that the key to understanding BAT AND BALL is to think of our minds as containing two systems, a fast thinking System 1 and a slow thinking System 2. System 1

- operates automatically and quickly, with little or no effort, and no sense of voluntary control
- generates impressions, feelings, and inclinations which, when endorsed by System 2 become beliefs, attitudes, and intentions
- is biased to believe and confirm
- focuses on existing evidence and ignores absent evidence
- generates a limited set of basic assessments.

In contrast, System 2

- has beliefs, makes choices, and decides what to think about and what to do
- allocates attention to effortful mental activities
- is associated with the subjective experience of agency, choice and concentration
- constructs thoughts in an orderly series of steps.

---

[1] This is one of three questions which make up Shane Frederick's Cognitive Reflection Test (CRT). See Frederick 2005 and Kahneman 2011: chapter 3 for further discussion. All three CRT problems generate an incorrect intuitive answer. The CRT was administered over 26 months to 3,428 respondents, mostly undergraduates. A startling proportion of respondents got all three questions wrong.

System 1 is fast but lazy, System 2 is slow but deliberate, orderly and effortful. System 1 'operates as a machine for jumping to conclusions' (2011: 85) and is 'radically insensitive to both the quality and the quantity of the information that gives rise to impressions and intuitions' (2011: 86). It often fails to allow for the possibility that critical evidence is missing and doesn't seek out such evidence; as far as System 1 is concerned, 'what we see is all there is' (2011: 87).

In terms of this framework it's easy to understand the results of BAT AND BALL. Some problems are so complicated that System 1 doesn't come up with an answer; there is no intuitive answer and the only way to find a solution is to deploy one's System 2. However, in BAT AND BALL there is an intuitive (but wrong) answer, and that is the answer which System 1 gives. At this point, several things can happen. One possibility is that System 2 kicks in, checks the answer delivered by System 1 and corrects it. Despite the impression that the answer is 10 cents one doesn't end up believing that the answer is 10 cents. However, as is clear from the results, this is often not what actually happens. Instead, the answer '10 cents' is endorsed by System 2, and one ends up believing that the ball costs 10 cents.

What this brings out is that even System 2 isn't always as effortful as one might think. It often endorses the deliverances of System 1 automatically and without careful checking. System 2 is *capable* of a systematic and careful approach to the evidence but 'most of the time it adopts the suggestions of System 1 with little or no modification' (2011: 24). So when Kahneman says that System 1 intuitions 'become beliefs' when endorsed by the effortful System 2 he certainly isn't suggesting that belief-formation always requires effort. There is such a thing as effortful belief-formation, as when a person comes to believe that P as a result of carefully checking the evidence for P, but this is often not what happens. For example, in BAT AND BALL, 'we know a significant fact about anyone who says the ball costs 10 ¢: that person did not actively check whether the answer was correct, and her System 2 endorsed an intuitive answer that it could have rejected with a small investment of effort' (2011: 44; cf. 2011: 31).

How prevalent is fast thinking? To ask the same question another way: how active is System 1 in our lives compared to System 2? Both systems are active when we are awake but System 2 is 'normally in a comfortable low-effort mode, in which only a fraction of its capacity is engaged' (2011: 24). In contrast, System 1 is continuously generating suggestions for System 2 and is the origin of most of what System 2 does. Our default mode of thinking is fast thinking, and System 2's role is to take over 'when a question arises for which System 1 does not offer an answer' (2011: 24) or when things get difficult for System 1 in some other way. System 2 is the 'conscious, reasoning self' (2011: 21). It is the system we identify with when we think of ourselves. However, in cinematic terms, it is System 1 that is the hero; System 2 is merely 'a supporting character who believes himself to be the hero' (2011: 31).

It's clear that what Burge calls 'critical reasoning' is a form of what Kahneman calls 'slow thinking'. *Homo philosophicus* only thinks carefully and 'slowly' and the prevalence of fast thinking among humans confirms the impression that there is a significant Disparity in this respect between *homo philosophicus* and *homo sapiens*; much of the time, our reasoning isn't guided by an appreciation, use, and assessment of reasons and reasoning as such. We are reluctant to criticize our reasons, and we do not guard against possible sources of bias. Most of us are too busy, lazy, or complacent to do much critical reasoning. It does not follow, however, that we reason blindly much of the time. In giving the '10 cents' response to BAT AND BALL you are saying what strikes you as intuitively correct, and you aren't flummoxed when asked why you gave that answer.[2] In genuinely blind reasoning to the conclusion that P you have no idea why you concluded that P. The reasoning that led you to the conclusion that the ball cost 10 cents was flawed but not all flawed reasoning is blind in this sense. 'Critical' and 'blind' reasoning aren't the only options, and a lot of human reasoning is neither.

It would also be a mistake to assume that fast thinking is necessarily irresponsible or irrational. The human predicament is one in which both time and energy are frequently in short supply, so what we implicitly rely on is what Kahneman and Tversky call 'heuristics' in fast thinking.[3] A heuristic is a rule of thumb, 'a simple procedure that helps find adequate, though often imperfect, answers to difficult questions' (2011: 98). When time is short we need shortcuts, which is exactly what heuristics are. Here are three examples of heuristics:

(a) *Representativeness*: when asked how likely it is that A belongs to category B people answer by answering a different question: how similar is A to their image or stereotype of B? For example, suppose you're told that Steve is shy and withdrawn, invariably helpful but with little interest in people or

---

[2] This also explains why fast thinking isn't sub-personal information processing. If it were you presumably would be at a loss to explain why you came up with '10 cents' in response to BAT AND BALL. You aren't at a loss, and that is because the fast thinking which resulted in your answering '10 cents' was something *you* did rather than a piece of sub-personal processing. Thanks to David Finkelstein for getting to me say something about why I don't think that fast thinking is sub-personal.

[3] It should be acknowledged that Kahneman and Tversky's so-called 'heuristics and biases' approach to human reasoning is not without its critics. See Gigerenzer 1996 and the response in Kahneman and Tversky 1996. For a helpful overview, see Sturm 2012. I don't believe that my story about the Disparity turns on the details of the debates and disagreements described by Sturm.

the world of reality. A meek and tidy soul, he has a need for order and structure and a passion for detail. Do you believe Steve is more likely to be a librarian or a farmer? If you say librarian that's because Steve's personality is that of a stereotypical librarian. Yet there are 20 male farmers for every male librarian so your judgement that Steve is more likely to be a librarian is insensitive to highly relevant statistical considerations.

(b) *Availability*: humans assess the probability of an event by the ease with which instances can be brought to mind. Asked to judge the rate of divorce among professors in your university you judge by the ease with which instances of divorced professors come to mind. Again, you are ignoring relevant statistical considerations.

(c) *Anchoring*: people make estimates of various kinds by starting from an initial value that is adjusted to yield the final answer. For example, a panel of experienced German judges read a description of a woman who had been caught shoplifting, and then rolled a pair of dice that were loaded so that every roll resulted in either a 3 or a 9. As soon as the dice came to a stop the judges were asked to specify the exact prison sentence they would apply in this case: 'on average, those who had rolled a 9 said they would sentence her to 8 months; those who had rolled a 3 said they would sentence her to 5 months' (2011: 126).

The essence of heuristics is *substitution*: 'when faced with a difficult question, we often answer an easier one instead, usually without noticing the substitution' (Kahneman 2011: 12). For example, the target question might be: 'Is Steve more likely to be librarian or a farmer?' The heuristic question you end up answering instead is: 'How similar is Steve to the stereotype of a librarian?' If the target question is 'How happy are you with your life right now?' the corresponding heuristic question might be: 'What is my mood right now?' *Homo philosophicus* would answer the target question but this might be completely impractical for *homo sapiens*. If you are human, you may have a poor understanding of logic and statistics, and may not be equipped to give a reasoned answer to the target question even if you have the time. However, humans 'aren't limited to perfectly reasoned answers to questions' (2011: 98). They have 'a heuristic alternative to careful reasoning, which sometimes works fairly well and sometimes leads to serious errors' (2011: 98). Where there isn't a lot at stake, and time is short, it's not irresponsible or irrational to rely on heuristics.

In describing System 1 as a 'machine for jumping to conclusions', Kahneman also by implication attributes to humans a 'bias to believe' (2011: 80). This is a further aspect of the Disparity. Suppose that *homo philosophicus* has never previously considered the question whether P; when he considers this question he looks at the evidence, and doesn't believe that P unless he finds evidence or grounds that are sufficient to justify the belief that P. The search for evidence comes first, and the belief that P only comes into being if the search is successful. In contrast, jumping to the conclusion that P means believing that P in advance of finding good reasons; jumping to conclusions 'is efficient if the conclusions are likely to be correct and the costs of an occasional mistake acceptable' (2011: 79). But it's not just a matter of efficiency since it is also plausible that understanding a statement must begin with the attempt to believe it.[4] The initial attempt to believe is an automatic operation of System 1; in contrast, doubt or disbelief require mental effort, and are therefore the domain of System 2.

It's sometimes claimed that the bias to believe helps explain why, as Michael Shermer puts it, 'people believe weird things'.[5] For example, a 2009 poll of 2,303 Americans revealed that 32% believed in the existence of UFOs, 42% in ghosts, and 72% in the existence of angels. In contrast, only 45% endorsed Darwin's theory of evolution.[6] In 2008, a global poll of over 16,000 people found that fewer than half believed that al Qaeda was responsible for the 9/11 attacks, with a significant number attributing the collapse of the World Trade Center towers to a controlled demolition by the US government rather than aircraft impacts.[7] Shermer suggests that we can understand how people can believe such things if we suppose that 'beliefs come first; reasons for belief follow' (Shermer 2011: 157). This can't be right since it doesn't explain why the bias to believe kicks in when people are considering conspiracy theories about 9/11, UFO landings in Roswell, and the assassination of JFK but not when presented with official denials of such theories. The problem is not that people aren't capable of being sceptical, but that they are often sceptical about the wrong things.

This suggests that if we want to explain why people believe weird things we will have to appeal to more than the bias to believe. For example, we will need to explain the peculiar appeal of conspiracy theories, and the role of other non-rational factors in belief-formation, including such things as wishful thinking.[8]

---

[4] Daniel Gilbert develops this insight, which he gets from Spinoza, in Gilbert 1991.

[5] *Why People Believe Weird Things* is the title of a book by Michael Shermer (Shermer 2007).

[6] These are the results of a Harris poll quoted by Michael Shermer. See Shermer 2011: 3.

[7] The poll was carried out by WorldPublicOpinion.org. A press release summarizing the poll results is available at: <http://www.worldpublicopinion.org/pipa/pdf/sep08/WPO_911_Sep08_pr.pdf>.

[8] When it comes to explaining the appeal of conspiracy theories one factor might be the difficulty many people have in getting their minds around the possibility that small causes can produce large effects. Commenting on conspiracy theories about the assassination of President Kennedy Richard Nisbett and Timothy Wilson write: 'The notion that small causes can produce large effects probably

The important point, however, is this: whatever the complete story about the origins of 'weird' beliefs there seems little doubt that human belief-formation *is* influenced by non-rational factors, including a bias to believe. The role of non-rational factors in human belief-formation is another powerful illustration of the Disparity. The seductive image of the careful, thorough, and sceptically minded *homo philosophicus* is far removed from what most ordinary humans are like. Perhaps we *ought* to be more like *homo philosophicus* but that's a different matter. As far as the Disparity is concerned, the issue is not how we ought to be but how we are.

Turning, next, to the extent to which our beliefs and other attitudes are able to survive evidential discrediting, this is the phenomenon of 'belief-perseverance' which I mentioned in the last chapter. Here is an example from Harman: Karen has taken an aptitude test and has just been told her results show she has a considerable aptitude for science and music but little aptitude for history and philosophy.[9] She concludes that her reported scores accurately reflect her actual aptitudes even though they don't correlate perfectly with her previous grades. Days later she is told that she had been given someone else's scores and that her own scores were lost. You might think that Karen ought now to give up her new beliefs about her aptitudes but Harman points out that 'Karen would almost certainly keep her new beliefs' (1986: 35); she would continue to believe that she has a considerable aptitude for science and music but little aptitude for history and philosophy even though the basis for this belief has been undermined by the revelation that she was given the wrong scores. It might seem obvious what Karen *should* do, but what she *would* do in the circumstances Harman describes is a completely different matter. What she would do is different from what *homo philosophicus* would do.

This example, which I will refer to as KAREN, is fictional, but what Harman's verdict about what Karen would believe post-undermining accords with extensive empirical research on belief-perseverance reported by Nisbett and Ross. In their words 'people tend to persevere in their beliefs well beyond the point at which logical and evidential considerations can sustain them' (1980: 192). How, then, is belief-perseverance possible? How can Karen fail to see that her new beliefs have been undermined, and fail to revise them accordingly? One explanation appeals to the existence of a *confirmation bias* among humans, their tendency to 'seek out, recall, and interpret evidence in a manner that sustains

---

develops very late and never attains very great stability. It is outrageous that a single, pathetic, weak, figure like Lee Harvey Oswald should alter world history' (1977: 252). See, also, Aaronovitch 2009.

[9] The example is from Harman 1986: 33.

beliefs' (Nisbett and Ross 1980: 192). Another explanation trades on the import-ance of what Harman calls 'clutter avoidance'. Subjects like Karen hold on to their new beliefs in face of evidential discrediting because they fail to recognize that their beliefs have been discredited:

[P]eople simply do not keep track of the justification relations among their beliefs. They continue to believe things after the evidence for them has been discredited because they do not realize what they are doing. They do not understand that the discredited evidence was the *sole* reason why they believe as they do. They do not see that they would not have been justified in forming those beliefs in the absence of the now discredited evidence. (Harman 1986: 38)

Failing to keep track of justification relations among one's beliefs, or the sources of grounds of one's beliefs, might appear to be a form of epistemic malpractice but it serves the purpose of reducing clutter in one's beliefs; it's important not to clutter one's mind with unimportant matters, and 'this means that one should try not to keep track of the local justifications of one's belief' (1986: 42). The forgetting or failing to keep track of one's justifications which makes belief-perseverance possible serves a very useful purpose in the cognitive economy of *homo sapiens*, and brings to light the possibility that belief-perseverance 'serves goals that may be more fundamental and important than holding correct views of particular issues' (Nisbett and Ross 1980: 192). If we suppose that belief-perse-verance is not an issue for *homo philosophicus* that can only be because clutter avoidance isn't an issue for him, and that can only be so if there is no limit to what he can remember and put into long-term storage.

Before moving on, it's worth noting two key features of Harman's plausible account of belief-perseverance. The first is the importance of self-ignorance; Karen goes on believing that she has an aptitude for science and music but not history or philosophy because she does not realize that her belief has been discredited, and she doesn't realize that it has been discredited because she doesn't realize that the discredited evidence was the sole evidence for her belief. In other words, she lacks a proper grasp of *why* she believes that she has an aptitude for science and music but not history or philosophy. Not knowing why she believes this is a form of self-ignorance and helps to account for the perseverance of her belief. Self-ignorance is another aspect of the Disparity, and it's important to see how different aspects of the Disparity are interrelated.

The second point to notice about Harman's account is that it points to a fundamental distinction between the phenomenon of belief-perseverance and what I have referred to as the phenomenon of belief-recalcitrance. Whereas in belief-perseverance you simply don't realize your attitude has been undermined, in recalcitrance you *know* you have no good reason to have the particular attitude which you know you have. This makes attitude-recalcitrance a far more puzzling phenomenon than belief-perseverance. Indeed, recalcitrance is so puzzling that one might wonder whether it is a genuine possibility, even for humans. If it is, then it certainly distinguishes us from *homo philosophicus*, so the next questions are: is attitude-recalcitrance a genuine phenomenon and, if so, how is such a thing possible?

The most compelling examples of recalcitrance involve attitudes other than belief. In the last chapter I gave the example of fear of spiders. In this example, you continue to fear the spider in your bathtub even though you know you have no reason or grounds for fearing it. It isn't that you have failed to keep track of your reasons for fearing the spider but that your fear is impervious to all reasons or reasoning. This form of recalcitrance is easy to understand but limited in scope: your never reasoned yourself into a fear of spiders so it's hardly surprising that your fear is impervious to reasons or reasoning. You didn't come to fear spiders because you genuinely thought they were dangerous, so the thought that they are harmless makes no difference to your fear. Your attitude in this case is judgement-insensitive, in the sense that it is unresponsive to your judgement about whether you are warranted in having it. We should not be in the least surprised that judgement-insensitive attitudes can be recalcitrant because this possibility is built into the very idea of judgement-insensitivity.[10]

It's harder to understand how beliefs can be recalcitrant because it's natural to think of belief as judgement-sensitive. Consider the following variation on KAREN: suppose that P is the proposition that she has an aptitude for science and music, but not for history or philosophy. She knows that her reported test result was her sole reason for believing that P, and that she was given someone else's results. She judges that she is no longer warranted in believing P but she still believes that P. How can that be? Here is one explanation: imagine that it takes a long time for it to emerge that she had been given the wrong result. Meanwhile, she plans her life on the basis of her belief that P. When the question arises whether P she is disposed to think that P. The thought that P produces in her a feeling of conviction, and she is disposed to use this thought as a premise in

---

[10]   Scanlon says that a judgement-sensitive attitude is one for which reasons in a certain sense can be asked for and given. See Scanlon 1998: 18–22. This isn't quite the notion I am after. An attitude of yours can be one for which reasons in the relevant sense can be asked for and given and yet unresponsive to your judgement about whether you are warranted in having it. However, Scanlon says other things about judgement-sensitivity which are much more in line with what I have in mind. I owe a lot to his discussion.

reasoning and deciding what to do.[11] Suddenly, she receives the news about the foul-up in the distribution of the test scores. It's not that she does not get the significance of this news, but it doesn't have an immediate impact on her beliefs about her aptitudes. These beliefs have become established habits of thought and, to quote Harman again, 'once a belief has become established, considerable effort might be needed to get rid of it, even if the believer should come to see that he or she ought to get rid of it, just as it is hard to get rid of a bad habit' (1986: 37).

So we now have the following explanation of recalcitrance: beliefs are something like habits or dispositions to think in certain ways and such habits or dispositions can become so deeply embedded that they become unresponsive to one's judgements. You can judge, and indeed know, that you aren't warranted in believing that P and yet continue to believe that P because your judgement doesn't have the effect that it should have on what you believe; you fail to take your judgement to heart. The more long-standing and deeply embedded your belief that P the harder you may find to shake it off when confronted by evidence which you realize undermines it. The problem is not that you don't recognize undermining evidence when you see it but that thinking that you should not believe that P has a limited impact on whether you do believe that P.

This account of recalcitrance raises difficult questions which I will come back to in later chapters. For example, it might be thought that if Karen genuinely judges that she ought not to believe that P then it follows that she doesn't believe that P. By the same token, if she judges that she ought to believe that P then she judges that P, and if she judges that P then it follows that she takes P to be true and so believes that P. So how can what she believes be unresponsive to what she judges? One response to this would be to argue that judging isn't the same as believing, and that the sense in which you take P to be true when you judge that P doesn't entail that you believe that P.[12] It doesn't entail that you believe that P because it doesn't entail that you form the habit of thinking and acting as if P. Another response would be to argue that what happens in recalcitrance cases isn't that you judge that P but somehow don't believe that P. What happens is rather that you judge, and so believe, that you ought rationally to believe that P without *actually* believing (or judging) that P. There is a mismatch between what you believe and what you judge, but the

---

[11] Here as elsewhere I'm drawing on Scanlon's account of belief in *What We Owe to Each Other*. As Scanlon points out, 'a person who believes that P will tend to have feelings of conviction about P when the question arises, will normally be prepared to affirm P and to use it as a premise in further reasoning, will tend to think of P as a piece of counterevidence when claims incompatible with it are advanced, and so on' (1998: 21).

[12] I defend this conception of the relationship between judging and believing in Cassam 2010. For a different view, see Boyle 2011a.

judgement to which your belief fails to conform is specifically a judgement about what you ought rationally to believe. I will have a lot more to say about all this in Chapter 9.

Before moving on to the last of the five aspects of the Disparity I want to discuss here, it would be worth saying something about the bearing of the discussion so far on the issue of whether our attitudes are as they ought rationally to be. Remember that I stipulated in the last chapter that *homo philosophicus* believes what he ought rationally to believe, wants what he ought rationally to want, fears what he ought rationally to fear, and so on. I conceded that it is hard to say in general terms when you ought rationally to have a given attitude, but it can still be clear in practice when someone's attitude is not as it ought rationally to be. Are the various Disparities I have so far described clear-cut examples of our attitudes not being as they ought rationally to be?

Recalcitrant attitudes are not as they ought rationally to be. In the case in which Karen judges that she ought not to believe that P but can't get rid of this belief, her belief is not as it ought rationally to be even by her own lights. Indeed, this conflict between what she believes and what she judges she is warranted in believing is a form of irrationality in a strict sense of that term. As Scanlon puts it, irrationality in the clearest sense 'occurs when a person's attitudes fail to conform to his or her own judgements' (1998: 25). This is the sense in which Karen's belief is irrational. In contrast, mere belief-perseverance isn't irrational per se; in the original version of KAREN she doesn't believe what she thinks she shouldn't believe. By her own lights, there is no question of her failing to believe what she ought to believe. We might think that she should no longer believe that P post-evidential discrediting, but this 'should' is relative to what *we* know about her grounds for believing that P, not relative to what *Karen* knows. The most that can be said is that Karen is open to rational criticism but being open to rational criticism is not the same as being irrational.[13]

BAT AND BALL is another case in which a person's belief isn't strictly irrational but is nevertheless not as it ought rationally to be. The test subjects who came up with the answer '10 cents' should have done better. A less straight-forward case is one in which the subject's reasoning is, in a sense, impeccable but where they are still open to rational criticism. Some 'bias to believe' cases are of this kind. Consider the example of a conspiracy theorist who I will call Oliver:

Oliver has an unhealthy obsession with 9/11. He spends much of his spare time reading about what he calls the 9/11 conspiracy and he regards himself as something of an expert

[13] Cf. Scanlon 1998: 27.

in the field of 9/11 studies. He thinks that the 9/11 attacks were not carried out by al Qaeda and that the collapse of the World Trade Center towers on 11 September 2001 was caused by explosives planted in the buildings in advance by government agents rather than by aircraft impacts and the resulting fires. As far as Oliver is concerned, the collapse of the twin towers was the result of a controlled demolition.[14]

Suppose that P is the proposition that the collapse of the twin towers on 9/11 was caused by explosives installed in the building in advance rather than by aircraft impact. In believing that P does Oliver believe something that he ought rationally not to believe? The answer depends in part on the basis on which Oliver believes P. Suppose he believes P because he believes that aircraft impact *couldn't* have caused the towers to collapse and that eye witnesses on the day heard explosions just prior to each tower going down. Call this conjunctive proposition Q. Oliver thinks there is good evidence for Q and he believes P on the basis that Q supports P. Now consider this principle from Sebastian Rödl:

If P follows from Q, then someone who believes Q *rationally* ought to believe P. (2007: 88)

In OLIVER P doesn't follow logically from Q but Q supports P. In reasoning from Q to P, and coming to believe P on that basis, Oliver can't be accused of bad reasoning but there is a clear sense in which, in believing that P, Oliver believes something he ought not to believe.

One of the things that is going on in cases like OLIVER is that the subject's belief has what might be called an *undermining non-epistemic explanation*. Oliver believes propositions such as P and Q, and ignores or dismisses evidence to the contrary, because he is biased to believe conspiracy theories and is perhaps generally gullible.[15] It all starts to make sense if we discover that Oliver believes

---

[14] Oliver is a fictional character but real-world Olivers are depressingly numerous. Hopefully few readers of the present work will need convincing not just of the absurdity of such conspiracy theories but the harm they do. If you do need convincing then the account in Aaronovitch 2009 is well worth reading though, of course, conspiracy theorists tend to regard all attempts to convince them of the error of their ways as part of the conspiracy. To get a sense of what really happened on 9/11 Kean and Hamilton 2012 is essential reading.

[15] Gullibility is an example of an intellectual character trait. While there might be epistemically acceptable forms of gullibility, the specific type of gullibility which Oliver displays is an example of what Linda Zagzebski calls an 'intellectual vice'. Her other examples of such vices are intellectual pride, negligence, idleness, cowardice, conformity carelessness, rigidity, prejudice, wishful thinking, closed-mindedness, insensitivity to detail, obtuseness, and lack of thoroughness (1996: 152). I'm taking it that an explanation of Oliver's beliefs about 9/11 by reference to an intellectual vice is a non-epistemic explanation. Sceptics about the existence of character traits (e.g. Harman 1999) argue that the positing of such traits is explanatorily redundant and that our behaviour is better explained by situational factors. I'm taking it that Oliver doesn't have his crazy beliefs about 9/11 because of situational factors but because he is the kind of person he is. Being that kind of person is partly a matter of his intellectual character.

many other conspiracy theories and has been the victim of low-grade internet scams. To explain Oliver's belief that P not by reference to rational linkages among his beliefs but by reference to his gullibility or a bias to believe conspiracy theories is to call that belief into question. The implication is that Oliver is wrong to believe that P, and not just because P is false.

What examples like OLIVER bring out is the complexity of the notion of 'believing what you ought rationally to believe'. I will come back to this point in later chapters. Another interesting feature of OLIVER is this: we can explain Oliver's belief that P by reference to his believing Q, or by reference to non-epistemic factors such as bias or gullibility. It's hard not to think that such non-epistemic explanations of Oliver belief that P are somehow deeper, but they are also explanations which Oliver himself can't know or accept. One person who can't think 'Oliver believes that P because he is gullible' is Oliver.[16] This brings us to the last aspect of the Disparity, self-ignorance. In particular, it points to the need to distinguish two kinds of self-ignorance in relation to one's attitudes corresponding to two kinds of self-knowledge. On the one hand, there is knowing, or failing, to know *what* you believe, want, etc. The issue here is *knowing what*. On the other hand, there is knowing or failing to know why your attitude is as it is. The issue here is not knowing what but *knowing why*. Oliver knows that he believes that P but there is an important sense in which he does not know why he believes that P. He thinks he knows why he believes that P but his own conception of why he has this belief fails to get to the heart of the matter.

Not knowing why is a pervasive form of self-ignorance among humans.[17] What about not knowing what in relation to our own propositional attitudes? There is the straightforward case of not knowing whether you believe that P simply because you haven't made up your mind about P. What about the possibility of believing that P but not realizing that you believe that P? If you are *homo philosophicus* then there is no such possibility, any more than there is a possibility of your belief that you believe that P being mistaken. However, it's not obvious that these possibilities are ruled out for *homo sapiens*. We may have attitudes we find it hard or embarrassing to acknowledge, and attributions of attitudes to ourselves aren't immune to error. These claims are controversial, and

---

[16] The point here is that our believing some proposition depends on our not being committed to a certain type of explanation of why we believe that proposition. Ward Jones calls this the First-Person Constraint on Doxastic Explanation and defends this constraint on the basis that 'seeing oneself as having a belief is inconsistent with offering a non-epistemic explanation of that belief' (2002: 233).

[17] There is much more on the pervasiveness of this form of self-ignorance in Nisbett and Wilson 1977.

I'll have more to say about them in Chapter 14, when I get around to talking about self-ignorance in more detail.

It's much less controversial that we may lack what I referred to in the last chapter as 'substantial' self-knowledge. There is no guarantee that you are a good judge of your abilities or character or emotions, and neither error nor ignorance is ruled out in such matters. Indeed, it might seem that the possibility of error and ignorance is part of what makes substantial self-knowledge substantial, in which case there is a question about the distinction between substantial and trivial self-knowledge. For if you can be wrong about what you believe then shouldn't we refrain from describing knowledge of your own beliefs as 'trivial'? In that case, what does the distinction between trivial and substantial self-knowledge come to? These are questions for the next chapter.

As far as the present chapter is concerned, here is a summary of where we have got to: when we reflect on the way we think, form attitudes, and respond to evidence that discredits our attitudes it's hard not to conclude that there is a Disparity between *homo sapiens* and *homo philosophicus*, and that the Disparity is extensive. The things we do that differentiate us from *homo philosophicus* are not all forms of epistemic malpractice, though several of them are. The disparities I have identified in this chapter are respects in which we are human—all too human, as Nietzsche might have said. I've suggested that the Disparity is a potential problem for TM so it's no surprise that rationalist and other philosophers who rely heavily on TM in their accounts of self-knowledge try to play down the Disparity. They argue that humans can't be as different from *homo philosophicus* as I've been suggesting. I will assess this damage limitation exercise on behalf on TM in Chapter 6, but our interim conclusion has to be that philosophical accounts of self-knowledge which implicitly regard *homo sapiens* as *homo philosophicus* are just not on.

3

Substantial Self-Knowledge

I'm no barefoot philosopher. I'm wearing a pair of socks, and know and believe that I'm wearing socks. If you ask me whether I believe I am wearing socks I hear you as asking me whether I am wearing socks. And that's a question I have no difficulty answering. It takes special effort, or a peculiar frame of mind, to hear your question as concerned with my state of mind, with what I believe. Perhaps I will hear your question that way if you follow up with 'Is that what you really believe?' Unless there is something quite odd about the context of our dialogue I will probably be puzzled by your asking me this but the answer is still obvious: yes, I believe I am wearing socks. It's plausible that I answer the question 'Do you believe you are wearing socks?' by answering the question 'Are you wearing socks?', but that might be because I hear the first of these questions as a funny way of asking the second question.

Only a philosopher would think of calling my knowledge that I believe I am wearing a pair of socks 'self-knowledge'; it's certainly far removed from anything that the ancients or, for that matter, ordinary humans would recognize as self-knowledge.[1] Still, if I have the belief that I am wearing socks, and I know that I have that belief, then it's undeniable that I thereby know something about my state of mind vis-à-vis my state of dress. If we want to call this 'self-knowledge' that is fine, but it seems a pretty boring and trivial example of self-knowledge when compared with what I referred to in Chapter 1 as substantial self-knowledge.[2] If I know that I have a talent for dealing with awkward colleagues or that I'm prone to prolonged bouts of self-pity then I have what looks like substantial self-

---

[1] As Charles Griswold points out, Socrates wanted to connect self-knowledge with 'leading a morally right life' (1986: 3). Knowing that I believe I'm wearing socks doesn't have a whole lot to do with that. There is much more to be said about self-knowledge in ancient philosophy, but only by someone who knows more about it than I do.

[2] Philosophical discussions of self-knowledge tend not to make much of the distinction between boring and interesting self-knowledge but Schwitzgebel 2012 is a notable exception. There is more on Schwitzgebel coming up.

knowledge, self-knowledge worth having, but why should anyone care why or how I know that I believe I am wearing socks?

No doubt philosophers have their reasons for concentrating on trivial self-knowledge—I will discuss these reasons in the next chapter—but a prior issue is whether there is anything to the distinction between trivial and substantive self-knowledge. One philosopher who says something about this is Eric Schwitzgebel. In his paper 'Self-Ignorance' he mentions what he calls 'fairly trivial attitudes' such as a preference for vanilla ice cream over chocolate or one's general belief that it does not rain much in California in April (2012: 191). The Delphic oracle's injunction to 'know thyself' was presumably not concerned with knowledge of such attitudes: 'to the extent the injunction to know oneself pertains to self-knowledge of attitudes, it must be attitudes like your central values and your general background assumptions about the world and about other people' (2012: 191). About such matters, Schwitzgebel argues, our self-knowledge is rather poor.

Schwitzgebel's discussion raises two obvious questions:

1. What would count as substantial, as distinct from trivial, self-knowledge?
2. What makes a given piece of self-knowledge substantial?

Here are some examples of substantial self-knowledge:

- Knowing that you are generous (knowledge of one's character).
- Knowing that you are not a racist (knowledge of one's values).
- Knowing that you can speak Spanish (knowledge of one's abilities).
- Knowing that you are a good administrator (knowledge of one's aptitudes).
- Knowing why you believe a controlled demolition brought down the World Trade Center on 9/11 (knowledge of one's attitudes in the 'knowing why' rather than in the 'knowing what' sense).
- Knowing that you are in love (knowledge of one's emotions).
- Knowing that a change of career would make you happy (knowledge of what makes one happy).

The distinction between 'substantial' and 'trivial' self-knowledge is a matter of degree rather than hard and fast, and the self-knowledge in some of these examples is more 'substantial' than in others. Still, if there is a substantial/trivial distinction then it seems a reasonable supposition that the items I have listed are at the more 'substantial' end of the spectrum.

To understand why this might be, we need to turn to the second of my two questions. There are many different characteristics of substantial self-knowledge. To get the ball rolling I will list ten. Although I will occasionally refer to these characteristics as 'conditions' of substantial self-knowledge, the way to think about them is not as constituting a set of strict necessary and sufficient conditions but rather as giving a rough indication of the sorts of consideration that are relevant to determining whether a particular kind of self-knowledge is substantial. The point of saying that knowledge of, say, your own character is substantial self-knowledge is to indicate that it has at least some of the characteristics I have in mind. The more of these characteristics it has the more substantial it is.

Here is my list:

(i) The Fallibility Condition: with substantial self-knowledge there is always the possibility of error. It's not just a theoretical possibility that you are mistaken about, say, whether you are generous but an actual, real-life possibility. There isn't even a presumption that you aren't mistaken about such things because it might be a psychological fact about us humans that we are generally prone to thinking well of ourselves even if an objective view of the evidence would support a harsher assessment. It's comforting to think that you are a generous person even though your close friends can hardly fail to have noticed your tendency to make yourself scarce when it's your turn to buy the next round of drinks.

(ii) The Obstacle Condition: the possibility of error in such cases is a reflection of the fact that for humans there are familiar and reasonably well-understood obstacles to the acquisition of substantial self-knowledge. Such obstacles include repression, self-deception, bias, and embarrassment. Some of us find it hard to be honest with ourselves about our own limitations and that can make it hard to acquire some types of substantial self-knowledge.

(iii) The Self-Conception Condition: the existence of such obstacles to substantial self-knowledge is related to the fact that, as Schwitzgebel puts it, this kind of knowledge often 'tangles with' a person's self-conception (Schwitzgebel 2012: 191). To know that you have a particular character you have to believe you have that character, and it might be hard for you to believe that if your having that character is at odds with your self-conception.

(iv) The Challenge Condition: substantial self-knowledge can be challenged even in normal circumstances. For example, if you assert that you have an aptitude for dealing with difficult colleagues or that a change of career would make you happy there is room for the question, 'Why do you think that?', or for the retort 'You must be joking'. No doubt you have your reasons for thinking you have an aptitude for dealing with difficult colleagues, but your reasons are not immune to criticism and correction.

(v) The Corrigibility Condition: substantial self-knowledge is corrigible, and its corrigibility is related to the fact that we are not necessarily authoritative about the matters to which such knowledge relates. You may not be in the best position to know about such matters and others might know better; your spouse may well have a much deeper insight into your character than you do.

(vi) The Non-Transparency Condition: substantial self-knowledge can't be got by employing the Transparency Method (TM). You can't determine whether you are kind by determining whether you ought rationally to be kind, just as you can't determine whether you are really happy with your new apartment by determining whether you ought rationally to be really happy with it. Maybe you ought to be really happy with it but aren't.

(vii) The Evidence Condition: substantial self-knowledge is based on evidence. Many different kinds of evidence bear on substantial self-knowledge. If the question is whether you are in love with X, the evidence might include how you behave in the presence of X, how you feel in their presence (does your heart go pitter patter?) and what people who know you tell you about your state of mind. If the question is whether you are a racist the evidence will include how you behave towards, and think about, people who belong to racial groups different from your own.

(viii) The Cognitive Effort Condition: acquiring substantial self-knowledge requires a degree of cognitive effort. For example, you don't 'just know' your own character or aptitudes; you have to work it out by reflecting on the behavioural evidence and on what other people tell you about you. The level of effort may be different in different cases but substantial self-knowledge can't literally be effortless. If it were it would scarcely be 'substantial'.

(ix) The Indirectness Condition: in the terminology of Chapter 1, substantial self-knowledge is neither psychologically immediate nor epistemically immediate. It isn't psychologically immediate because, as the Cognitive Effort Condition suggests, it requires reasoning or inference. It isn't epistemically immediate because it depends on your having justification for believing other, supporting propositions. For example, you can't know that you are generous if you aren't justified in believing a range of supporting propositions about your actions. To know that you are generous it isn't enough that you act generously; you also need to believe, and be justified in believing, that this is how you act.

(x) The Value Condition: substantial self-knowledge *matters* in a practical or even a moral sense. If you are planning a trip to Spain it helps to know whether you can speak Spanish. As King Lear discovered, not knowing what will make you happy can result in your making bad choices, and we think of some forms of self-ignorance not just as cognitive but also as moral defects. Being unkind is bad in itself but made morally worse if it is combined with the belief that one is kind.

With this list in mind, it's easy to see why knowing you have a preference for vanilla over chocolate ice cream doesn't look like a substantial piece of self-knowledge. It's not that there is no possibility of being mistaken about whether you prefer vanilla but it's a lot harder to imagine circumstances in which you get this wrong than circumstances in which you have mistaken beliefs about your own character or aptitudes. If it is regarded as bad form to prefer vanilla in your social group then that might make it harder for you to believe, and so to know, that you prefer vanilla but there aren't usually obstacles to knowing that you prefer vanilla. Your preference for a particular flavour of ice cream is unlikely to be a significant part of your self-conception, and it would be fairly unusual for others to challenge your assertion that you prefer vanilla. It would be presumed that you know best about such matters. It's true that you cannot come to know that you prefer vanilla by asking whether you ought rationally to prefer vanilla but that doesn't make knowing that you have a preference for vanilla a piece of substantial self-knowledge. All it does is to bring out the limitations of TM even with respect to non-substantial self-knowledge. Your knowledge that you prefer vanilla is usually effortless, relatively direct, and not based on behavioural evidence or what other people tell you. As for the value of knowing your flavour preferences, not knowing which flavour you prefer might be a practical problem for you when ordering dessert but it's hardly a moral defect.

Turning now to substantial self-knowledge, how do the various examples given above fare in relation to the ten characteristics? It would be tedious to go through each of the examples in relation to each of the ten characteristics but there are a few points that are worth noting. With regard to knowledge of one's character, one view is that there is no such thing as character, understood as something that explains one's choices and behaviour.[3] If there is no such thing as character then there is of course no such thing as knowing one's character but that still doesn't preclude one from having beliefs about one's character and knowing what one's beliefs are. However, knowing that one believes that one is generous is a very different thing from knowing that one is generous. This isn't really the place to get into a debate about the pros and cons of scepticism about character but the

---

[3] Harman 1999 and Doris 2002 are notable philosophical defences of scepticism about character.

existence of this form of scepticism can't be ignored by anyone who wants to make the case that knowledge of one's own character is an example of substantial self-knowledge. I will have more to say about this in Chapter 13.

The next question concerns the suggestion that knowledge of one's values is a form of substantial self-knowledge. Can this be right? Here is one reason why one might think not: to have knowledge of your values is to have knowledge of your beliefs and desires, in what I've called the 'knowing what' sense. But knowing what you believe or want isn't substantial self-knowledge, so how can knowledge of your values be substantive self-knowledge? There are two answers to this question: firstly, knowledge of your beliefs, desires, and other attitudes is necessary but not sufficient for knowledge of your values. Take the case of knowing that you are not a racist. Not being a racist isn't just a matter of believing that all races are equal or having the appropriate desires. It also has to do with how you act, that is, with whether you treat people differently according to race. So knowing that you aren't a racist is also partly a matter of knowing how you act, of knowing whether you put your money where your mouth is. But knowledge of how you treat people of different races can only be substantial, and that is why knowing that you are not a racist qualifies as substantial self-knowledge.

This is fine as far as it goes, but there is one respect in which it is too simple. The story so far suggests knowledge of your values has two components: knowledge of what you believe and desire and knowledge of how you act. There is the further implication that these two components are distinct and that only knowledge of the second, behavioural, component is substantial. However, knowing that you genuinely believe that all races are equal also has some of the characteristics of substantial self-knowledge. Whether you genuinely believe that all races are equal doesn't just depend on whether you *say* that all races are equal but also on your unguarded behaviour, implicit assumptions, and spontaneous emotional reactions. You may confidently ascribe to yourself the belief that you are not a racist but your self-ascription is neither infallible nor incorrigible. It can be challenged if there is evidence that it is at odds with your behaviour, assumptions, and spontaneous emotional reactions, and you only count as knowing that you believe in racial equality if you have taken these factors into account. Taking these factors into account requires cognitive effort and means that any resulting self-knowledge is based on evidence. In all of these respects, knowing that you believe that all races are equal is very different from knowing that you believe you are wearing socks; the latter might be trivial self-knowledge but knowing that you believe that all races are equal is anything but trivial. What this shows is that there is no rule that knowledge of your own beliefs in the 'knowing what you believe' sense is always trivial; it all depends on the content of the belief, just as knowing what you want can be trivial or substantial depending on the content of your desire; knowing that you want vanilla rather than chocolate ice cream is no big deal from an epistemological standpoint but figuring out whether, say, you want another child is unlikely to be quite as straightforward.

One response to such supposedly 'hard' cases of knowing what you want or believe might be to argue that they confuse two quite different things. What is hard in these cases is the *forming* of the belief or desire, not *knowing* your formed belief or desire; in other words, it is making your mind up that requires cognitive effort, not knowing your own mind once it is made up. If you already have children and the question arises whether you want another child you may well find it hard to decide what you want. But once you have decided that you do want another child, knowing that this is what you have decided requires no extra cognitive effort. The same goes for knowing what you believe. The really hard question in some cases is whether *to* believe that P, and the difficulty of figuring out whether to believe that P should not be confused with the difficulty of establishing whether you believe that P *given* that this is what you believe.

Here is how to respond to this line of thinking: the question whether to believe that P is the question whether, given the evidence available to you, you ought rationally to believe that P. Take the case in which this is an easy question for you to answer; for example, you ought to believe that all races are equal and you know that this is what you ought to believe. In this sense, you have no difficulty working out whether *to* believe that all races are equal. However, the question remains whether you *do* believe that all races are equal, that is, whether your recognition that you ought rationally to believe that all races are equal has the appropriate impact on your thinking and behaviour. You don't get the answer to *this* question for free, but not because you find it a hard question whether to believe that all races are equal; you don't find this a hard question, so there is no risk of confusing the difficulty of answering one question with the difficulty of answering another. In other cases, deciding what to want or believe might be much harder but the challenge of *knowing* your mind is still additional to the challenge of *making up* your mind. I'll come back to this point later in this book, because it has direct bearing on a certain way of understanding TM.

The notion that knowledge of your abilities is substantial self-knowledge also raises some interesting questions. A character in a P. G. Wodehouse novel is asked whether she can speak Spanish and replies 'I don't know: I've never tried'.[4] The point here is that in order to know that you can't speak Spanish you don't need to have tried and failed to speak Spanish. You know without trying that you

---

[4] The novel is *Ring for Jeeves*. There is more about this example in Dummett 1993.

can't speak Spanish (assuming you can't), and this might lead to the idea that knowledge of your abilities is insubstantial at least to the extent that it isn't based on evidence. You 'just know' that you can't speak Spanish, or that you can speak English, and it is far from obvious what might stand in the way of your knowing these things. So isn't there a case for removing knowledge of one's abilities from the list of 'substantial' self-knowledge?

It certainly wouldn't be a disaster if this is how things turn out as there is no shortage of other examples of substantial self-knowledge. Still, it's important not to exaggerate the extent to which you 'just know' that you can't speak Spanish. To know that you can't speak Spanish you don't need to have tried and failed to speak Spanish but what if you know that you can't speak Spanish on the basis that you have never learned Spanish or been brought up to speak it? If you know that you have never learned Spanish that is evidence that you don't speak Spanish, and it's not incoherent to suppose that you know that you don't speak Spanish at least in part on the basis of that evidence. You can certainly be wrong about whether you speak Spanish *well*, and even wrong about whether you can speak Spanish at all. Perhaps you are fluent in a language which you take to be Spanish but which is actually Portuguese. In the case of other abilities, the possibility of error is even more straightforward. You think you can swim because you had swimming lessons some years ago but when you jump into the water you soon discover that you can no longer swim. Or you think you can't swim, perhaps because you have never been taught to swim, and yet when thrown into the deep end you find yourself swimming. In these, and in other respects, knowledge of your own abilities (or lack of them) has a lot in common with other, more straightforward examples of substantial self-knowledge, even if it has one or two epistemological peculiarities which are certainly worth noting.

The remaining examples of substantial self-knowledge are relatively straightforward, in that they all display a significant proportion of what I have identified as the characteristics of substantial self-knowledge. With respect to each example of substantial self-knowledge we can ask the same three basic questions that can be asked about self-knowledge generally:

- The Sources Question—what is its source?
- The Obstacles Question—what are the obstacles, if any, to our acquiring or having it?
- The Value Question—what is its value?

There clearly isn't a single answer to the Sources Question that works for all substantial self-knowledge. How one knows one's character might be different from how one knows one's abilities, and there are multiple pathways even to knowledge of any one of these things. Still, it's striking how much we rely on testimony, inference, and reflection in acquiring different kinds of substantial self-knowledge. You gain a much better understanding of your character, aptitudes, and values by talking to people who know you well and learning how they perceive you. Inference plays a part because of the role of evidence in substantial self-knowledge. You infer from your judgement that all races are equal that you believe that all races are equal, and you infer that you are a poor swimmer from the fact that you have never been taught to swim. Your inferences in these cases are inferences from the evidence available to you, and the idea that your self-knowledge in these cases is inferential goes with the idea that it requires effort to acquire it. As for reflection, the idea here is that in order to know your own values or what will make you happy you usually need to think about it. You don't 'just know', and what I'm calling 'reflection' is the kind of slow thinking that is normally required for substantial self-knowledge.

Just as there are different pathways to substantial self-knowledge so there are different obstacles to substantial self-knowledge; there isn't a single answer to the Obstacles Question. For example, the possibility of self-deception or repression might be more of a threat to some kinds of substantial self-knowledge than to others; thus, with respect to any given example of substantial self-knowledge there is scope for an investigation of what might prevent us from having it. Of course, such an investigation is only worth the effort on the assumption that the self-knowledge in question is worth having and therefore that the obstacles to our having it are worth overcoming. This brings us to the Value Question. I have assumed that substantial self-knowledge is valuable and that its value is either moral or practical or both. There are variations in how different kinds of substantial self-knowledge matter to us, and in how much they matter to us, but it is difficult to conceive of substantial self-knowledge being totally worthless. Perhaps the hardest case is knowing why you have a particular belief or desire. What is the value of that? The thought here is that it matters to us to have the attitudes we have for the right reasons; we don't want to be like Oliver, the conspiracy theorist who believes a particular theory about what happened on 9/11 for all the wrong reasons. What we value is precisely the kind of self-insight that Oliver lacks, and the hard question is not whether it's *important* for us to have this kind of insight into our own attitudes but whether it is *possible* for humans to have this kind of insight. I'll come back to this question Chapter 14.

This, then, is where we have got to: starting with an intuitive distinction between so-called trivial and substantial self-knowledge I've tried to explain the basis of this distinction and make the case that substantial self-knowledge includes knowledge of things that actually matters to ordinary humans. There is much more to be said about *why* it is important to know one's own character, values, abilities, and fundamental attitudes but easy to see *that* it matters. Given the wide range and intrinsic importance of substantial self-knowledge one might have thought that it would be the focus of the philosophy of self-knowledge. In fact, nothing could be further from the truth. Instead, the recent philosophy of self-knowledge has concentrated on explaining such things as knowing that you are in pain or knowing that you believe that it is raining. This is a little strange, and it's worth asking why the focus has been on trivial self-knowledge. This is next question I want to address.

4

Self-Knowledge for Philosophers

In her entry on self-knowledge for the *Stanford Encyclopedia of Philosophy*, Brie Gertler says this:

In philosophy, "self-knowledge" commonly refers to knowledge of one's particular mental states, including one's beliefs, desires and sensations. It is also sometimes used to refer to knowledge about a persisting self—its ontological nature, identity conditions, or character traits. At least since Descartes, most philosophers have believed that self-knowledge is importantly different from knowledge of the world external to oneself, including others' thoughts. (Gertler 2008)

On this account, the philosophical understanding of self-knowledge comes over as extremely limited. Indeed, in some ways it's even more limited than Gertler suggests. I haven't so far said anything about the philosophical interest in the nature of the self but this tends to be pursued as an issue in metaphysics rather than as a question about self-knowledge. Gertler also mentions knowledge of one's character traits, which is an example of what I have been calling substantial self-knowledge, but in reality there is little interest in this topic when compared with the huge philosophical interest in what I'm going to call *particular self-knowledge*, that is, knowledge of our 'particular mental states'. This, as Gertler's summary suggests, is where most of the action has been, at least as far as recent analytic philosophy of self-knowledge has been concerned.

Even when it comes to knowledge of particular self-knowledge, it's worth noting three respects in which the interest at least of analytic philosophers has been limited in scope:

(a) In the context of explaining knowledge of our own propositional attitudes the focus has tended to be on a fairly narrow range of propositional attitudes, with a particularly strong emphasis on knowledge of our beliefs and desires. The question 'How does one know one's own beliefs?' has been extensively discussed but not the question 'How does one know one's own hopes?'

(b) Even when it comes to knowledge of our own beliefs, the chosen examples have been remarkably bland. At least until recently, the attention lavished on explaining a person's knowledge that he believes it is raining has far exceeded the attention paid to explaining whether and how he knows that he truly believes that men and women are equal or that God exists. All the emphasis has been on explaining self-knowledge of relatively trivial attitudes.

(c) Knowledge of one's particular beliefs and desires could mean knowledge of *what* one believes or wants, or knowledge of *why* one believes what one believes or wants what one wants. For the most part, philosophers of self-knowledge have tried to explain self-knowledge of attitudes in the 'what' rather than in the 'why' sense.

Presumably it's not a coincidence that so much of the philosophy of self-knowledge has, in all these different ways, been so limited in scope. A natural question, therefore, is: why has the focus been on trivial rather than substantial self-knowledge? Is this just an historical accident or is there a deeper explanation of this phenomenon?

Usually when philosophers spend a lot of time trying to explain a particular kind of knowledge, it's either because they think that knowledge of that kind is especially important or valuable or because they think it is distinctive in a way that is puzzling or just interesting. So we now have two questions: is particular self-knowledge especially important or valuable, and is it distinctive in a way that makes it puzzling or interesting? Gertler implies that it is the distinctiveness of particular self-knowledge, the fact that it is different from knowledge of the world external to oneself, which explains why so many philosophers have been so interested in it. That might be right, but first I want to look at the suggestion that it is the importance of particular self-knowledge, including supposedly 'trivial' self-knowledge, which explains what the fuss is all about.

Why would anybody think that it is important, or that it matters, whether you know what you believe or desire? In particular, why would anybody suppose that if you believe it is raining it is important for you to know that you believe it is raining? If you are about to go for a walk it's obviously going to be useful for you to know that it is raining but how is it useful to know, in addition, that you believe it is raining? Where does knowing that you believe it is raining get you? One historically important answer to this question is given by so-called foundationalists in epistemology. Their idea is that our beliefs have a pyramid structure, with basic beliefs forming the foundation, and all other justified beliefs being supported by reasoning that traces back ultimately to basic beliefs.[1] What makes basic beliefs basic is, on one reading, the fact that they are infallible. On a different reading, it is the fact that they are non-inferentially justified. Either way, old-fashioned foundationalism holds that basic beliefs are beliefs about our particular mental states, and that our beliefs about our particular mental states are justified in a way that makes it the case that we *know* our particular mental states. On this account, knowledge of our particular mental states turns out to be foundational with respect to the rest of our knowledge, and that is why particular self-knowledge, including knowledge of relatively trivial attitudes, is important.

I agree that talking about foundationalism might help to explain why particular self-knowledge has in the past been seen as important but it's less clear that it casts any light on why this kind of self-knowledge continues to be seen as important. There are two points here. Historically, the particular self-knowledge which interested foundationalists was knowledge of our own sensations. They weren't that interested in the foundational status of knowledge of our own beliefs and desires, and it's not even clear whether they would have regarded this form of self-knowledge as foundational. A second and more obvious point is that few philosophers nowadays would be happy to be described as foundationalists. To the extent that epistemologists discuss the topic at all they tend to think that foundationalism is false but that hasn't led to any change in focus as far as the philosophy of self-knowledge is concerned. This might be a reflection of philosophers of self-knowledge failing to see that knowledge of one's particular mental states is only important in the context of foundationalism, but there is another possibility: the other possibility is that foundationalism is a red herring and that there are independent reasons for thinking that particular self-knowledge, especially knowledge of our own propositional attitudes, is important.

For an influential non-foundationalist account of the importance of particular self-knowledge we need look no further than Tyler Burge's account of critical reasoning. As we have seen, critical reasoning is guided by an appreciation, use, and assessment of reasons and reasoning as such. To be a critical reasoner 'one must be able to, and sometimes actually, use one's knowledge of reasons to make, criticize, change, confirm *commitments* regarding propositions—to engage explicitly in reason-induced changes of mind' (1998: 248). On this conception, critical reasoning requires thinking about one's thoughts; you can't critically evaluate your own thoughts without thinking about your thoughts. In fact, you don't just need to be able to *think* about your thoughts in order to engage in critical reasoning. You also need to *know* you thoughts. As Burge puts it, for critical

---

[1] See, for example, Pollock and Cruz 1999: 29.

reasoning to be possible one's thinking about one's own thoughts must be 'normally knowledgeable' (1998: 248); to check, weigh, criticize, and confirm one's reasons 'one must know what one's reasons, thoughts, and reasoning are' (1998: 248). What is more, this knowledge 'must take a distinctive, non-observational form' (1998: 248); the problem with merely observational knowledge of one's thoughts is that it would 'entail a dissociation between cognitive review and the thoughts reviewed that is incompatible with norms of epistemic reasonability' (1996: 256).

What Burge is offering is, in effect, a 'transcendental argument' for the importance of self-knowledge.[2] In brief, the argument is: critical reasoning occurs among us, particular self-knowledge is necessary for critical reasoning, so we have particular self-knowledge. The self-knowledge that is necessary for critical reasoning includes so-called trivial self-knowledge. Even the belief that you are wearing socks is open to criticism, confirmation, and reason-induced change. For this to be possible you need to know that you believe you are wearing socks, and that is why this kind of self-knowledge matters. From the standpoint of critical reasoning what matters is not so much the content of your beliefs but your ability to assess them, so there is no reason to be dismissive of attempts to explain trivial self-knowledge; even trivial self-knowledge matters.

It's one thing to say that critical reasoning occurs among us and another to say that it is prevalent among humans or central to our cognitive lives. I argued in Chapter 2 that we are often too lazy, distracted, or complacent to do much critical reasoning and that much of our reasoning takes the form of non-critical, or not very critical, 'fast thinking'. If full-fledged critical reasoning plays a relatively small part in the cognitive lives of most humans then showing that a particular type of self-knowledge is indispensable for critical reasoning is not the same as showing that it is important for humans. More worryingly, it's not even clear that self-knowledge *is* necessary for critical reasoning. It's certainly necessary, by stipulation, for what Burge calls 'critical reasoning' but it's not necessary for any reasoning that involves the assessment of relations of support, consequence, and evidence among one's beliefs and other attitudes. Here is an example from Peacocke which makes the point:

Suppose you come home, and see that no car is parked in the driveway. You infer that your spouse is not home yet... Later, you may suddenly remember that your spouse mentioned in the morning that the brakes of the car were faulty, and wonder whether she may have taken the car for repair. At this point, you suspend your original belief that she is not home yet. For you come to realize that the absence of the car is not necessarily good

---

[2] I talk about transcendental arguments in chapter 2 of Cassam 2007.

evidence that she is not home. If the car is being repaired, she would have returned by public transport. Then finally you may reach the belief that she is home after all, given your next thought that she would not have taken any risks with faulty brakes. (1998: 276)

As Peacocke points out, nothing in this little fragment of thought requires the self-ascription of belief. The thoughts that it involves all seem to be thoughts about the world, not about the thinker's thoughts. Peacocke labels this kind of thinking *second-tier thought* since 'it involves thought about relations of support, evidence or consequence between contents, as opposed to first-tier thought, which is thought about the world where the thought does not involve any consideration of such relations between contents' (1998: 277). Although second-tier thought is 'critical' it doesn't require self-knowledge. Self-knowledge is only necessary for a specific form of critical reasoning, and this is another reason for not going along with the idea that being necessary for critical reasoning in Burge's sense is what makes knowledge of one's particular attitudes valuable or important.

Perhaps, in the light of this discussion, the point to press isn't that particular self-knowledge is *necessary* but that it is *unavoidable*. For example, it might be claimed that you can't be in pain without knowing that you are in pain, and that you can't believe you are wearing socks without knowing that you believe you are wearing socks. On this account, our sensations, beliefs, and other attitudes are *self-intimating*, which is another way of saying that we can't avoid knowing about them. The 'self-intimation thesis' obviously needs to be qualified in various ways. For a start, being in pain can only bring with it the knowledge that you are in pain if you have the concept of pain, and believing that you are wearing socks can only bring with it knowledge that you believe you are wearing socks if you have the concept of belief. Another way the self-intimation thesis might need to be qualified is to build in the concession that when you are in a particular mental state you only need to be *in a position* to know that you are in that state; you can be in a position to know something without actually knowing it. Finally, it might be added that our own attitudes are only necessarily self-intimating insofar as we are rational. If you believe that you are wearing socks, are rational, and you have the appropriate concepts then you can't avoid knowing, or at least being in a position to know, that you believe that you are wearing socks.

Even with these qualifications, the self-intimation thesis is hard to swallow. It's not just false but obviously false for attitudes other than belief. To use an example of Timothy Williamson's, I believe I don't hope for a particular result to a match but 'my disappointment at one outcome reveals my hope for another' (2000: 24). I can hope that P without being in a position to know that I hope that P, and I can want that P without being in a position to know that I want that P; my desire might be so repressed as to be inaccessible, but it still motivates me to act so as to satisfy it. Among the attitudes, belief is the most promising candidate for being self-intimating, but still not a good candidate. As Williamson remarks, 'the difference between believing P and merely fancying P depends in part on one's dispositions to practical reasoning and action manifested only in counterfactual circumstances, and one is not always in a position to know what those disposi-tions are' (2000: 24). Of course, it's also true that if our particular mental states were necessarily self-intimating, that *still* would not explain why it's important to have knowledge of them; why couldn't self-knowledge be both unavoidable and worthless?

This is as far as I want to go with the idea that knowledge of one's particular mental states deserves the philosophical attention it has received because it is an especially important or valuable form of knowledge. I want to move on to the more promising suggestion that it is the epistemological distinctiveness of par-ticular self-knowledge, including 'trivial' self-knowledge, which explains and justifies all the attention. One traditional idea, which is often attributed to Descartes, is that particular self-knowledge is infallible and incorrigible. Let's start with infallibility. Suppose that you believe that you believe that P. The belief that P is your first-order belief, and your belief that you believe that P is your second-order belief. The infallibility thesis says that your second-order belief can't be mistaken if formed on the basis of introspection. Applied to desires the infallibility thesis says that your introspectively based beliefs about your desires can't be mistaken. Incorrigibility is a different matter. To say that introspectively based beliefs about your own attitudes are incorrigible is to say that they can't be corrected, where what this means is that no one else can have good grounds for correcting them. Incorrigibility is not the same as infallibility; in theory, it could be the case that your beliefs about your own beliefs and desires are not immune to error but that no other person could have grounds for correcting them.

If particular self-knowledge is infallible and incorrigible then this would distinguish it from knowledge of the external world, knowledge of other minds, and also from substantial self-knowledge. Your belief that there is a tomato in your refrigerator can be mistaken and another person can have grounds for correcting it. The same goes for your belief that *I* think that there is a tomato in your refrigerator, and for your belief that you are generous. Particular self-knowledge would stand out as highly distinctive, and it would be entirely understandable that philosophers of self-knowledge should make it their business to explain how particular self-knowledge is possible given its distinctiveness. The sense in which it is distinctive is that it is epistemically privileged, and the epistemic privileges of particular self-knowledge are what need explaining.

Substantial self-knowledge looks less interesting, and less in need of philosophical attention, because it isn't epistemically privileged; there just isn't a deep asymmetry between your knowledge that you are generous and your knowledge that another person is generous, as there is between your knowledge that you believe that P and your knowledge that someone else believes that P.

To argue in this way is to allow the agenda for the philosophy of self-knowledge to be set by quite narrow epistemological concerns. Self-knowledge for philosophers becomes self-knowledge that is epistemically privileged rather than the substantial but far from infallible or incorrigible self-knowledge that matters to most reflective humans. One might wonder about the wisdom of allowing the peculiar epistemology of particular self-knowledge to play such a major role in shaping the philosophy of self-knowledge but a prior question is whether it is even true that particular self-knowledge is infallible or incorrigible. Although I have already dismissed the self-intimation thesis you could in principle regard particular self-knowledge as infallible and incorrigible even if you don't think that it is knowledge of mental states that are self-intimating. However, as many philosophers have pointed out, there isn't much to be said for the notion that knowledge of your own beliefs and desires is infallible and incorrigible. It is implausible, for example, that your belief that you want another child can't be mistaken or that others might not have grounds for correcting the assertion that you want another child ('No you don't, you are deceiving yourself if that's what you think you want'). Beliefs are no different; there is no guarantee, as we saw in the last chapter, that your beliefs about what you believe can't be mistaken; you believe that you believe in racial equality but there might be strong independent evidence that your second-order belief is mistaken.

One reaction to such examples might be to suggest that while there are some attitudes with respect to which your self-knowledge isn't infallible or incorrigible there are other cases in which you really can't be wrong or corrected. Maybe you can be wrong about whether you want another child but not about whether you want vanilla rather than chocolate ice cream for dessert. This would explain the concentration on bland or trivial particular self-knowledge: trivial self-knowledge is interesting because it is most likely to be epistemically privileged in ways that make it distinctive. However, the problem with this is that there is no immunity to error even when it comes to self-ascriptions of trivial attitudes. You think you want vanilla but when the waiter brings it you realize that you wanted chocolate. You were wrong about what you wanted, and indeed your spouse might have had good grounds for correcting your assertion that you wanted vanilla. Of course, it's possible that you *did* really want vanilla but no longer want it when it arrives but it's hard to know whether you were wrong about your initial desire or whether you have simply changed your mind. Not only are you sometimes wrong about what you want or believe, you also find it hard on occasion to work out whether or not you have changed your mind about what you want or believe.[3]

A common philosophical reaction to this kind of argument is to accept that infallibility and incorrigibility are too strong but to hold on to the idea that particular self-knowledge is distinctive in other ways. The usual suggestion is that while particular self-knowledge might not be infallible or incorrigible it is *authoritative*. When you self-attribute beliefs, desires, and other attitudes, you are authoritative in at least two senses: there is a presumption that your self-attribution is not mistaken, and your self-attribution isn't normally open to challenge by others.[4] In addition, your particular self-knowledge is *direct* or *immediate* in two related senses: it isn't based on evidence and it isn't inferential. As Paul Boghossian puts it:

In the case of others, I have no choice but to *infer* what they think from observations about what they do or say. In my own case, by contrast, inference is neither required nor relevant. Normally, I know what I think—what I believe, desire, hope or expect—without appeal to supplementary evidence. Even where such evidence is available I do not consult it. I know what I think directly. I do not defend my self-attributions; nor does it normally make sense to ask me to do so. (1998: 150–1)

So here we have a revised account of the privileges of particular self-knowledge, together with the suggestion that these privileges are what distinguish it from knowledge of others. It's still the case on this account that particular self-knowledge is epistemologically distinctive.

There is certainly room for argument about the directness of self-knowledge. It is true that I do not normally know what I want or believe on the basis of behavioural evidence, that is, on the basis of what I do and say, but this leaves it open that other kinds of evidence are implicated in particular self-knowledge. I will explore this possibility later in this book. The intuition that particular self-knowledge is direct is really the intuition that it's psychologically immediate, that I don't normally have to engage in conscious reasoning or inference to know what I want or believe, but this leaves the epistemological issues wide open. Even if I don't consciously infer that I believe that P it could still be true that I'm only justified in believing that I believe that P if I have justification for believing other,

---

[3] This is one illustration of what Peter Carruthers calls the 'opacity of mind'. See Carruthers 2011.

[4] Davidson writes: 'When a speaker avers that he has a belief, hope, desire or intention, there is a presumption that he is not mistaken, a presumption that does not attach to his ascriptions of similar mental states to others' (2001: 3).

supporting propositions. This would make particular self-knowledge epistemologically indirect despite being direct in the psychological sense. Again, this is something I will come back to later, when I get round to giving my own positive account of particular self-knowledge.

For the moment, let's agree that particular self-knowledge is direct and authoritative. As with infallibility and incorrigibility, the least controversial examples of authoritative and direct particular self-knowledge are ones in which one is self-attributing relatively trivial attitudes. The point is not that only trivial self-knowledge is authoritative and direct, but that it's best in the context of philosophical discussion to concentrate on straightforward examples of epistemically privileged self-knowledge. The philosophical challenge is then understood as the challenge of explaining how authoritative and direct self-knowledge is possible in these cases, with the adequacy of particular accounts of self-knowledge being assessed in large part according to whether they are able to account for the authority and directness of trivial self-knowledge. In this context, examples of particular self-knowledge that do not appear to be authoritative or direct are dismissed as departures from the norm that can be safely ignored. This also makes it easy for philosophy to ignore substantial self-knowledge, on the basis that it is neither direct nor authoritative. What is there to say about substantial self-knowledge other than that, like knowledge of other minds and of non-mental reality, it isn't epistemically privileged? For if what makes self-knowledge *philosophically* interesting is the fact that it is epistemically privileged and substantial self-knowledge is not epistemically privileged then the obvious conclusion is that substantial self-knowledge is not philosophically interesting, however important it might be in other ways.

This line of thinking does a good job of accounting for the way the philosophy of self-knowledge has developed. In particular, it accounts for the concentration on relatively bland particular self-knowledge at the expense of any serious engagement with the epistemology of substantial self-knowledge. It explains the self-imposed limitations of many philosophical accounts of self-knowledge, and even to some extent justifies them. Insofar as particular self-knowledge is epistemologically distinctive it is in order for philosophers to try to explain its distinctiveness, regardless of whether knowing what you believe or desire has any intrinsic value or importance. Even if it's difficult to see the value of knowing that you believe that you are wearing socks, it's still a reasonable question how this self-knowledge can be direct and authoritative (assuming that it is).

However, there are also dangers in allowing the whole issue of epistemic privilege to play such a dominant role in setting the agenda for the philosophy of self-knowledge.

1. It can lead to a kind of philosophical myopia. It is one thing to think that particular self-knowledge is philosophically interesting because it (or some of it anyway) is epistemically privileged but it certainly doesn't follow that self-knowledge that is not epistemically privileged isn't philosophically interesting in other ways. Even if the epistemology of substantial self-knowledge is as simple as is often assumed, there are other questions about substantial self-knowledge which the philosophy of self-knowledge should tackle. These include questions about its value, its sources, and obstacles to its acquisition. There is no excuse for ignoring substantial self-knowledge, especially given that this is the self-knowledge which reflective humans who don't do philosophy for a living tend to find interesting. Whereas trivial self-knowledge can seem interesting because it is so *easy* to get, what is striking about substantial self-knowledge is that it can be so *hard* to get. It is the *elusiveness* of substantial self-knowledge, and the resultant threat of self-ignorance, which accounts for some (but not all) of its philosophical interest.

2. It can result in a tendency to lump together different varieties substantial self-knowledge without taking account of important differences between them. As we saw in the last chapter, the epistemology of substantial self-knowledge isn't in fact as straightforward as philosophical legend has it, and there are subtle differences between different forms of substantial self-knowledge which are clearly worthy of philosophical attention.

3. It can promote a highly selective and distorted view of particular self-knowledge. Knowledge of one's particular mental states has been the focus of philosophical attention on the assumption that it is epistemically privileged but not all particular self-knowledge is epistemically privileged. If the issue of epistemic privilege is allowed to dominate the agenda the risk is that the complexities of particular self-knowledge will be ignored or down-played in just the way that the complexities of substantial self-knowledge are often ignored or downplayed.

In relation to the first point, it's interesting to compare two different perspectives on self-knowledge. From one perspective, self-knowledge is all too easy when compared with other kinds of knowledge; indeed from this perspective, it's so *easy* to know your own mind that self-knowledge of this kind barely qualifies as a cognitive achievement at all. This is an *optimistic* view of self-knowledge. From a different perspective self-knowledge is difficult to get. It can be hard to know your own mind, and considerable effort may be required to work out, say, what you really want or your true feelings about your nearest and dearest, and self-ignorance is a real possibility. This is a *pessimistic* view of self-knowledge. You can be both an optimist and a pessimist as long as you are not an optimist and pessimist about the same things. A balanced account of self-knowledge will be one that combines the right degree of optimism with the right degree of pessimism, and this means paying attention to the respects in which self-knowledge, including some particular self-knowledge, is far from easy as well as the respects in which some self-knowledge is epistemically privileged. Focusing on trivial self-knowledge can make one excessively optimistic about self-knowledge and ignore all the respects in which self-knowledge, including a lot of self-knowledge that really matters to us, is far from straightforward. This is the philosophical myopia I have described, and it accounts for the barrenness of a lot of philosophizing about self-knowledge.

I have talked about the philosophical view of self-knowledge but what about the naïve view, if there is such a thing? One way of describing the naïve view would be to say that it oscillates between thinking of self-knowledge as easy and thinking of it as hard. A different way of describing it would be to say that it strikes an appropriate balance between optimism and pessimism. On the one hand, there is the intuition that only you can really know what you think and feel, whereas other people can only conjecture. Even if others can in some sense know your mind, it's a form of knowledge that is less secure than the knowledge you have of your own mind. This is the notion of privileged access to your own mind, and it isn't a philosophical invention; it is built into the naïve view of self-knowledge. At the same time, the naïve view also recognizes that self-knowledge can be a hard-won cognitive achievement and that one is, in some respects, opaque to oneself. In *this* context the real challenge isn't to explain the special authority of self-knowledge, since it has no such authority, but to make it plausible that there can be self-knowledge. From this perspective, a fundamental question is: how is self-knowledge possible? But what gives this question its philosophical bite is not the assumption that self-knowledge is epistemically privileged in ways that need explaining but rather the concern that self-knowledge of the kinds in question might not be possible after all. A theory of self-knowledge for humans will be a balanced view of which does justice to both aspects of the naïve view.

The point about not lumping together different varieties of substantial self-knowledge is straightforward. If you think that what makes self-knowledge philosophically interesting is the fact that it is epistemically privileged then if you are not careful you may find yourself having very little to say about other varieties of self-knowledge beyond pointing out that they aren't epistemically privileged. To the extent that you have anything positive to say about the epistemology of substantial self-knowledge it might well be something along the lines of: it's based on behavioural evidence just as, on some views, knowledge of other minds is based on behavioural evidence. But this would be a travesty. As we saw in the last chapter, substantial self-knowledge is not all the same, and there are subtle and interesting differences between, say, the basis on which you know that you are in love and the basis on which you know that you can speak Spanish. In neither case is it remotely plausible to think that's it's just a matter of how you behave, and it's all too easy to ignore the rich epistemology as well as the value of substantial self-knowledge if you insist that epistemically privileged self-knowledge is where all the philosophical action is.

Finally, when I talk about the concentration on the supposed epistemic privileges of self-knowledge promoting a highly selective and distorted view of particular self-knowledge I have two things in mind. First, there is the danger that all particular self-knowledge is viewed as direct and authoritative but there are many examples of particular self-knowledge which seem not to be privileged in these ways. Second, when it comes to answering the Sources Question one may find oneself neglecting sources of self-knowledge, even sources of particular self-knowledge, which don't sustain the picture of self-knowledge as direct and authoritative. In real life, for example, I may come to realize that I believe that the present government will be re-elected, or that I don't want another child, in all sorts of different ways. There are multiple pathways to self-knowledge, and there can be no justification for ignoring pathways to self-knowledge that aren't pathways to epistemically privileged knowledge of what one wants or believes.

Indeed, once the Disparity is taken into account, even the concession that particular self-knowledge is normally direct as well as authoritative starts to look questionable. Given all the respects in which humans aren't model epistemic citizens is there really a presumption that our self-attributions of beliefs and other attitudes aren't mistaken? If there is, how strong is this presumption? As for the idea that particular self-knowledge is normally direct, this is hard to reconcile with many philosophical accounts of self-knowledge, especially accounts that represent knowledge of one's own mind as the product of reasoning. So there are two issues here: is it a genuine datum that a significant class of self-knowledge is authoritative, and do philosophical accounts of self-knowledge succeed in explaining this datum? I'll have much more to say about these questions as I go along, but it is hard to avoid the suspicion that the datum is much less robust than many philosophers suppose, and that influential attempts by philosophers to explain this datum do no such thing.

Be that as it may, the important point for the moment is this: even if, as Gertler suggests, it is the epistemological distinctiveness of self-knowledge that makes it interesting to philosophers, the human interest in self-knowledge is much more broadly grounded. What I am suggesting is that philosophy needs to be more respectful of the human interest in self-knowledge. Most philosophers who write about self-knowledge will have had the experience of trying in vain to explain to incredulous non-philosophers why they are interested in figuring out how it's possible to know that you believe that it's raining. It's easy to dismiss the incredulity of the initiated as being of no philosophical relevance but this would be a mistake. The incredulity with which the uninitiated respond to the philosophical interest in trivial self-knowledge is the result of thinking that self-knowledge matters and that it *couldn't* matter if it is what many philosophers seem to think it is, namely, knowledge of one's particular mental states. No doubt there are all sorts of ways in which this reaction is flawed but there is also *something* right about it. The challenge is to talk about self-knowledge in a way that speaks to the concerns of the philosophically uninitiated as well as the concerns of epistemologically minded philosophers. Whether this challenge can be met remains to be seen.

5

Reality Check

So far in this book I have talked a lot about the Disparity, that is, the respects in which *homo sapiens* and *homo philosophicus* are different. *Homo philosophicus* is, of course, a mythical species. Members of this species are model epistemic citizens who reason critically, believe what they ought rationally to believe, and don't suffer from self-ignorance. I have talked about the many respects in which real human beings aren't like this, and have claimed that the distinction between *homo sapiens* and *homo philosophicus* matters a great deal not just for the philosophy of self-knowledge but for philosophy more generally. It's tempting when thinking about self-knowledge to assume that humans and *homo philosophicus* have much more in common than they really do, and this can distort our understanding of the kinds of self-knowledge which humans actually have and the kinds of self-knowledge they think it is worth having.

To see how the distinction between *homo sapiens* and *homo philosophicus* might matter for a proper understanding of self-knowledge we need look no further than TM.[1] The idea behind TM is that you can determine whether you believe that P by determining whether you ought rationally to believe that P.[2] Since this assumes that what you believe is what you ought rationally to believe I suggested in Chapter 1 that the Transparency Method is tailor made for *homo philosophicus*. Since *homo philosophicus* only believes what he rationally ought to believe he can use TM to determine what he believes. The resulting knowledge of his own beliefs may not be direct, since it is the product of reasoning, but it's still *knowledge*. However so-called Rationalists about self-knowledge think that TM is not only a pathway to self-knowledge for *homo philosophicus*, it is also a pathway to self-knowledge for *us*.[3] And surely that can be true only if we are in the relevant respects like, or sufficiently like, *homo philosophicus*, that is, only if our attitudes

---

[1] TM is the Transparency Method introduced in Chapter 1.
[2] This is David Finkelstein's gloss on TM, as described in Chapter 1.
[3] From my perspective Richard Moran is the paradigm contemporary Rationalist about self-knowledge.

are as they rationally ought to be. But we aren't in this respect like *homo philosophicus*; the implication of the Disparity is that our attitudes are not always, or even mostly, as they ought rationally to be, so TM is not a pathway to self-knowledge for humans.

The underlying point is that any account of human self-knowledge, and indeed other kinds of human knowledge, needs to be subjected to a reality check. The question that always needs to be asked is: is the proposed account of human knowledge, or human self-knowledge, psychologically realistic? Does it presuppose a conception of how humans think, reason, and form attitudes that accords with what we actually know about how humans think, reason, and form attitudes? If not, then that's a major problem. The objection to Rationalism about self-knowledge is that it ignores or underestimates the Disparity and so ends up with a highly unrealistic conception of human self-knowledge. It fails as an account of self-knowledge for humans because it doesn't pass the reality check.

As we saw in Chapter 1, there is quite a lot that Rationalism can say in response to this line of attack. It can question both the extent and the significance of the Disparity, and I will have more to say about each of these strategies in a moment. However, I'd like to begin by noting how my account of the philosophical relevance of the distinction between *homo sapiens* and *homo philosophicus* is similar to an account of the relevance for economics of the parallel distinction between *homo sapiens* and *homo economicus*. Economics tries to model and explain human behaviour. In particular, it tries to model and explain the economic behaviour of humans, and the question is whether economics makes psychologically realistic assumptions about the human economic subject. As Thaler and Sunstein put it in their book *Nudge*, 'many people seem at least implicitly committed to the idea of *homo economicus*, or economic man—the notion that each of us thinks and chooses unfailingly well, and thus fits the textbook picture of human beings offered by economists' (2008: 7). The problem is that this picture of human beings seems obviously false. We don't think and choose unfailingly well. Real human beings can't think like Einstein and they lack the willpower of Mahatma Gandhi; in Thaler and Sunstein's terminology, they are not Econs but Humans.

Recognition of the disparity between Econs and Humans has led in recent years to the development of a new approach to economics. This approach tries to increase the explanatory power of economics by 'providing it with more realistic psychological foundations' (Camerer and Loewenstein 2004: 3). It calls itself 'behavioural economics' and sees itself as a rival to neo-classical economics. Here is an amusing account of the rise of behavioural economics:

The discipline of economics is built on the shoulders of the mythical species *Homo economicus*. Unlike his uncle, *Homo sapiens*, *H. economicus* is unswervingly rational, completely selfish, and can effortlessly solve even the most difficult optimization problem. This rational paradigm has served economics well, providing a coherent framework for modelling human behaviour. However, a small but vocal movement has sought to dethrone *H. economicus*, replacing him with someone who acts "more human". This insurgent branch, commonly referred to as behavioural economics, argues that actual human behaviour deviates from the rational model in predictable ways. Incorporating these features into economic models, proponents argue, should improve our ability to explain observed behaviour. (Levitt and List 2008: 909)

In my terminology, the basic claim of behavioural economics is that neo-classical economics is in need of a reality check, and that the way to improve the explanatory and predictive power of economics is to take on board the disparities between Humans and Econs. What we should be after is an economics for Humans, and that means an economics that doesn't represent us as living embodiments of *homo economicus*.

There are obvious parallels between what I have been saying about the right way to explain self-knowledge and what behavioural economists say about the right way to explain economic behaviour. There are also parallels between how Rationalism responds to the threat of the Disparity and how neo-classical economists have responded to the rise of behavioural economics. In both cases there are questions about the true extent and the relevance of the differences between Humans and their rational counterparts. Starting with the economic case, sceptics about behavioural economics object that many of its central claims about human behaviour are based on empirical evidence drawn from laboratory experiments and that 'there are many reasons to suspect that these laboratory findings might fail to generalize to real markets' (Levitt and List 2008: 909). In the real world, these critics allege, the behavioural anomalies between *homo sapiens* and *homo economicus* are less extensive than behavioural economists assume. And if they are less extensive than behavioural economists assume then they must also be less relevant from the perspective of economic theorizing; the behaviour of humans in real markets at least approximates to the behaviour of *homo economicus*.

It's interesting to compare Levitt and List's response to behavioural economics with Daniel Dennett's response to the question 'How rational are we?' in his paper 'Three Kinds of Intentional Psychology'. Again, the emphasis is on the limitations of the research that has led psychologists to conclude that we are only minimally rational. Dennett objects that this jaundiced view 'is an illusion engendered by the fact that these psychologists are deliberately trying to produce situations that provoke irrational responses' (1987: 52). I will have more to say about Dennett in Chapter 6. Rationalists in philosophy can certainly avail themselves of Dennett's objections to arguments from empirical psychology in support of the Disparity, but they typically go further. They also question the extent of the Disparity on the grounds that the supposition of an extensive Disparity makes it hard to think of humans as having beliefs, desires, and other propositional attitudes.

Why do Rationalists think that there can't be an extensive Disparity if humans are to be thought of as having beliefs and desires? Because they think that, as Bill Child puts it, 'if a subject has attitudes at all, the relations amongst her attitudes, perceptions, and actions must be by and large rational' (1994: 8).[4] On this account, it is a necessary condition for humans to have beliefs, desires, and other propositional attitudes that their attitudes are, or approximate to being, as they rationally ought to be. All sorts of local irrationality are intelligible but what we believe, want, fear, etc. must be at least *roughly* what we ought rationally to believe, want, fear, etc. This isn't just how things are but in some sense how they have to be; there *can't* be as large a Disparity between *homo sapiens* and *homo philosophicus* as I have claimed since this would call into question the idea that humans even *have* propositional attitudes. This is of course very different from how Levitt and List argue against behavioural economics but the end result is the same: just as neo-classical economists insist that when the chips are down real humans aren't all that different from *homo economicus* so Rationalists insist that real humans can't be, and so are not, all that different from *homo philosophicus*.

Here we have one kind of damage limitation exercise on behalf of Rationalism. The focus is on the extent of the Disparity between *homo philosophicus* and *homo sapiens*, and the upshot is a form of what I will call Psychological Rationalism. Whereas I have painted a picture of humans as only distantly related to *homo philosophicus* Psychological Rationalism regards the two species as closely related. If there can only be a relatively small gap between *homo philosophicus* and *homo sapiens* then that obviously limits the damage the Disparity can do to Rationalism. This is damage limitation with a 'transcendental' twist. The twist is that Psychological Rationalism bases its conception of the relationship between *homo sapiens* and *homo philosophicus* on what it sees as conditions of the

---

[4] Child is here describing one aspect of what he calls 'interpretationism', that is, the account of the nature of the mental given by philosophers such as Donald Davidson and Daniel Dennett. Interpretationism says that 'we can reach an understanding of the nature of propositional attitudes by reflection on the procedure for *interpreting* a subject's attitudes and language' (1994: 1), and that 'in ascribing beliefs, we should seek to optimize agreement between what S believes and what she ought rationally to believe, in the light of her situation, her other attitudes, and the available evidence' (1994: 8). Interpretationists are, in my terms, 'Psychological Rationalists'. There is more on this below.

possibility of having beliefs, desires, and other such attitudes. The implication is that Rationalism is not psychologically unrealistic and so has nothing to fear from a reality check. I will discuss Psychological Rationalism in the next chapter.

If it's true that I have exaggerated the *extent* of the Disparity then that would also be a reason for questioning the *relevance* of the Disparity for Rationalism. However, there are also independent reasons for thinking that the Disparity is less of a threat to Rationalism than I've claimed. There are different ways of making the point. One is to argue that Rationalism about self-knowledge is primarily concerned with what is *normal* for humans, with how things are *supposed* to go for humans, and that it's irrelevant that things sometimes or even often don't go the way they are supposed to go. On this interpretation, Rationalism is a normative rather than a psychological doctrine. According to Normative Rationalism, it is normally possible for you to determine what your attitudes are by determining what they ought rationally to be. I will discuss Normative Rationalism in Chapter 7.

Another way of questioning the relevance of the Disparity for Rationalism is to draw attention again to a point I first made in Chapter 1. There I pointed out that in cases of belief-perseverance you still believe what you ought rationally to believe by your own lights so you can still determine what you believe in such cases by determining what you think you ought rationally to believe. Yet belief-perseverance was supposed to be an aspect of the Disparity; since *homo philosophicus* keeps track of justification relations among his beliefs he would realize when his beliefs are undermined. We don't always realize when our beliefs have been undermined but this doesn't stand in the way of our coming to know our own beliefs by using TM. This is what I referred to in Chapter 1 as a 'compatibilist' response to the Disparity. I will talk about this in Chapter 9.

One thing this discussion brings out is that the notion of a reality check is far from straightforward in philosophy, just as in economics. It's all too easy to criticize Rationalism and neo-classical economics on the grounds that they are psychologically unrealistic but it's not as simple as that. In both cases it's hard to determine the psychological facts, and it's just as hard to figure out what assumptions about humans are strictly necessary for explanatory purposes in philosophy and economics. However, having said all that, it's clearly right that if you want to explain the economic behaviour of humans, or human self-knowledge, you had better make assumptions about what we are actually like that bear some relation to reality. In explaining human behaviour or human knowledge a degree of idealization is inevitable, but there is also a point at which idealization tips over into fantasy. This is the also the point at which reality checks come into their own. However tricky it is to work out whether the assumptions which disciplines like philosophy and economics make about humans are right, there is no getting away from the need to address questions about the relationship between *homo sapiens* and *homo philosophicus* or *homo economicus* and *homo sapiens*.

I believe that reflection on the relationship between *homo philosophicus* and *homo sapiens* causes genuine problems for Rationalism in general, and specifically for Rationalism about self-knowledge. Both Psychological and Normative Rationalism face serious problems, and neither doctrine rescues Rationalism about self-knowledge. I also have doubts about compatibilism; it has something going for it when it comes to explaining how we know our own beliefs but little going for it as far as our self-knowledge of attitudes other than belief is concerned. Putting all this together, the inescapable conclusion is that Rationalism fails as an account of self-knowledge for humans, and that we need to look elsewhere for an account of how humans, with all their cognitive shortcomings as well as their strengths, are able to know their own minds.

In drawing this part to a close I want to make a comment on the way I've been talking about 'self-knowledge for humans'. When I claim that a particular philosophical approach such as Rationalism fails as an account of self-knowledge for humans there are several ways of understanding this. An account of self-knowledge for humans could be:

1. An account of self-knowledge that applies to humans, that is, an account that explains if and how humans have self-knowledge. This is the *application sense* of self-knowledge for humans.
2. An account of how humans conceive of self-knowledge, that is, an account of what humans take self-knowledge to be or to mean. This is the *conception* sense of self-knowledge for humans.
3. An account which provides guidance to humans who seek self-knowledge either by providing answers to their questions about the self or showing them how to go about answering their questions. This is the *guidance* sense of self-knowledge for humans.

A natural way of understanding the accusation that a philosophical theory such as Rationalism fails as an account of self-knowledge for humans is that it fails to deliver in the application sense. This is how I see things; part of the point of harping on about the Disparity is to question the applicability of Rationalism about self-knowledge to human self-knowledge given the way we humans are. However, it's not clear that the 'self-knowledge' which such theories try to explain would be understood as self-knowledge in the ordinary sense. As I've remarked previously, only a certain kind of philosopher would describe my knowledge that I believe I am wearing socks as 'self-knowledge'. This is not to say it *isn't* self-knowledge, but it isn't self-knowledge in the ordinary human sense. Self-knowledge in the ordinary sense is what I have been calling 'substantial' self-knowledge, and accounts of self-knowledge which don't have anything substantial to say about substantial self-knowledge are neither accounts of how humans ordinarily conceive of self-knowledge nor accounts of self-knowledge as we ordinarily conceive of it. They are not accounts of self-knowledge in the conception sense.

That leaves the guidance sense of self-knowledge. By and large philosophers—or at least contemporary philosophers—who write about self-knowledge don't see it as their job to provide humans with practical guidance or practical advice on how to attain self-knowledge; they leave that to the 'self-help' industry. There are exceptions; Stephen Hetherington's book *Self-Knowledge* is a good example of an account of self-knowledge for humans in the guidance sense; it rightly sees self-knowledge as both a philosophical and a practical issue, and one of its chapters is even called 'How Might Self-Knowledge Be Gained?'[5] In my view there is a lot to be said for this approach, but giving advice on how self-knowledge might be gained presupposes that (a) you conceive of self-knowledge in the same way that those you are advising conceive of it, (b) you think of self-knowledge as worth gaining, and (c) you regard the lack or absence of self-knowledge as a serious possibility. Few philosophers who talk about self-knowledge clearly satisfy all of these conditions, and that might explain their inability, as well as their reluctance, to engage with the project of developing an account of self-knowledge for humans in the guidance sense.

My own engagement with this project will centre on the identification of pathways to substantial self-knowledge and sources of self-ignorance. When it comes to the substantial self-knowledge that really matters to humans, self-ignorance is a real possibility. By the same token, the overcoming of self-ignorance is a genuine challenge. I will have more to say about all this, and about the value of self-knowledge, in later chapters. But first I want to complete my discussion of Rationalist accounts of particular self-knowledge. Whatever one makes of the project of explaining knowledge of one's own attitudes, it is one that has attracted a lot of philosophical interest. In addition, this kind of self-knowledge may well be indispensable for substantial self-knowledge. As I have represented things, the Disparity has a major bearing on how we know our own attitudes, as well as on other forms of self-knowledge, so it's now time to consider in detail the damage limitation strategies in relation to the Disparity which I have been describing in this chapter.

---

[5] Hetherington 2007.

6

Psychological Rationalism

In the last chapter I introduced Psychological Rationalism as a view about the extent of the Disparity. When I talk about the Disparity that is shorthand for the various respects in which *homo sapiens* differ from *homo philosophicus*. I've been arguing that the Disparity is extensive, at least extensive enough to put pressure on Rationalism about self-knowledge.[1] If we are as different from *homo philosophicus* as I have been maintaining then it's not usual for our propositional attitudes not to be as they ought rationally to be, and that makes it hard for us to determine what our attitudes are by determining how they ought rationally to be. In reply, Psychological Rationalists question the grounds for positing an extensive Disparity, and offer their own grounds for thinking that there can't be an extensive Disparity. As far as Psychological Rationalism is concerned we are sufficiently similar to *homo philosophicus* for Rationalism about self-knowledge to be a viable account of how we know our own beliefs, desires, and so on. I will refer to this as Psychological Rationalism's *Similarity Thesis*.

Psychological Rationalism has antecedents in the history of philosophy. In his book *The Mind of God and the Works of Man*, Edward Craig discusses how what he calls 'The Similarity Thesis' influenced many of the great, dead philosophers, including Berkeley, Spinoza, and Leibniz. Craig's Similarity Thesis emphasizes the closeness between God and the individual human being; it says that 'man was made in God's image' (1987: 14). No doubt there are countless differences between man and God but the nature of their reason is one point where 'the human mind and the mind of God naturally coincide' (Craig 1987: 46). Since God is presumably a model epistemic agent whose reasoning is flawless and whose beliefs are as they ought rationally to be, the claim that humans and God naturally coincide in respect of their reason implies that we generally reason well and that our beliefs are generally as they ought rationally to be. This suggests that

---

[1] As I've already argued, the Disparity puts pressure on Rationalism about self-knowledge because it puts pressure on the Rationalist's idea that a basic way of coming to know what your beliefs and other attitudes are is by coming to know what they ought rationally to be.

the Similarity Thesis I am attributing to Psychological Rationalism is in the same ballpark, and has some of the same implications, as the thesis that Craig attributes to a bunch of seventeenth-century rationalists.

With Craig's discussion in mind, the model epistemic citizen I have been referring to as *homo philosophicus* can be viewed as a representation of some of the epistemic virtues traditionally attributed to God. By the same token, placing emphasis on the Disparity can be viewed as a way of emphasizing the discontinuities between man and God as traditionally conceived. Indeed, these discontinuities might be even greater than is implied by talk of a 'Disparity'; for God to believe what he ought to believe it would have to be assumed that God has beliefs, and that isn't an uncontroversial assumption.[2] Presumably, there is also a sense in which God doesn't really reason; he sees instantly what follows from what and so doesn't have to move from premises to conclusions. God only reasons if genuine reasoning can be instantaneous. We can avoid such complications by reframing the Similarity Thesis in terms of the relationship between *homo sapiens* and *homo philosophicus* rather than the relationship between man and God.

Why would anyone believe the Similarity Thesis in my sense? You might think that it is an empirical question how close we are to the ideal of *homo philosophicus*. If there is empirical evidence that much of our reasoning isn't critical, that we are self-ignorant and biased to believe, and that our attitudes tend to survive evidential discrediting then there is, to that extent, empirical evidence against the Similarity Thesis. By the same token, it would seem to follow that the best way to defend the Similarity Thesis and attenuate the Disparity is to produce evidence that we do by and large reason critically, that we aren't generally self-ignorant or biased to believe, and that our attitudes do not on the whole survive evidential discrediting and aren't recalcitrant. Such empirical evidence against the Disparity would also amount to empirical grounds for thinking that our attitudes are more or less as they ought rationally to be.

In fact, this isn't how Psychological Rationalists argue. It's not that they do not regard empirical arguments for the Disparity as questionable in their own terms but that they don't regard the Similarity Thesis as one that should be defended on piecemeal empirical grounds. The alternative is to defend the thesis on 'transcendental' grounds. What I mean by a transcendental defence of the Similarity Thesis is one that focuses on the question: what are the necessary conditions for a subject to have propositional attitudes at all? Suppose it turns out that for a subject to have attitudes at all the relations among his attitudes, perceptions, and

---

[2] See Alston 1986 for more on this.

actions must be *by and large* rational. This would be a positive argument for the Similarity Thesis, since *homo philosophicus* is by stipulation a being whose attitudes are as they ought rationally to be. Indeed, the result of this transcendental argument is not just that *our* attitudes must approximate to being as they rationally ought to be but that *any* being that has attitudes must in this respect be like *homo philosophicus*. As for the specific elements of the Disparity, there are now two ways of dealing with these other than on piecemeal grounds: one is to argue that however widespread phenomena like belief-perseverance and self-ignorance may be they do not show that relations among our attitudes, perceptions, and actions aren't by and large rational. The other would be to view the transcendental argument for the Similarity Thesis as an argument against the possibility of such phenomena being widespread. I'll come back to this.

Before looking in detail at how a transcendental argument for the Similarity Thesis might go I'd like to say something about my use of the term 'transcendental'. The notion of a transcendental argument is associated with Kant, who saw such arguments as 'a priori' rather than empirical. A transcendental argument tries to establish the truth of some proposition P by arguing that the truth of P is necessary for knowledge, thought, or experience. As far as Kant was concerned, such necessary conditions can only be established non-empirically, by means of a priori philosophical reflection, but there is no need to follow Kant in this respect. You *could* think that there are highly general necessary conditions of thought, knowledge, or experience that can only be established by philosophical reflection but that what we appeal to when we engage in such reflection are high-level empirical considerations. In addition, claims about what is and isn't necessary for thought, knowledge, or experience are certainly liable to empirical refutation. Seen in this way, so-called 'transcendental' arguments for the Similarity doesn't have to be a priori though they can be; it's one thing to say that a necessary condition for a subject to have attitudes is that his attitudes are largely rational, and another to say that this isn't an 'empirical' truth, whatever that means.

The next question is: is it *true* that having attitudes that are mostly rational, mostly as they ought rationally to be, is a necessary condition for one to have attitudes at all? There is a discussion of this issue in Dennett's paper 'Three Kinds of Intentional Psychology'. Dennett argues that we approach each other as what he calls 'intentional systems', that is, as entities whose behaviour can be predicted by the method of attributing beliefs, desires, and rational acumen according to the following principles:

1. 'A system's beliefs are those it *ought to* have, given its perceptual capacities, its epistemic needs, and its biography' (1987: 49).
2. 'A system's desires are those it *ought to have*, given its biological needs and the most practicable means of satisfying them' (1987: 49).
3. 'A system's behaviour will consist of those acts *it would be rational* for an agent with those beliefs and desires to perform' (1987: 49).

On this account, the notion of a propositional attitude is fundamentally an *explanatory* notion. We ascribe beliefs and desires to give reason-giving explanations of actions, and beliefs and desires can themselves be given rational explanations; we make it intelligible that S believes that P by explaining why S ought to believe that P in these circumstances. This is presumably also what McDowell is getting at when he says that concepts of propositional attitudes have their 'proper home in explanations of a special sort: explanations in which things are made intelligible by being revealed to be, or to approximate to being, as they rationally ought to be' (1998: 328).[3]

What Dennett means by 'ought to have' in 1 and 2 is 'would have if it were ideally ensconced in its environmental niche'. This gives us 'the notion of an ideal epistemic and conative operator or agent' who recognizes all the dangers and vicissitudes in its environment and desires all the benefits relative to its needs. An 'ideal epistemic operator' sounds like a good description of *homo philosophicus* but not of *homo sapiens*, 'for surely we are not all that rational' (1987: 50). Nevertheless, Dennett insists, we treat each other *as if* we are rational agents, and that this 'works very well because we are *pretty* rational'; while we are not ideal epistemic and conative agents we 'approximate to the ideal version of ourselves exploited to yield predictions' (1987: 51). This is Dennett's version of the Similarity Thesis. Folk psychological attributions of propositional attitudes predict what we will believe, desire, and do 'by determining what we ought to believe, desire, and do' (1987: 52).

The original question was: is it a necessary condition for having attitudes at all that the relations among our attitudes, perceptions, and actions are by and large rational? But what Dennett argues is that we have to *assume* that our attitudes are as they rationally ought to be when we *attribute* attitudes to one another. Even if his argument works it doesn't look like an answer to the original question; just because we have to assume that our attitudes are a certain way as a condition for attributing attitudes it doesn't follow that we couldn't so much as have attitudes

---

[3] This is McDowell's gloss on what Davidson regards as the 'constitutive ideal of rationality' (1980: 223) in shaping our thinking about propositional attitudes.

unless they *are* that way. Indeed, Dennett explicitly describes our rational agent-hood as a 'myth', and the fact that this myth 'structures and organizes our attributions of belief and desire to each other' (1987: 52) doesn't make it true that we are rational. The claim that we are 'pretty rational' can only be established on empirical grounds, but then there is no longer anything 'transcendental' about this defence of the Similarity Thesis.

What this objection fails to take to take into account is Dennett's 'interpreta-tionism'. This is roughly the view that what makes it true that a subject S believes or desires that P is that S can be interpreted as believing or desiring that P on the basis of what he says and does. So there isn't a gap between what is necessary for S to have propositional attitudes and what is necessary for S to be interpreted as having propositional attitudes, that is, what is necessary for such attitudes to be attributed to S on the basis of his verbal and non-verbal behaviour. It is at this point that rationality comes into the picture; in attributing beliefs and desires to S, the sense in which we have to assume that S's attitudes are by and large as they ought to be is that the ideal of rationality has a 'constitutive role' in interpretation. Here is Bill Child's lucid summary of all this:

> When we interpret someone, we explain her actions in terms of her reasons. So the idea of a reason-giving explanation is central to the interpretationist conception of the mental. Internal to that form of explanation, and thus to the interpretationist conception, is the notion of rationality; the ideal of rationality has a constitutive role in propositional attitude psychology. To say that is to say (amongst other things) that if a subject has attitudes at all, the relations amongst her attitudes must by and large be rational. No actual individual is perfectly rational; so all sorts of local irrationality in thought and action are intelligible. But what is not intelligible is that a subject might have a set of attitudes that were absolutely irrational. . . . with an individual like that, the idea of explaining actions in terms of reasons could have no application. (1994: 8)

On this account, the assumption that we are 'pretty rational' has a transcendental justification; our being pretty rational is a necessary condition of interpretability, and being interpretable as having beliefs, desires, and other attitudes is *what it is* for one to have such attitudes. If we have beliefs and desires then by and large they must be as they ought to be.

I'm going to call this argument for the Similarity Thesis the 'argument from above' since it relies on highly abstract claims about the nature and explanatory role of propositional attitudes to show that insofar as we have beliefs and desires we must approximate to the ideal of *homo philosophicus*. The contrast is with what might be called an 'argument from below' for the Similarity Thesis, that is, one that defends this thesis on piecemeal empirical grounds. As I've already indicated, the argument from above needn't be conceived of as non-empirical since the interpretationist account of the mental could in principle be regarded as a high-level but nevertheless ultimately empirical theory of mind. However, there is also no denying that it is more natural to interpret the argument from above as relying on a series of 'a priori' claims about the nature of mental states and the constitutive ideal of rationality.

Whatever the status of the argument from above, the important question is: is it any good? Here are three reasons why you might be sceptical about this argument:

(a) You might have a problem with interpretationism.
(b) You might question the supposed 'constitutive role' of the ideal of rationality in interpretation. The aim of interpretation is to make people intelligible and predict their behaviour but doing these things does not require the supposition that their attitudes are as they rationally ought to be.
(c) You might accept the argument from above, including what it says about the constitutive role of rationality, but think that the argument only looks plausible because it is vacuous; the Disparity consists of a bunch of highly specific respects in which humans typically fall short of *homo philosophicus*, and the very abstract guarantee of rationality supplied by the argument from above does nothing to attenuate the Disparity; for all that this argument shows the various phenomena which make up the Disparity could still be widespread among normal humans.

I'm not going to get into a discussion about (a), beyond pointing out that it is a fact that the considerations in support of the Similarity Thesis that are put forward by writers like Dennett, Davidson, and McDowell are interpretationist considerations, and that interpretationism isn't uncontroversial; it certainly wouldn't and shouldn't be accepted by anyone who thinks that propositional attitudes are internal states.[4] I'm going to concentrate instead on (b) and (c), both of which raise serious questions about the argument from above.

Starting with (b), let's go back to the case of Steve from Kahneman's *Thinking, Fast and Slow*.[5] You will recall that Steve has been described as shy and withdrawn, as invariably helpful but with little interest in people or the world of reality. This is the description you have been given, and I'm trying to decide whether you believe that he is more likely to be a farmer or a librarian. Let's suppose also that you know that there are many more farmers than librarians.

---

[4] Child notes that interpretationism 'stands opposed to the view of propositional attitudes as internal states' (1994: 4).

[5] Kahneman 2011: 6–7.

The sense in which you 'know' this is that if I were to ask you to compare the number of farmers with the number of librarians in the country you would say that there are many more farmers. If you know that there are many more farmers then you ought rationally to believe that Steve is more likely to be a farmer but do I think that this is what you are more likely to believe? Not at all. Even without detailed knowledge of Kahneman's discussion of the role of the representativeness heuristic in human thinking I might suspect that you are in fact more likely to believe that Steve is likely to be a librarian. You are more likely to believe this because Steve's personality is that of a stereotypical librarian rather than a stereotypical farmer.

In this example the belief I attribute to you is that Steve is more likely to be a farmer, and this is the belief I attribute to you because I know enough about human psychology to know that in making judgements of probability people are prone to ignoring highly relevant statistical considerations; indeed, it's not just that people ignore such considerations but that large sections of the population seem not to have a grasp of even the most elementary statistical principles. Unless I know that you are a particularly careful thinker with a grasp of statistics it's a fair bet that my description of Steve will have led you to form the belief that Steve is more likely to be a librarian. So that is the belief I ascribe to you even though it is not the belief you ought rationally to have. I don't determine what you believe by determining what you ought to believe, and the basis of my ascription isn't the 'constitutive ideal of rationality' but an explicit or implicit grasp of the power of the representativeness heuristic. BAT AND BALL is no different. You ought to think that the ball costs 5 cents but I don't suppose that this is what you do think. Again, there are two points: what you believe in this case isn't what you ought rationally to believe, and the myth of your rational agenthood isn't what structures and organizes my thinking about what you believe. The thing that does that is my sense of how fast-thinking humans are likely to approach problems like BAT AND BALL.

Other non-rational factors that need to be taken into account when attributing beliefs to others include the bias to believe, the attractions of conspiracy theories, and the prevalence of belief-perseverance and attitude-recalcitrance. The evidence supports the view that the 9/11 attacks were carried out by al Qaeda but one would have to be quite optimistic to think that what people believe about the 9/11 attacks is what they ought rationally to believe. In a case like this, the sociopolitical context of the attribution seems far more relevant than any considerations of rationality. Or take Harman's Karen example. Karen believes on the basis of her aptitude test scores that she has an aptitude for science and music but not for history or philosophy. Then she is told that she had been given someone else's test results. What would Karen now think? When Harman concludes that 'Karen would almost certainly keep her new beliefs' (1986: 35) he isn't appealing to the principle that what she would believe is what she ought rationally to believe. The basis on which he predicts Karen's belief is the prevalence of belief-perseverance. It doesn't matter what Karen ought rationally to believe because it isn't the thought of what she ought rationally to believe that is doing the explanatory work.

In none of these cases do we have any difficulty making believers and their beliefs intelligible other than on the basis of considerations of rationality. We don't even try to make it intelligible that S believes that P by explaining why S ought to believe that P. And when it comes to attitudes other than belief it's even clearer that intelligibility does not depend on rationality. You have no reason to fear the spider in your bathtub but it's intelligible that you fear the spider. My grounds for judging that you fear the spider have little to do with thinking that you ought rationally to fear it. As for the suggestion that a system's desires are the ones it ought to have given its biological needs and the most practicable means of satisfying them, this might be true of *homo philosophicus* but humans are a different matter. A desire to smoke cigarettes is one that many humans have but ought not to have given their biological needs, while a desire for exercise is one that many of us lack even though we ought to have it. In his discussion Dennett tends to oscillate between representing the 'ought' in 'S ought to desire P' as having to do with what is rational and as a matter of what promotes survival. These aren't the same thing but either way it's implausible that we can make sense of each other by thinking about what our attitudes 'ought' to be.

It might seem that the way for the interpretationist to deal with such cases is to point out that they are examples of the 'local irrationality' the existence of which interpretationism never sought to deny. Just because we sometimes interpret people as having attitudes other than the ones they ought rationally to have it doesn't follow that their attitudes aren't *by and large* as they rationally ought to be; it's unintelligible that someone who has beliefs and desires is absolutely irrational. This is what I mean when I describe the argument from above as a 'damage limitation exercise' or, more colourfully, as a transcendental damage limitation exercise. It allows that our beliefs sometimes persevere despite evidential discrediting, that our propositional attitudes are sometimes recalcitrant, and so on, but the suggestion is that such phenomena can't be widespread. They may amount to respects in which we are different from *homo philosophicus* but they don't falsify the Psychological Rationalist's Similarity Thesis because the limitations on the extent to which we can be different from *homo philosophicus* still allow us to determine what our attitudes are by determining what they ought rationally to be; the Disparity, such as it is, isn't a problem for rationalism about self-knowledge.

There are quite a few problems with arguing this way. Here is the first problem: let's agree that the argument from above succeeds in limiting the extent of the Disparity. But since there is no question of the argument completely *eliminating* the Disparity we then face the question: how much of a Disparity can Rationalism about self-knowledge live with? At least on the face of it, even a small Disparity is going to be a problem for Rationalism. Given that it is at least sometimes the case that your attitude towards something isn't as it rationally ought to be, the method of determining what your attitude is by determining what it ought rationally to be will sometimes lead you astray. For example, you will sometimes conclude that you want something that you don't actually want because you judge it is what you ought to want. But how can use of an unreliable method give you *knowledge* of your own attitudes?

It's hard to assess this objection without getting into a wide-ranging epistemological discussion that is well beyond the scope of this chapter. The obvious thing to say is that just because use of a particular method for forming beliefs about our attitudes sometimes leads us astray it clearly doesn't follow it's an unreliable method or not reliable enough to be a source of knowledge. The reliability required for knowledge isn't perfect reliability so you can still discover what your attitudes are by determining what they ought to be as long as using this method will generally give you the right answer. It will generally give you the right answer as long as your attitudes are generally as they ought to be, which is precisely what the argument from above claims. So the real issue is whether this argument is capable of limiting the scale of the Disparity in the way that it claims. Just how similar to *homo philosophicus* do we have to be if we are to be interpretable as having propositional attitudes?

The problem the argument from above faces at this point is perfectly illustrated by the passage from Bill Child quoted above. On Child's interpretation of interpretationism, what it rules out is that 'a subject might have a set of attitudes which were absolutely irrational, for none of which she has any reasons at all, and which it was impossible to relate intelligibly to her action' (1994: 8). The interpretationist may be right that this would be unintelligible but ruling out the possibility of an absolutely irrational subject of propositional attitudes doesn't do much to limit the scale of the Disparity since you can have many attitudes that aren't as they ought rationally to be without being 'absolutely irrational'. When Oliver thinks that the collapse of the twin towers on 9/11 was caused by a controlled demolition, or when Karen continues to insist that she has an aptitude for science and music, it's not that they don't have reasons for what they believe.

They have their reasons, in the light of which their attitudes are intelligible. To be sure, their reasons aren't very *good* reasons but that doesn't make Karen or Oliver absolutely irrational. Their attitudes are not as they rationally ought to be, and they may be open to rational criticism, but these aren't examples of the kind of extreme irrationality that the argument from above rules out. Saying that a person's attitudes can't be absolutely irrational is one thing; saying that they must be by and large as they rationally ought to be is another.

To put it another way, the argument from above establishes something much weaker than Psychological Rationalism needs. Psychological Rationalism says that we approximate to ideal epistemic agents, that is, to *homo philosophicus*, but the argument from above only shows that if we have propositional attitudes we can't be totally irrational. But there's a very big difference between not being totally irrational and approximating to *homo philosophicus*. Ruling out extreme irrationality leaves open the possibility of an extensive Disparity between *homo sapiens* and *homo philosophicus*, certainly extensive enough to make it impossible for us to determine with any reliability what our attitudes are by determining what they ought to be. If this is right then the transcendental guarantee the argument from above provides is too weak to be of much use to Psychological Rationalism.

In any case, it's not just a question of *how much* epistemic malpractice is consistent with the argument from above. This way of putting things makes it sound as though the real problem with the argument from above is quantitative: what Psychological Rationalism can tolerate is only a *small* Disparity but the argument from above allows the Disparity to be *big*. This way of putting things is fine as far as it goes but it misses a deeper point about the basis on which we ascribe propositional attitudes to each other. The deeper point concerns the role of the ideal of rationality in attitude ascriptions. The impression you get from Dennett is that when we interpret other people we make the default assumption that their attitudes are by and large as they ought to be, and that this assumption is what enables us to predict the behaviour and attitudes of other people. However, it's only any use assuming that people generally have the attitudes they ought to have if it's clear what attitudes they ought to have, and that's just the problem: the notion of a person's attitudes being as they rationally ought to be is much more opaque than the argument from above assumes.

Here is a simple illustration of the point: you believe P and you believe that if P then Q. Should you believe that Q? Not necessarily. If you have independent evidence against Q then maybe you should revise your belief that P, or your belief that if P then Q. This is a point I made in Chapter 1: in practice, the question 'Does S believe that P?' is often much easier to answer than the question 'Ought

S to believe that P?', just as the question 'Does S fear that P?' is often much easier to answer than the question 'Should S fear that P?' This makes it implausible that the way to answer the first of these questions is to answer the second, since we would then be answering an easier question by answering a harder question. In addition, if we can answer the question 'Does S believe that P?' prior to answering the question 'Should S believe that P?' then we must have independent means of answering the former question, as indeed we do in many cases. This suggests that what is true in cases like KAREN and BAT AND BALL is true more generally: it's *inefficient* to predict a person's attitudes on the basis of what their attitudes ought to be because we are often so unclear what their attitude ought to be, and it's also *ineffective* to predict a person's attitudes on this basis because what people believe, want, fear, etc. is more often than not influenced by a wide range of non-rational psychological and contextual factors that are in danger of being ignored if the focus on is the 'constitutive ideal of rationality'. Once again, the inescapable conclusion is that the argument from above does very little in practice to attenuate the Disparity.

This discussion leads naturally to (c). Like (b), the effect of (c) is to call into question the argument from above's ability to limit the extent of the Disparity, but (c) does this in a different way from (b). Whereas (b) casts doubt on the role of the myth or ideal of rationality in structuring and organizing our attributions of belief and desire to each other, (c) makes the point that even if interpretation *is* governed by the ideal of rationality the net effect on the Disparity is negligible. How can that be? Because the various principles of rationality which interpretationists like Dennett propose are so lacking in substance as to be compatible with most of the phenomena which make up the Disparity. If this is right, then (b) and (c) are two horns of a dilemma for the argument from above: the first horn says that if the principles of rationality are substantial enough to rule out the Disparity then it's implausible that they structure and organize our attributions of belief and desire to each other. The second horn says that if Dennett's principles structure and organize our attributions of attitudes to each other then they can't be substantial enough to rule out the Disparity. Either way, the argument from above provides no effective transcendental guarantee that insofar as we have beliefs and desires we must be similar to *homo philosophicus*.

The point that interpretationism's principles of rationality aren't substantial enough to attenuate the Disparity or vindicate Psychological Rationalism can be illustrated by reference to the principle that 'a system's beliefs are those it *ought to* have, given its perceptual capacities, its epistemic needs, and its biography' (Dennett 1987: 49). Now consider Karen. Is her belief that she has an aptitude for science and music one that she 'ought' to have after she has been told about the mix up with the test results? I have been arguing that it's hard to know what the subject should or shouldn't believe in cases like KAREN but the other side of the coin is that there then isn't a clear-cut cut case for saying that her belief is one that she *oughtn't* to have given her capacities and biography. Among her capacities are her capacity to keep track of her justifications for her beliefs, but we know that this capacity is bound to be limited given the need for her to avoid too much mental clutter. Given that she might have lost track of her original justification for believing that she has an aptitude for science and music it could be argued that her belief is not in breach of Dennett's principle even though belief-perseverance after evidential discrediting is not something that *homo philosophicus* would ever be guilty of. In interpreting Karen as believing that she has an aptitude for science and music but not for history or philosophy you aren't interpreting her as believing anything other than what she ought to believe given further background assumptions about her.

Even in the variation on KAREN in which she has kept track of her justifications but still believes that she has an aptitude for science and music because she finds it hard to get rid of this belief, it's not absolutely clear that Dennett should find this objectionable. Who is to say that a certain degree of attitude-recalcitrance might not promote survival and be 'rational' at least to the extent that it isn't always worth the mental effort to get rid of one's entrenched beliefs? This doesn't mean, of course, that Karen is no different from *homo philosophicus*, or that there is no Disparity if her beliefs are those she 'ought to have' in Dennett's sense. Her beliefs can be those she ought to have in *this* sense even if the way she operates is different from the way that *homo philosophicus* would operate; your beliefs can be as they ought to be in Dennett's sense even if you aren't a model epistemic citizen.

Although it's easy to see the point of arguing in this way, my own view is that (b) is a more effective response to the argument from above than (c). What the latter does is to try to reconcile the Disparity with the role of the ideal of rationality in interpretation but it goes too far when it implies that the myth of our rational agenthood rules very little out when it comes to the differences between us and *homo philosophicus*. Although it's true that a system whose beliefs are those it ought to have can also be one whose beliefs sometimes persevere despite evidential discrediting, it's *not* true that principles like Dennett's rule nothing out. It's hard to maintain that your beliefs are as they ought to be in BAT AND BALL, or that Oliver's beliefs about 9/11 are in good order. It's even clearer with other attitudes, such as self-destructive desires or irrational fears, that something is seriously amiss from the standpoint of rationality. The thing to say about these cases is not that they are ones in which the subject's attitudes are as they ought to be, either from the standpoint of rationality or the standpoint of survival. The thing to say is that the fact that something is seriously amiss with such attitudes doesn't make it impossible or especially difficult to interpret ordinary humans as having them. However, this takes us back to (b), and to the suggestion that the argument from above doesn't limit the extent of the Disparity because many of our attitudes do not conform to demanding principles of rationality.

So much for the argument from above: it tries to vindicate Psychological Rationalism by means of a transcendental argument against the possibility of a substantial Disparity but the proposed argument is no good. What it shows is that there are limits to how irrational a being with propositional attitudes can be, but these limits do not in any sense vindicate the Similarity Thesis. That leaves the argument from below. When I introduced this argument I described it as an argument for the Similarity Thesis, but this is misleading. It's not so much a positive argument for this thesis as an attempt to deflect arguments against Psychological Rationalism. The idea is really very simple: the main line of attack on the Similarity Thesis has been to point out the various ways in which humans fail to approximate to the ideal of *homo philosophicus*. This is an empirical argument against the Similarity Thesis and is only as good as the empirical evidence for a substantial Disparity. This evidence takes the form of experiments that reveal all manner of human epistemic malpractice, but the issue is whether the various failings that emerge in contrived experimental situations tell us anything about *ordinary* human thinking and reasoning. The argument from below challenges the relevance of the supposed experimental evidence for the Disparity; it says that this evidence does not generalize, and doesn't show that that there is a substantial Disparity in real life.

I mentioned an argument along these lines Chapter 5. Just as behavioural economists argue that laboratory findings of economic irrationality fail to generalize to real markets, so Dennett objects on roughly similar grounds to empirical evidence from psychology against the Similarity Thesis:

How rational are we? Research in social and cognitive psychology . . . suggests we are only minimally rational, appallingly ready to leap to conclusions or be swayed by logically irrelevant features of situations, but this jaundiced view is an illusion engendered by the fact that these psychologists are deliberately trying to produce situations that provoke irrational responses—inducing pathology in a system by putting strain on it—and succeeding, being good psychologists . . . . A more optimistic impression of our rationality is engendered by a review of the difficulties encountered in artificial intelligence research. Even the most sophisticated AI programs stumble blindly into misinterpretations and misunderstandings that even small children reliably evade without a second thought . . . From this vantage point we seem marvellously rational. (1987: 52)

This, in essence, is the argument from below: not a grandiose transcendental argument from on high for the Similarity Thesis but a more prosaic empirical argument against the Disparity or, more accurately, an empirical argument against empirical arguments for the Disparity.

Is the argument from below any good? Talk of 'laboratory finds' and of psychologists trying to engineer irrational responses is well wide of the mark. Consider BAT AND BALL again. This problem figures in Shane Frederick's Cognitive Reflection Test (CRT) of one type of cognitive ability.[6] Frederick reports that CRT was administered to 3,428 people in 35 separate studies. Most respondents were undergraduates who were paid $8 to complete a 45-minute questionnaire. They were told only: 'Below are several problems that vary in difficulty. Try to answer as many as you can' (2005: 28). It's true that BAT AND BALL is specifically designed to produce an answer that is intuitive and wrong, and it makes a difference that the example is BAT AND BALL rather than, say, BAGEL AND BANANA: a banana and bagel cost 37 cents. The banana costs 13 cents more than the bagel. How much does the bagel cost? As Frederick points out, respondents miss the 'bat and ball' problem far more often than they miss the 'bagel and banana' problem. There is, to this extent, an element of experimental manipulation but this doesn't vindicate the argument from below; since the aim is to test our susceptibility to certain kinds of cognitive illusion, it's obvious that the chosen example needs to be one that is potentially illusion-generating. BAT AND BALL doesn't so much *provoke* as *evoke* a flawed response, and the fact that it does that is the point of the example.

Dennett's accusation is if anything even less pertinent in relation to Ross, Lepper, and Hubbard's early work on belief-perseverance.[7] Subjects were presented with the task of distinguishing between authentic and genuine suicide notes. Initially subjects were provided with false feedback indicating varying levels of success in the task, only to be told later that the initial feedback had been false. Subjects were then asked to fill out questionnaires asking them to estimate their actual performance at the task. The results showed a remarkable degree of post-debriefing perseverance, with subjects who had initially been given the false feedback that they were good at distinguishing authentic and fake suicide notes continuing to rate their abilities far more favourably than those who had initially been given negative feedback. As with BAT AND BALL there is little evidence here of illicit experimental manipulation or any attempt to 'induce pathology' by 'putting strain' on subject's belief systems. The tests *show* that test subjects' responses to undermining evidence are in some sense less than ideal; it

[6] Frederick 2005.   [7] Ross, Lepper, and Hubbard 1975.

doesn't *induce* them to respond 'irrationally', if that means that it gets them to respond in a way that is unrepresentative of how they and other humans would respond to such scenarios in real life. Anyway, as I've already argued above, it's not clear that belief-perseverance *is* irrational.

This leads on to another, related point about the argument from below: the argument represents the evidence for the Disparity as experimental evidence, and then raises questions about the extent to which the evidence generalizes. However, it's arguable that the idea of a significant Disparity is also part of folk psychology, and that there is plenty of evidence from everyday life that humans don't approximate to *homo philosophicus*. The psychological data only confirm what many people who haven't been influenced (or should that be corrupted?) by philosophy believe anyway; it isn't exactly news that our attitudes are in many cases not as they ought rationally to be, that we often reason carelessly, that most of us are no good at statistics, and that self-ignorance is a pervasive feature of human life. We don't really need experimental psychologists to tell us these things, though for those who believe there is a significant Disparity it's certainly reassuring that the scientific evidence supports their view.

The case of Oliver is particularly telling in this regard. We might be dismayed by the fact that there are so many real-world Olivers with bizarre views about 9/11 and little sense of why they think the weird things they think about such events. But are we surprised? Hardly. For those of us who don't start out with the touchingly optimistic and naïve vision of man as a model epistemic citizen made in the image of God, the natural reaction to OLIVER and even KAREN is: *of course* that's how it is. Why would you think otherwise? Dennett's attempt to discredit the empirical evidence for the Disparity therefore misrepresents the *source* of the evidence as well as its credentials: it doesn't all come from artificial laboratory experiments, and the simple reason it generalizes to the real world is that a lot of it is drawn from non-specialist observation of the real world.

No doubt there is much more to be said about all this but I hope I have said enough to justify concluding that the argument from below is no good. Its heart is in the right place since it's certainly a good idea to assess the Disparity by looking at the actual evidence for and against rather than by armchair reflection. If you are sceptical about the prospects for a transcendental deduction of the Similarity Thesis then the obvious alternative is to challenge the evidence against this thesis. The problem is that this evidence is really rather strong: it turns out that there are solid empirical grounds for positing a Disparity that is large enough to create problems for the Similarity Thesis.

Where do we go from here? When I introduced Psychological Rationalism at the start of this chapter I characterized it as the view that humans are sufficiently similar to *homo philosophicus* for Rationalism about self-knowledge, with its reliance on TM, to be a viable account of how we know our own beliefs and other attitudes. Most of this chapter has been about how far we are from being ideal epistemic agents, but a substantial Disparity might be something a Psychological Rationalist could live with at least to this extent: suppose it turns out that Rationalism about self-knowledge is compatible with a substantial Disparity. I called this position 'compatibilism' in Chapter 1, and if this turns out to be defensible then there is no need for Psychological Rationalism to try to show that we approximate to ideal epistemic agents. All it needs to show is that the Disparity, however substantial, still allows us to know our own attitudes by employing the Transparency Method.

I will come back to compatibilism in Chapter 9. Before then, there are a couple of other questions to consider. One is whether it's right to conclude from the Disparity that we are irrational or even, as has recently been claimed by the behavioural economist Dan Ariely, 'predictably irrational'.[8] This question, which I will discuss in the chapter after next, brings into focus an issue which I have mentioned a few times but not yet discussed in any detail: what is meant by the term 'irrational', and does the suggestion that we aren't much like *homo philosophicus* commit one to endorsing the view that we are irrational? The other question is this: I have represented Psychological Rationalism as a descriptive thesis, as a view about what humans are actually like. This makes Psychological Rationalism something of a hostage to empirical fortune, and that is the point I have been exploiting in this chapter. However, it's worth noting that there is a quite different way of thinking about Rationalism. The alternative is to represent it as a view about what is normal for humans, or with what we should be like, rather than with what we humans are actually like. So, for example, it could be normal for our beliefs not to survive evidential discrediting even if belief-perseverance isn't uncommon in practice.

The key to this response to the Disparity is the thought that what is normal for us isn't a statistical matter. This allows Rationalism to live with the Disparity because as far as the normative issue is concerned the Disparity is neither here or there. One question is: how do humans actually reason and revise their attitudes when faced with undermining evidence? A quite different question is: what is the normal or correct way for humans to reason and revise their attitudes in the face of undermining evidence? These questions can, of course, have quite different answers, and there is a form of Rationalism that concentrates on the second

---

[8] Ariely 2009.

question and deems the Disparity to be irrelevant for the purposes of answering this question. This form of Rationalism points out that what is normal for us may not be what is common. I'm going call this view Normative Rationalism. Is Normative Rationalism any good, and does it have anything useful to say about the sources, character, and value of our self-knowledge? These are among the questions I want to address in the next chapter.

7

Normative Rationalism

So far in this book I've been harping on about the Disparity, the respects in which we humans are different from *homo philosophicus*. I've suggested that how we reason and form and revise our attitudes is very different from how *homo philosophicus* would do these things and that we are a long way from being model epistemic citizens. I've also suggested that this is a problem for Rationalism about self-knowledge and maybe for rationalism more generally. In the last chapter I discussed and ultimately rejected a response which objects that I have exaggerated the extent of the Disparity. This Psychological Rationalist response says that we *aren't* as different from *homo philosophicus* as I've suggested because we *can't* be. This is the transcendental damage limitation strategy recommended by the likes of Davidson, Dennett, and McDowell. Their thought is it's a condition on having propositional attitudes at all that our attitudes are more or less as they ought rationally to be.

In this chapter I want to consider an alternative response to the Disparity. This response doesn't question the extent of the Disparity but rather its relevance. It recognizes the dangers of basing rationalism about self-knowledge on claims about what we humans are actually like and doesn't lay itself open to empirical refutation in the way that Psychological Rationalism is open to empirical refutation. Even if you argue transcendentally that we are a certain way because we have to be that way, you can still be refuted by evidence that suggests that we aren't the way you think we have to be. What kind of rationalism can possibly avoid this problem? How can the Disparity be so irrelevant to Rationalism about self-knowledge that it's not necessary for the Rationalist to question the extent of the Disparity?

Here is one answer to this question: suppose we interpret Rationalism not as a theory about what human beings are actually like but about how humans *ought* to be or how they are *supposed* to be. This is not Psychological but Normative Rationalism, and the Disparity is not problem for Normative Rationalism because saying that humans ought to be a certain way is perfectly consistent with admitting that they aren't in fact that way. For example, you could think it's some kind of normative requirement on us that our attitudes are responsive to our reasons or evidence without thinking that they are always responsive to our reasons or to our evidence. From this standpoint there is simply no need to question the extent of the Disparity because the actual Disparity between *homo sapiens* and *homo philosophicus* doesn't affect the idea *homo sapiens* ought to be, or should be, like *homo philosophicus*.

Normative Rationalism is related to but not the same as what I referred to in Chapter 1 as compatibilism. Compatibilism says that despite the Disparity between *homo philosophicus* and *homo sapiens* TM is still a viable source of self-knowledge for the latter. So far I haven't represented Normative Rationalism as saying anything about TM. So we now have two basic questions about Normative Rationalism and its relevance for TM, bearing in mind that TM is at the heart of Rationalism about self-knowledge:

1. Is there any justification for the view that we humans ought to, or are supposed to, approximate to *homo philosophicus*?
2. If we ought to approximate to *homo philosophicus*, does that mean that we can know our own attitudes by employing the Transparency Method?

The first of these questions asks what there is to be said for Normative Rationalism, while the second asks whether Normative Rationalism supports compatibilism. If it does, then that also helps Rationalism about self-knowledge.

What lies at the basis of Normative Rationalism is a certain view about the nature of philosophy. The view I have in mind says that philosophy is primarily a normative rather than a descriptive discipline. For example, when it comes to reasoning, the main aim of philosophy is not to describe how we do reason but to tell us how we should reason. How we do reason is a matter for empirical psychology not for philosophy. What this means is that we shouldn't think of *homo philosophicus* as a mythical species whose operations have nothing to do with us. Rather we should think of the idea of *homo philosophicus* as a regulative ideal, as setting the standard for *homo sapiens*: in stipulating how *homo philosophicus* does reason we are also saying something about how *homo sapiens* should reason. And if we humans think and reason as we should then it *would* be possible for us to know our attitudes by employing TM. To concentrate on our intellectual shortcomings is to miss the point of philosophy, which is to help us to overcome our shortcomings.

The idea that rationalism should represent itself as normative rather than descriptive is based on an important strand in the history of philosophy from Descartes to Alvin Goldman. For example, Descartes' *Rules for the Direction of the Mind* is explicitly not concerned with what people have thought but with the direction of our mind so as to enable it to form solid and true judgements.[1] In a similar vein, what Goldman calls 'epistemics' aims to 'regulate or guide our intellectual activities' and 'lay down principles or suggestions for how to conduct our cognitive affairs' (1978: 509). However, the guidance that epistemics provides doesn't come out of thin air; it must be grounded in a conception of how we *ought* to conduct our cognitive affairs, and that is what Normative Rationalism tries to flesh out.

On this view, psychology isn't irrelevant to philosophy's normative project but it only plays a subsidiary role. As Goldman points out, since 'ought' implies 'can', advice about how we ought to reason must take account of what is possible for us: 'it must take account of the powers and limits of the human cognitive system, and this requires attention to descriptive psychology' (1978: 510). In addition, to the extent that the regulative enterprise is concerned to correct flaws in human reasoning, it has to know what the flaws are. This again is where descriptive psychology might have a part to play. Nevertheless, descriptive psychology can't tell us how we ought to conduct our cognitive affairs or, for that matter, what counts as a flaw. These are things only normative philosophy can do.

In assessing the merits of Normative Rationalism, it's worth noting that this doctrine comes in two different varieties. It's one thing to talk about how we are *supposed* to conduct our cognitive affairs and another to talk about how we *ought* to conduct our cognitive affairs. One version of Normative Rationalism, call it NR_1, says that we are supposed to approximate to *homo philosophicus* in our thinking and reasoning. The other version, call it NR_2, says that we ought to approximate to *homo philosophicus*. The difference is subtle but will become a lot clearer once the notion of how humans are 'supposed' to operate has been explained. My aim in this chapter is to explain the difference between NR_1 and NR_2, explain why there are serious problems with both forms of Normative Rationalism, and argue that neither form of Normative Rationalism is of much use to Rationalism about self-knowledge. To put it another way, I will be arguing that the answer that the answer to questions 1 and 2 is 'no'.

Starting with NR_1, Matthew Boyle's paper 'Essentially Rational Animals' helps to clarify what I have in mind.[2] In this paper Boyle discusses what he refers to as the Classical View of man. One element of this view is that human beings are essentially rational animals or, as Boyle puts it, that 'rational animal' belongs to 'the specification of the *essence* of humankind' (2012: 399). Boyle points out that

---

[1] There is a translation of Descartes' *Rules for the Direction of the Mind* in Cottingham, Stoothoff, and Murdoch 1985.

[2] Boyle 2012.

the claim that man is a rational animal isn't meant as some sort of statistical generalization. It is rather 'a claim about our essential nature, about *what it is* to be a human being, and to say that it is in our nature to be rational is not necessarily to say that most members of our species draw rational inferences most of the time' (2012: 422). The underlying point is that to say what it is to be a human being is not to describe properties of *individuals* that make them human beings but rather to characterize the nature of the kind *human being.*

As Boyle observes, this mode of description is familiar from nature documentaries. Suppose you are watching a documentary about grizzly bears in which the voiceover says: 'The grizzly bear digs a den under rocks or in the hollow of a tree, or in a cave or crevice. It goes into its den between October and December and stays there until the early spring. It has a protective layer of fat that allows it to stay in its den while the weather is cold. It does not really hibernate and can be easily woken up in the winter...' Boyle comments:

These sentences describe, not what this or that grizzly bear does... but what is done by "the grizzly bear", or by grizzly bears in general—where "in general" is heard in a special register. These sentences do not necessarily describe what holds of *most* grizzly bears: it may be, for instance, that, given human encroachment on their habitat, most actual grizzlies are not in a position to build up the layer of fat that allows them to survive the winter. Even so, it would be a true description of how "the grizzly bear" lives to say that it goes into hibernation with a protective layer of fat. This truth seems to belong to a story about how things are *supposed* to go for grizzlies... Recognizing this, we might try saying that the sentences describe how things "normally" or "properly" go for grizzly bears. (2012: 404)[3]

The 'normally' in this formulation isn't statistical. Let's say that what is Normal (with a capital N) for grizzly bears is how things are supposed to be for grizzlies. What is normal (lower case n) is how things generally do go for them. In these terms, Boyle's point is that what is Normal for grizzly bears might not be normal.

The same goes for humans. The claim that it is in our nature to be rational can either be interpreted as the claim that humans are Normally rational or as the claim that they are normally rational. The first of these claims is unaffected by empirical arguments for the existence of widespread irrationality among humans. For example, in a paper called 'Could Man be an Irrational Animal?' Stephen Stich argues against the view that man is a rational animal on the grounds that human subjects 'regularly and systematically invoke inferential and judgemental strategies ranging from the merely invalid to the genuinely bizarre' (1985: 115).

---

[3] Boyle is drawing here and elsewhere in his paper on the work of Michael Thompson, especially Thompson 1998 and 2004.

Boyle objects that Stich's own argumentative strategy here is itself flawed. Stich wrongly assumes that the idea that man is a rational animal must be taken as 'a claim about how most men think' (2012: 421). If it isn't taken this way, how could it be an objection to the Classical View that humans regularly make invalid inferences? However, the Classical View of man is not concerned with how most humans think. It is a view about our *essential* nature, and so rejects the 'Quantificationalist Assumption' that statements about the nature of a certain kind of living thing 'must be read as involving an implicit quantification over (all or most) individuals of that kind' (2012: 422–3).

With Boyle's discussion in mind, we are now in a better position to understand NR$_1$. When NR$_1$ says that we are supposed to approximate to *homo philosophicus* in our thinking and reasoning what this means is that it is Normal (but not necessarily normal) for humans to think and reason like *homo philosophicus*. So, for example, critical reasoning is Normal for us but self-ignorance, belief-perseverance, and attitude-recalcitrance are not. When things go as they supposed to go we know our own attitudes, they conform to our judgements and they do not survive evidential discrediting. If, for whatever reason, things don't go as they are supposed to go the result is a Disparity between *homo philosophicus* and *homo sapiens* but the Disparity is no more a problem for NR$_1$ than the fact grizzly bears don't always hibernate in the winter is a problem for the view that grizzlies are 'supposed' to hibernate in the winter. Whether or not we want to characterize the various elements of the Disparity as amounting to examples of *irrationality*—I say more about this in the next chapter—they have no bearing on Normative Rationalism as I am now interpreting this doctrine.

The obvious next question is: is NR$_1$ actually correct? However, before tackling this question I want to say something about NR$_2$. What is the difference between saying that we are *supposed* to think and reason like *homo philosophicus* and saying that we *ought* to reason like *homo philosophicus*? If it is Normal for us to think and reason in a certain way then there is a sense in which we 'ought' to reason that way. This is a *teleological* 'ought', the point being that we ought to do what it is Normal for us to do, or what it is in our nature to do. However, not all 'oughts' are like this. For example, the suggestion that we ought to give money to charity doesn't depend on thinking that it's in our nature to give money to charity. This 'ought' is a moral ought, and there are many other examples of 'oughts' which needn't be grounded in a conception of what is Normal for us: we ought to exercise regularly whether or not it is Normal for us to do so in anything like the way that it's Normal for grizzly bears to hibernate in the winter. If this is right then you could think that humans ought to reason like *homo philosophicus* regardless of whether this is what we are 'supposed' to do. This is what NR$_2$ says, and the challenge is to explain what kind of ought is at issue here if it isn't a teleological ought.

We can now return to the question whether NR_1 is any good, before going on to ask the same question about NR_2. Consider, to begin with, critical reasoning. If you are impressed by the Disparity then you will be happy to acknowledge the extent to which critical reasoning isn't prevalent among humans. Much of our thinking is fast rather than critical. In response, NR_1 says: well, that may be so, but it's still true that critical reasoning is Normal for us, and that 'proper' human reasoning is critical reasoning. But why should we think that? If we realize that humans have limited time and intellectual resources it's hard not to conclude that fast thinking is not just normal but Normal for us. This is the implication of Kahneman's view that the human mind contains a fast-thinking, automatic, System 1 as well as a slow-thinking and effortful System 2. As Kahneman writes, 'when all goes smoothly' System 2 adopts the suggestions of System 1 with little or no modification (2011: 24). 'Goes smoothly' means goes as things are supposed to go, and it's no great mystery that when even our minds operate as they are supposed to operate much of our thinking and reasoning still isn't critical. There is no mystery because the division of labour between System 1 and System 2 is highly efficient: 'it minimizes effort and optimizes performance' (Kahneman 2011: 25).

The same goes, in some ways, for belief-perseverance and self-ignorance. As we saw in Chapter 2, belief-perseverance after evidential discrediting is made possible by our failure to keep track of the justification relations among our beliefs, and it's not obvious that this failure constitutes a departure from how we are supposed to operate, or from what is Normal for humans. It is both impractical and inefficient for us to keep track of all the justification relations among our beliefs and, as Nisbett and Ross speculate, it might turn out that belief-perseverance serves a range of 'higher order epistemic goals' (1980: 191). Clutter avoidance is one such goal. Maintaining stability in one's belief system might be another. A degree of self-ignorance might also serve a range of epistemic and non-epistemic goals in such a way as to make it Normal for humans; we are not 'supposed' to know all there is to know about our attitudes, aptitudes, character, and so on. Knowing all there is to know about these things would consume vast amounts of energy and storage, and would serve no obvious purpose. In contrast, it's easy to see how, for beings as psychologically fragile as humans tend to be, a degree of self-ignorance might serve a useful purpose: there are some things about ourselves we are better off not knowing.

What this discussion brings out is just how difficult it is to make the case that we are supposed to think and reason like *homo philosophicus*. If, cognitively speaking, so much of what is Normal for us would be far from Normal for *homo philosophicus* how can it possibly be true that we are 'supposed' to be like *homo philosophicus*? All the indications are that it is not in our nature to approximate to *homo philosophicus* and that it is in our nature not to be, or even come close to being, model epistemic citizens. Does this mean that we have to reject the Classical View of man as essentially a rational animal? Not at all. What I have just been arguing is not at odds with this view, which is not to say that it is one we should go out of our way to endorse.

There are a couple of points to notice. The first is that the elements of the Disparity I have been describing as Normal aren't all forms of irrationality. For example, neither belief-perseverance nor fast thinking are irrational, though a person whose belief that P persists after evidential discrediting might be open to rational criticism for continuing to believe that P. If fast thinking isn't irrational, then the fact that it is Normal for humans has no bearing on whether man is a rational animal. A different case is continuing to believe that P even when one recognizes that one isn't warranted in believing that P. This really is irrational but even if it is Normal for some of our attitudes to be 'recalcitrant' in this sense it still wouldn't follow that we aren't essentially rational; it would only follow that it isn't in the nature of man to be perfectly rational.

It's also worth noting that the Classical View, at least as Boyle understands it, doesn't directly support NR_1. On Boyle's reading, the key to the Classical View is that it doesn't see rationality as a particular power that rational animals are equipped with. Rationality is rather a distinctive manner of having powers. Here is an example: both rational and non-rational animals have the power to act but 'there is a sense of "doing something" that applies only to rational creatures' (2012: 414). Only rational creatures can act intentionally, where this is a matter of acting knowingly. A rational creature acts knowingly and intentionally 'in virtue of exercising its power to determine what ends are worth pursuing and how to pursue them' (2012: 414). Belief is another concept that applies differently to rational and non-rational creatures; non-rational animals have beliefs, but the ascription of beliefs and other attitudes to rational animals presupposes an ideal of rationality. This doesn't mean that a rational animal's beliefs are for the most part rational but that the fundamental employment of concepts like *belief* and *action* 'is one in which they figure in representations of a subject as believing and acting for adequate reasons, grasped as such, as exercising *powers* to get things right in the distinctive way in which rational creatures can get things right' (Boyle 2012: 423).

From the fact that we are essentially rational animals and that rationality is a *manner* of having powers rather than a power in its own right it doesn't follow that we are supposed to approximate to *homo philosophicus*, or that it's Normal (or normal) for us to think and reason like *homo philosophicus*. *Homo philosophicus* isn't just rational but hyper-rational, and there is no reason to believe that rational animals are 'supposed' to be hyper-rational, or that having powers in the distinctive manner that rational animals have powers means that we 'should' be like *homo philosophicus* when nothing else gets in the way. Like other rational animals (if there are any), humans are not *homo philosophicus* manqué, and the respects in which we aren't like *homo philosophicus* are quite Normal (as well as normal) for creatures like us.

NR$_2$ can be dealt with more briefly: the question is whether we ought to be like *homo philosophicus*, where 'ought to be' doesn't mean 'supposed to be'. What else could it mean to say that we ought to be like *homo philosophicus*? It would be absurdly moralistic to read this as a moral 'ought'. Even if, contrary to what I've argued, all elements of the Disparity are epistemic failings, epistemic failings aren't moral failings. It's not a sin to think fast or to fail to revise one's beliefs after they have been discredited by new evidence. Perhaps, in that case, the 'ought' in NR$_2$ is a pragmatic 'ought': we will live and work more effectively and happily if we approximate to *homo philosophicus*. This is just implausible. For example, fast thinking is a highly effective responsive to many of the problems we face even if it sometimes leads us astray. No doubt there are particular circumstances in which we 'ought' to reason slowly and critically; as Burge points out, the ability to reason critically is crucial in enterprises such as giving a proof or engaging in debate but these are not exactly things which many of us spend a lot of time doing.[4] Most of the time, fast thinking works just fine, and there is no general truth of the form 'humans ought to reason critically'. It all depends on the circumstances.

Other elements of the Disparity are no different. Would we be better off or happier if we are never biased or self-ignorant, or if our attitudes never survive evidential discrediting? Not necessarily. I've already mentioned the various epistemic and non-epistemic goals served by belief-perseverance and self-ignorance, and it's because they serve such goals that we can make sense of such phenomena. For example, a fair degree of stability in one's attitudes is a good thing not just epistemically but also in respect of one's psychological well-being: it's no good being the kind of person whose attitudes are totally impervious to new evidence but it's also disruptive and unsettling to be constantly revising one's attitudes, however insignificant, in response to every piece of undermining evidence. There is something to be said for sticking to one's guns (in moderation,

---

[4] Burge 1998: 247.

of course) but this is something that *homo philosophicus* would never do in the absence of evidential support. This might not bother him but it would bother us; being a model epistemic citizen can't be much fun, and it's simply not clear why and in what sense we 'ought' to be model epistemic citizens. Indeed, if 'ought' implies 'can' and it's not possible for humans to be much like *homo philosophicus* then NR₂ is wrong to say that we 'ought' to approximate to *homo philosophicus*. The most that can be said is that there are specific times and contexts where we ought to behave ourselves epistemically.

To sum up, I've distinguished two versions of Normative Rationalism and argued that they are both problematic in related ways. They both respond to the Disparity by arguing that whether or not we are actually like *homo philosophicus* we should, in different senses of 'should', be like *homo philosophicus*. I've argued that the relevant senses of 'should' are hard to pin down and that both forms of Normative Rationalism seriously underestimate the extent to which it is *appropriate* for human beings not to approximate to *homo philosophicus*. It's easy, especially for philosophers, to be seduced by the vision of humans striving to be model epistemic citizens but there is also a downside to perfect rationality which shouldn't be forgotten. But even if you are not convinced, there is another point which you will hopefully find convincing: even if Normative Rationalism is plausible, it doesn't help Rationalism about self-knowledge. Let me conclude this chapter by explaining why.

Rationalism about self-knowledge says that it's possible for us to know our own attitudes by employing the Transparency Method. TM says that you can determine what your attitude is in a given case by determining what it ought rationally to be. This requires the assumption that your beliefs and other attitudes *are* as they ought rationally to be, but what if they aren't? There are many ways of dealing with this problem which I'll discuss further in a later chapter: if your attitudes are *roughly* as they ought rationally to be then determining how they ought to be can still serve as a more less reliable guide to how they are. Alternatively, it might be argued that determining that you ought rationally to believe that P *makes it the case* that you believe that P and thereby enables you to know that you believe that P. Whatever the problems with these approaches they do at least address the question raised by the Disparity between what our attitudes are and what they ought rationally to be. But pointing out that we *should* be such that our attitudes are as they ought rationally to be is no help at all. If we were the way that Normative Rationalism says we should be then it would be possible for us to use TM to know our attitudes but the problem is that we aren't that way.

The point is this: Rationalism about self-knowledge isn't just a view about how in an ideal world it would be possible for us to know our own attitudes; it's a view about how we can *actually* know our own attitudes. The key is therefore whether our attitudes are *actually* as they rationally ought to be and, if not, whether this matters to TM. In contrast, Normative Rationalism is *not* concerned with whether our attitudes are actually how they ought to be. It is only concerned with how our attitudes ought to be, and we can all agree that our attitudes rationally ought to be as they rationally ought to be. This is no use to TM because it doesn't tackle the Disparity. Unlike Psychological Rationalism, Normative Rationalism doesn't try to attenuate the Disparity. Unlike compatibilism, Normative Rationalism doesn't try to show that TM is still usable despite the Disparity. What Normative Rationalism says is that TM would be usable by us if we approximated to *homo philosophicus* but that is plainly not the issue. For all that Normative Rationalism says about how humans should think and reason, it remains totally mysterious how on this account we actually are able to know our own attitudes.

I started this chapter by asking these questions: is there any justification for the view that humans ought to, or are supposed to, approximate to *homo philosophicus*? If we ought to approximate to *homo philosophicus*, does that mean that we can know our own attitudes by employing the Transparency Method? It should now be clear that the answer to both is 'no'. If the answer to the second question were 'yes' then Normative Rationalism would support what I have been calling 'compatibilism', but in reality Normative Rationalism does no such thing. Although insisting that we 'should' be like *homo philosophicus* is compatible with admitting that we aren't like *homo philosophicus*, this doesn't explain how our not being like *homo philosophicus* is compatible with our being able to know our own attitudes by using the Transparency Method. These are two different types of 'compatibility', and they need to be clearly distinguished.

Given the limitations of Psychological and Normative Rationalism the best bet for rationalism about self-knowledge is to explore the second type of compatibility, that is, the possibility that the Disparity is compatible with our actually being able to know our attitudes by means of TM. This is 'compatibilism' as I understand it, and I will have more to say about it in Chapter 9. First, there is another matter that needs to be resolved. I have repeatedly said in this chapter and in previous chapters that not all the elements of the Disparity are forms of irrationality. This raises an obvious question: how exactly should the notion of 'irrationality' be understood? This question is worth asking because, apart from its relevance for the Classical View of man and Rationalism about self-knowledge, it has become fashionable in recent years for non-philosophers to talk about the extent to which humans are 'irrational'. Behavioural economists, in particular, tend to go on about this but I want to argue that the concept of rationality isn't well understood by people who argue in this way, and that however struck we are by the Disparity we should refrain from describing human beings as constitutionally irrational.

8

Predictably Irrational?

Predictably Irrational is the title of a bestselling book by the behavioural econo-mist Dan Ariely.[1] This is one of many such books, all of which are about the ways in which we are irrational or less than perfectly rational. Yet, while behavioural economists like Ariely regard irrationality as endemic in our lives, many philo-sophers continue to the impressed by human rationality. It's not that irrationality isn't a topic in philosophy; philosophers do discuss such things as self-deception and weakness of the will, and are prepared to view these as forms of irrationality. However, what makes irrationality philosophically interesting is that fact that it is a departure from what is seen as the norm: in the terminology of the last chapter, rationality is normal (as well as Normal) for humans, and that's why irrationality needs explaining. In contrast, the impression you get from writers like Ariely is that irrationality is the norm, and that human beings are not just irrational but predictably irrational.

It's possible that philosophers and behavioural economists are to some extent talking at cross purposes. What behavioural economists mean when they describe us as 'irrational' might turn out to be consistent what philosophers mean when they describe man as a rational animal. In addition, not all behavioural econo-mists would accept Ariely's formulations. Some of the key papers in the history of behavioural economics were written by Daniel Kahneman and the late Amos Tversky, and it's telling that in *Thinking, Fast and Slow* Kahneman says this:

Irrational is a strong word, which connotes impulsivity, emotionality, and a stubborn resistance to reasonable argument. I often cringe when my work with Amos is credited with demonstrating that human choices are irrational, when in fact our research only showed that Humans are not well described by the rational agent model. (2011: 411)

The 'rational agent model' is at the basis neoclassical economics; it is the model of humans as what Thaler and Sunstein call 'Econs', beings who think and choose unfailingly well, and fit the textbook picture of rational agents offered by

---

[1] Ariely 2009.

economists.[2] Kahneman's point is that just because you believe that there is a significant disparity between *homo sapiens* and *homo economicus* that doesn't commit you to thinking that human beings are irrational. Indeed, it's not just that you aren't committed to thinking this but that describing humans as 'irrational' is potentially misleading and unhelpful.

The question raised by all of this is: just what is it to be rational or irrational? How are these notions to be understood? Is Kahneman right that 'irrational' connotes impulsivity, emotionality, and a stubborn resistance to reasonable argument? Is this what Ariely means by 'irrational'? If not, what does he mean? It's important for my purposes to get clear about all of this since I've claimed that fast thinking and belief-perseverance aren't irrational whereas attitude-recalci-trance is. What does 'irrational' mean in this context? I have also talked at various times about:

Whether a person's attitudes are irrational
Whether a person's attitudes are as they ought rationally to be
Whether a person's attitudes are open to rational criticism

How are these things related? For example, I said in Chapter 2 that belief-perseverance might be open to rational criticism even if it isn't irrational. But in what sense can your belief that P be open to rational criticism if it's not irrational for you to believe that P? Can your attitude fail to be as it ought rationally to be without it, or you, being irrational? Notice also that only some of these epithets apply to both attitudes and people. Both you and your attitudes can be irrational and open to rational criticism but only your attitudes can fail to be as they ought rationally to be. This might lead one to wonder whether the most basic use of 'irrational' and 'open to rational criticism' is in relation to people or to their attitudes.

Before explaining my own view of these matters, I'd like to spend a bit more time on Ariely, since his books provide a good illustration of some of the pitfalls we need to take care to avoid. It's striking how hard it is in a book called *Predictably Irrational* to figure out what Ariely means by 'irrational'. He writes at one point that his book is about 'human irrationality—about our distance from perfection' (2009: xxix). The perfection referred to here is exemplified by *homo economicus* but it's far from obvious that not thinking and choosing like *homo economicus* makes us irrational. Even if we agree that *homo economicus* is ideally or perfectly rational, it's implausible that not being ideally or perfectly rational makes us *irrational*. Indeed, it's striking that many of Ariely's examples of human

---

[2] Thaler and Sunstein 2008: 7.

irrationality don't even come close to exemplifying the phenomenon. For example, he devotes an entire chapter in the sequel to *Predictably Irrational* to what he calls 'adaptation', the human ability to get used to new environments, pain, and 'almost everything else' (2011: 168) but it's never clear from the discussion what this has to do with our being irrational.

A slightly better example for our purposes is one that Ariely uses to illustrate what he calls 'the truth about relativity'. He describes an advert for the *Economist* which offers three subscription choices:

1. Internet-only subscription for $59.
2. Print-only subscription for $125.
3. Print-and-internet subscription for $125.

In a survey of MIT Management students, 84% went for option 3, 16% for option 1, and none for option 2. But when option 2 was removed, 68% chose the internet-only option and only 32% chose the combined print-and-internet option. What is going on here? In the original list, option 2 was functioning as a 'decoy'. Option 3 looks good compared to option 2, and lots of students chose option 3 as a result. Remove the decoy, which no one chose, and suddenly option 3 doesn't look so good.

The lesson of this case, which I will call SUBSCRIPTION, is that 'we are always looking at the things around us in relation to others' (Ariely 2009: 7). This is the relativity that helps to explain our responses to the *Economist* offer but why is it irrational to be influenced by considerations of relativity? The problem, according to Ariely, is not just that we are often influenced by factors that are themselves irrational but that we do not realize how often we are influenced by such factors:

If I were to distil one main lesson from the research described in this book, it is that we are pawns in a game whose forces we largely fail to comprehend... Each of the chapters in this book describes a force (emotions, relativity, social norms, etc.) that influences our behaviour. And while these influences exert a lot of power over our behaviour, our natural tendency is to vastly underestimate or completely ignore this power. These influences have an effect on us not because we lack knowledge, lack practice, or are weak-minded. On the contrary, they repeatedly affect experts as well as novices in systematic and predictable ways. (2009: 243)

This suggests that our fundamental problem is *self-ignorance*, ignorance of what Ariely calls 'The Hidden Forces that Shape our Decisions'.[3] Uncovering these forces is in turn 'the real goal of behavioural economics' (2011: 9); the hope is that we will make better decisions if we understand the forces that influence us.

---

[3] This is actually the subtitle of Ariely 2009.

We now have two quite different ways of understanding the claim that human beings are irrational. On one reading, we are irrational in being influenced by forces (hidden or not) that are in themselves irrational. On another reading, the suggestion is that we are irrational to the extent that we are ignorant of the forces that influence our decisions. However, there are problems with Ariely's account on either reading. Mere self-ignorance is not itself irrational on any recognizable conception of irrationality: if in a case like SUBSCRIPTION you simply don't realize that your choices are being influenced by the presence of decoys why does that make you irrational? There might be something to the charge of irrationality if the influence of such factors is something we ought to realize but there isn't any case for saying that; we are *supposed* not to realize what is going on so it can't just be our ignorance of the various forces that shape our decisions that makes us irrational. These forces would themselves have to be 'irrational forces' (2011: 9), and then we are back with the problem of having to explain in what sense each of the factors whose influence is described by Ariely counts as 'irrational'.

What this discussion brings out is the paramount importance of being absolutely clear at the outset about the concept of irrationality, and the distinction between this concept and other concepts like that of self-ignorance. It's no good going on about 'human irrationality' unless you have a decent account of the concept of irrationality, and this is what is Ariely and others like him plainly do not have. The account of irrationality I favour is Scanlon's account in *What We Owe to Each Other*.[4] With this in mind, my plan for the rest of this chapter is this: I'm going to start by listing five platitudes about the notions of 'rationality' and 'irrationality' which I think need to be respected by any viable account of these notions. This will lead into a discussion of Scanlon. He defends a narrow account of irrationality which pays due respect to the platitudes but is more restrictive than other accounts, such as Derek Parfit's. I will explain why I think the narrow view is better and how it accounts for some of the phenomena I've been discussing. Finally, after using the narrow account to explain what is wrong with Ariely's discussion, I will conclude with a short discussion of a paper I mentioned in the last chapter, Stephen Stich's 'Could Man be an Irrational Animal?'[5] Stich is a notable example of a philosopher who, unlike the rationalists I have been criticizing, plays up rather than plays down the scale of human irrationality. Although I'm sympathetic to the spirit of 'Could Man be an Irrational Animal?', I believe that some of my criticisms of Ariely also apply to Stich's vastly superior discussion. In my terms, what Stich does is to draw

---

[4] Scanlon 1998.   [5] Stich 1985.

attention to the Disparity, but this has little to do with man being an 'irrational' animal.

Here are the platitudes:

(a) 'Rational' and 'irrational' are terms that apply to many different things, including people, beliefs, desires, fears, and choices. They don't apply to sensations like pain and hunger. If you've just eaten a big meal and are still hungry your hunger might be odd or surprising but not irrational; you can't be irrationally hungry. When it comes to arguments or inferences it's not clear whether they can be said to be rational or irrational. It might be 'rational' to infer one proposition from another which entails it but we don't tend to describe bad arguments as 'irrational', as opposed to 'invalid' or 'fallacious'.

(b) When we talk about beliefs and other attitudes as rational or irrational what we are thinking of as rational or irrational is the *having* of the attitude. The belief that the present government will be re-elected is one that you and I can both have, and it can be irrational for you to believe that the present government will be re-elected even if it isn't irrational for me to have the very same belief. Your evidence and other beliefs might be different from mine. It isn't 'the belief that the government will be re-elected', understood as something that different people can have, that is rational or irrational but rather *believing* that the government will be re-elected, given one's other beliefs and the available evidence.

(c) Even rational beings are sometimes irrational, in the sense that they sometimes have attitudes and make choices that are irrational. This is an elementary point but it's significant because it suggests that the mere fact that some of your choices and attitudes are irrational isn't sufficient to make you irrational, though there must be limits to how irrational your attitudes can be without also calling your rationality into question.

(d) People and their attitudes can both be irrational but the sense in which a person is irrational is different from the sense in which one of his attitudes is irrational. Saying that a person is irrational implies some kind of systemic failure, and that is why the fact that some of your attitudes are irrational doesn't necessarily make you irrational: some of your attitudes can be irrational without implying the kind of systemic failure that would justify the conclusion that you are irrational.

(e) Saying that a person or attitude is irrational is different from saying that they are open to rational criticism. 'Irrational' is harsher but also narrower in application. If you are a poor logician and produce a fallacious argument for some conclusion you are open to rational criticism but not irrational. You might be open to rational criticism for not knowing things you should know given the evidence available to you but not knowing what you should know is not necessarily irrational.

One of the attractions of Scanlon's account is that it does justice to these platitudes. The focus of Scanlon's discussion is what he calls reasons in the 'standard normative sense'.[6] Reasons in this sense are what are at issue if you assert that P and I ask you what reason there is to think that P. A good reason for thinking that P is a consideration that counts in favour of thinking that P. The class of attitudes for which reasons in the standard normative sense can sensibly be asked for is the class of *judgement-sensitive attitudes*. These are attitudes that 'an ideally rational person would come to have whenever that person judged there to be sufficient reasons for them and that would, in an ideally rational person, "extinguish" when that person judged them not to be supported by reasons of the appropriate kind' (Scanlon 1998: 20). Belief, fear, admiration, and respect are judgement-sensitive attitudes and are in this sense 'in the space of reasons'. Hunger is not, which might explain why it's not the kind of thing that can properly be described as 'rational' or 'irrational'.

In these terms, 'a rational creature is, first of all, a reasoning creature – one that has the capacity to recognize, assess, and be moved by reasons, and hence to have judgement-sensitive attitudes' (1998: 23). When a rational creature judges that a certain attitude is warranted she generally comes to have this attitude, and 'when a rational creature judges that the reasons she is aware of count decisively against a certain attitude, she generally does not have that attitude, or ceases to have it if she did so before' (1998: 24). The sense in which the rationality of a person is a systemic matter is that it involves systematic connections between aspects of the person's thought and behaviour. And what makes it intelligible that 'rational creatures are sometimes irrational' (1998: 25) is the fact that these connections need not hold in every case.

Having explained what it is for a creature to be rational or irrational Scanlon says the following about what it takes for one's attitudes to be irrational:

Irrationality in the clearest sense occurs when a person's attitudes fail to conform to his or her own judgements: when, for example, a person continues to believe something (continues to regard it with conviction and take it as a premise in subsequent reasoning) even though she judges there to be a good reason for rejecting it, or when a person fails to

---

[6] Scanlon 1998: 19.

form and act on an intention to do something even though he or she judges there to be an overwhelmingly good reason to do it. These are clear cases of irrationality because the thought or action they involve is in an obvious sense "contrary to (the person's own) reason": there is a direct clash between the judgements a person makes and the judgements required by the attitudes he or she holds. Irrationality in this sense occurs when a person recognizes something as a reason but fails to be affected by it in one of the relevant ways. (1998: 25)

On this account there is a distinction between an attitude's being irrational and its being mistaken or open to rational criticism. Someone who is hasty or careless in arriving at the conclusion that P may be open to rational criticism but isn't irrational. Mistaken or misguided beliefs are open to rational criticism but 'not every mistaken belief is one that it is irrational to hold' (1998: 25). BAT AND BALL is a very good illustration of this point: if you believe as a result of fast thinking that the ball costs 10 cents then you are wrong and open to rational criticism. However, it's not *irrational* to think the ball costs 10 cents as long as there is no conflict between what you believe (that the ball costs 10 cents) and what you take yourself to have good reason to believe (that the ball costs 10 cents). It might be 'contrary to reason' to believe that the ball costs 10 cents but it isn't contrary to *your* reason.

Scanlon describes his account of irrationality as 'narrow' and it's easy to see why. On his account, irrationality is a kind of inconsistency. Critics object that Scanlon's view is too narrow and that 'irrationality' in the ordinary sense is a much broader notion, meaning 'open to rational criticism'. Parfit observes that in Scanlon's sense the term 'irrational' applies 'only to people who fail to respond to what they themselves believe to be reasons' (2011: 123). On Parfit's preferred broader construal, the term also applies to those who fail to respond to what *are* reasons, and not just to those who fail to respond to what they themselves *acknowledge* to be reasons. On this account, our beliefs are irrational 'when we are failing to respond to clear and strongly decisive epistemic reasons not to have these beliefs' (2011: 122). For Parfit, 'irrational' in the ordinary sense means 'deserves strong criticism of the kind we also express with words like "foolish", "stupid", and "crazy"' (2011: 123). This claim is directly at odds with my final so-called platitude.

One problem with the broad construal of irrationality is that it makes it tough for us to draw straightforward distinctions between different types of cognitive failing. If 'irrational' means 'open to rational criticism' then in the case of the poor logician and BAT AND BALL we would have to say that the subject's attitude is irrational but that's wrong. If there is a lot at stake in giving the right answer to BAT AND BALL (you'll be shot if you make a mistake) then it would undoubtedly be foolish to judge that the ball costs 10 cents but still not strictly irrational. The narrow construal of irrationality also does better with phenomena like belief-perseverance and attitude-recalcitrance. I argued in Chapter 2 that whereas recalcitrance is irrational, belief-perseverance is not. The narrow account of irrationality makes sense of this verdict and also allows us to say that belief-perseverance is open to rational criticism without being irrational. The broad account ends up lumping together phenomena that clearly should not be lumped together; the sense in which belief-perseverance is open to rational criticism is plainly different from the sense in which attitude-recalcitrance is open to rational criticism, and the obvious way to mark this distinction is to say that only the latter is irrational.

It's easy to see why, on the narrow account, recalcitrance counts as irrational. In Chapter 1, I gave the example of fear as a recalcitrant attitude: in this example, call it SPIDER, you are afraid of the spider in your bathtub despite knowing that you have no reason to be afraid of it. Fear is your attitude and it isn't extinguished by your judgement that there is good reason to reject it. Understood in this way, your fear is 'irrational' in the narrow sense. It's also irrational in the broad sense of irrational if anything that is irrational in the narrow sense is also irrational in the broad sense; unless you have a phobia it is 'foolish' or 'stupid' to fear the spider in your bathtub when you judge that there is no reason to be afraid of it. However, we now run into the following problem: fear is supposed to be judgement-sensitive but in SPIDER your fear is judgement-insensitive. Isn't this a problem for the narrow account, and isn't the obvious conclusion that there are in fact two varieties of fear, judgement-sensitive and judgement-insensitive fear? However, once we think of recalcitrant fear as judgement-insensitive it looks as though it can't be irrational. We don't think of other judgement-insensitive states of mind such as hunger as irrational (or rational) so how can judgement-insensitive fear be irrational? Surely the right thing to think is that it isn't in the space of reasons, and that terms like 'rational' and 'irrational' don't apply to it.

This argument misunderstands Scanlon's judgement-sensitive/judgement-insensitive distinction. In fact, there is no basis for distinguishing between two varieties of fear, or for claiming that recalcitrant fear isn't judgement-sensitive. Remember that judgement-sensitive attitudes are ones that an ideally rational person (*homo philosophicus*?) would come to have whenever that person judged there to be sufficient reasons for them. In that case your fear is judgement-sensitive, for whenever an ideally rational person judged there to be sufficient reason to fear spiders he *would* fear them. Your fear is also judgement-sensitive in another sense: it belongs to the 'class of things for which reasons in the standard normative sense can sensibly be asked for or offered' (Scanlon 1998: 21); you can sensibly be asked why you are afraid of the spider in your bathtub. The point is that judgement-sensitive attitudes must be *generally* responsive to the agent's judgements about the adequacy of the reasons for having them but the fact that in this case your attitude isn't responsive to your reasons is consistent with its being the *kind* of attitude that is generally reason-responsive.

Why, on the narrow construal of irrationality, is belief-perseverance *not* irrational? Let's consider KAREN again: on the basis of her reported test results, she believes that P, the proposition that she has an aptitude for science and music but not for history and philosophy. When she finds out that she was given the wrong results, she continues to believe that P. On the broad construal of irrationality, whether this belief is irrational depends on whether Karen is failing to respond to clear and decisive epistemic reasons not to believe that P after the discrediting of her evidence. You might think that the discrediting of her evidence is itself a clear and decisive epistemic reason for her not to believe that P. On the other hand, it could also be argued that the discrediting of her evidence only means that she has lost one clear and decisive epistemic reason to believe that P, and that this is not the same as having a clear and decisive epistemic reason not to believe that P; maybe Karen has, or thinks she has, other reasons for believing that P. There remains the question whether Karen is 'foolish', 'stupid', or 'crazy' to continue to believe that P but it's not entirely clear what the answer to the question is.

Unlike the broad account of irrationality, the narrow account has no trouble giving the right verdict in KAREN. As I've said, the right verdict is that her continuing to believe that P is not irrational because she doesn't judge there to be a good reason for rejecting this belief. Her believing that P isn't contrary to her own reason because she doesn't realize her belief has been discredited by the discovery that there was a mix-up over the test results. This is something she can fail to realize as long as she doesn't realize the discredited evidence was the sole evidence for her belief that P. She doesn't realize this because, like most of us, Karen is bad at keeping track of her original reasons for her beliefs. It would be irrational for Karen still to believe that P if she is aware that her sole evidence has been discredited but this would turn the example into a case of recalcitrance and not mere perseverance.

Is Karen nevertheless open to rational criticism for continuing to believe that P? Yes, on the basis that her belief is mistaken and misguided. Another consideration is whether, after the discrediting of her evidence, Karen believes what she ought rationally to believe. At least by her own lights she does because she doesn't *realize* that her belief has been discredited. But the fact is that her belief *has* been discredited, and her failure to recognize this doesn't get her off the hook epistemologically speaking. So perhaps what we should say about Karen is this: her continuing to believe that P after her sole evidence for P has been discredited is *in fact* a case of her believing what she ought no longer to believe, even though she doesn't realize it. Her failure to realize that her evidence has been discredited means that she is open to rational criticism rather than strictly irrational for continuing to believe that P. This take on KAREN exploits Scanlon's distinction between being irrational and being open to rational criticism. At the same time, it links Karen's being open to rational criticism to her believing what she ought not to believe.

Another case which brings out the importance of distinguishing between a belief's being irrational and its being open to rational criticism is OLIVER. Oliver believes that P (the collapse of the twin towers on 9/11 was caused by explosives planted in advance rather than by aircraft impact and the resulting fires) because P follows from various other things he believes on the basis of what he regards as 'evidence'. Suppose that Q is the proposition from which Oliver infers P. Q might be the proposition that aircraft impacts couldn't have caused the towers to collapse and that eye witnesses heard explosions just before the collapse of each tower. In these circumstances, is Oliver's belief that P irrational? Notice that there is nothing wrong with Oliver's reasoning from Q to P, and no clash between his judgements and the judgements required by the attitudes he holds. In this sense his attitudes are not irrational. Is his belief that P nevertheless irrational in the sense that it fails to respond to strongly decisive epistemic reasons not to have it? Even that isn't clear. Oliver is, of course, aware of official denials of P but his response is 'They would say that, wouldn't they?' He doesn't just ignore the official denials of P but has a story to tell about why such denials are not to be trusted.

One advantage of the narrow over the broad construal of irrationality is that it delivers a clear, as well as a plausible, verdict in cases like OLIVER. The clear and plausible verdict is that Oliver's belief that P is foolish, stupid, and open to rational criticism but not irrational. The next challenge is to explain why his belief is open to rational criticism despite not being irrational. In Chapter 2, I quoted Sebastian Rödl as claiming:

If P follows from Q, then someone who believes Q *rationally* ought to believe P. (2007: 88)

If this is right then in believing P Oliver believes what he ought rationally to believe. In that case, how can he be open to rational criticism? The reply to this is that he is open to rational criticism because he shouldn't believe that Q. If he shouldn't believe that Q then he shouldn't believe that P, given that he infers P from Q. The delicate question is: what's wrong with believing that Q? Again, the issue isn't whether it's irrational to believe that Q. Consider the claim that aircraft impacts couldn't have caused the towers to collapse. This claim has (I take it) been refuted by a National Institute of Standards and Technology (NIST) study, but Oliver dismisses the NIST study and attaches much greater weight to claims by conspiracy theorists that explosive residues were found in the debris of the twin towers.[7] What has gone wrong is that Oliver attaches too much weight to such claims and not enough weight to the NIST report. Given the NIST report Oliver shouldn't believe that Q and is open to rational criticism for believing that Q. However, attaching too much weight to one piece of evidence and too little to another isn't strictly irrational, even though it is something for which Oliver deserves criticism.

I hope I've said enough to convince you of the following:

- There's rather a lot to be said for construing irrationality narrowly rather than broadly. The narrow construal does justice to the five platitudes and delivers the correct verdict on examples like SPIDER, BAT AND BALL, KAREN, and OLIVER. In some of these cases the broad construal gives the wrong verdict or no clear verdict.
- Whereas attitude-recalcitrance is irrational, belief-perseverance per se is not. If you don't realize your evidence for P has been discredited you aren't irrational for continuing to believe that P though you might be open to rational criticism.
- In such cases being open to rational criticism is linked to your believing what you shouldn't believe. The fact that you *think* your beliefs are as they ought rationally to be doesn't mean that they *are* as they ought rationally to be or that they aren't open to rational criticism.

Bearing these points in mind, along with the five platitudes, we can now go back to Ariely. As a behavioural economist he is primarily concerned with the extent to which our choices and behaviour are irrational rather than with the irrationality of our beliefs. One issue, therefore, is whether the choices and behaviour he describes are really irrational, and not just flawed in some other way. Another is whether, if they are examples of irrationality, Ariely is justified in concluding that *we* are predictably irrational. On the first issue, I've already made the point that there is no clear sense in which the choices made by the majority of

---

[7] See Lew, Bukowski, and Carino 2005. The report found no evidence that the towers were brought down by controlled demolition using explosives planted prior to 11 September 2001. The absurdity of Oliver's theory is also brought out by the 9/11 Commission Report. See Kean and Hamilton 2012.

subjects in SUBSCRIPTION are irrational; just because you aren't aware that your choices are being influenced by a decoy that doesn't make them irrational. On a narrow interpretation of irrationality they would only be irrational if they are inconsistent with your own sense of what you have reason to choose. This can happen: if you are trying to lose weight you know perfectly well that you should not have the chocolate dessert but might still choose to have it. Knowingly choosing the high fat dessert is irrational but SUBSCRIPTION is different. You might be open to rational criticism for switching from option 3 to option 1 after the removal of option 2—though even that isn't completely obvious—but switching under the influence of relativity doesn't make you irrational: you aren't at any stage choosing something you know you have a good reason not to choose.

On the narrow construal of irrationality less of our behaviour and fewer of our choices are irrational than Ariely would have us believe. It's also important to keep in mind that even rational creatures can make irrational choices (this was my third platitude), so you can't jump directly from the claim that humans make irrational choices to the conclusion that humans are irrational. Given my fourth platitude, the real issue is whether our irrational choices, such as they are, are evidence of a systemic failure that is serious enough to call into question whether we are rational beings. If a rational being is one that has the capacity to recognize, assess, and be moved by reasons then examples like SUBSCRIPTION plainly do not show that we aren't rational beings. Even if we agree that we aren't being moved by 'reason' or 'reasons' in cases like SUBSCRIPTION, this doesn't show that we lack the *capacity* to be moved by reasons or to recognize and assess reasons; a creature can have the capacity to be moved by reasons and yet not be moved by them at all times. The inescapable conclusion is that nothing that Ariely says has any bearing on whether human beings are rational beings in the systemic sense. The most that he and other behavioural economists show is that we aren't *homo economicus* but not being *homo economicus* doesn't make us 'irrational'.

Turning, finally, to Stich, some of the things I've been saying about Ariely also apply to him. Stich's question is: could man be an irrational animal? His first move in tackling this question is to observe that human beings 'regularly and systematically invoke inferential and judgemental strategies ranging from the merely invalid to the genuinely bizarre' (1985: 115). He notes, however, that there are philosophers like Daniel Dennett who argue that 'empirical evidence could not possibly support the conclusion that people are systematically irrational'. Stich disagrees: 'my central thesis is that philosophical arguments aimed at showing that irrationality cannot be experimentally demonstrated are mistaken' (1985: 115).

The inferential and judgemental strategies Stich discusses include violations of basic principles of probabilistic reasoning as well as familiar examples of belief-perseverance. He reads Dennett as arguing that supposed experimental demonstrations of human irrationality are at odds with the inevitable rationality of believers: 'people must be rational *if they can usefully be viewed as having any beliefs at all*' (1985: 121). In response Stich argues that 'it is simply not the case that our ordinary belief and desire ascriptions presuppose full rationality' (1985: 121-2). When we ascribe propositional attitudes to others, we take it that they are 'in relevant ways, similar to ourselves' (1985: 122). We know that we make mistakes in our reasoning and so have no difficulty imagining that other believers do the same: in order to view other people as having beliefs we don't have to regard them as fully rational.

I think that Stich is right to this extent: what he objects to is pretty much the same as what I was objecting to in my discussion of Psychological Rationalism: the idea that we must approximate to *homo philosophicus* if we have beliefs, desires, and other such propositional attitudes. If 'full rationality' means operating like *homo philosophicus* then it's true, as Stich points out, that full rationality is not a necessary condition for having propositional attitudes; the fact that we regularly and systematically invoke inferential and judgemental strategies ranging from the invalid to the bizarre doesn't prevent us from having propositional attitudes. But does this show that man could be an irrational animal? Yes, if being an irrational animal means 'being prone to poor reasoning and having propositional attitudes some of which are irrational'. However, there is a deeper sense in which, like Ariely, Stich doesn't show that we are irrational: just because some of our reasoning is poor, it doesn't follow that we lack the capacity to recognize, assess, and be moved by reasons. This is just another example of my third and fourth platitudes in operation.

It's an interesting question what it would take to show that humans lack the capacity to recognize, assess, and be moved by reasons. Whether or not such a thing is possible, one thing is clear: if you really think that humans are incapable of being moved by reasons, there wouldn't be much point trying to persuade them of this. For doesn't the philosophical project of *arguing* for something presuppose that the person you are addressing is capable of being moved by rational argument, and therefore rational? But being rational in this sense has little to do with being a model epistemic citizen, with being *homo philosophicus*, and this brings us back neatly to the one of main themes of this book, namely, the Disparity. I think that the best and most generous way of reading people like Ariely and Stich is as drawing attention to the scale of the Disparity. Saying on the basis of the Disparity that 'man is an irrational animal' is just a piece of hyperbole. I think that Kahneman is absolutely right about this, and I hope that this chapter has explained why he is right: the problem is not that 'irrational' is a strong word which connotes impulsivity, emotionality, and a stubborn resistance to argument but that the description of humans, as distinct from some of their attitudes and choices, as 'irrational' implies a specific kind of systemic failure which just isn't at issue in behavioural economics or the psychological literature which Stich make so much of.

Suppose, then, that we cut out talking about humans as 'irrational' and talk instead about the Disparity between *homo sapiens* and *homo philosophicus*. Where does this leave us? It leaves us with the task of figuring out the consequences of the Disparity. Man may be a 'rational creature' in Scanlon's sense but still is a long way being *homo philosophicus*. I've suggested in previous chapters that this looks like a problem for Psychological Rationalism and for Rationalism about self-knowledge. I've already devoted a chapter to Psychological Rationalism so it's now time take a closer look at Rationalism about self-knowledge. What we need to figure out is: how can TM be a pathway to self-knowledge given the Disparity? This was the question which got my discussion going and it's now time to tackle it head-on.

9

Looking Outwards

Way back in Chapter 1, I talked about the Rationalist approach to self-knowledge. Rationalism tries to account for our knowledge of our beliefs, desires, fears, and other such 'intentional' states. The central idea of Rationalism is that using the Transparency Method (TM) is, for us, a basic source of 'intentional' self-knowledge, that is, knowledge of our own beliefs, fears, desires, etc. A lot of what I've been calling 'substantial' self-knowledge isn't accounted for by TM but that's not an objection to Rationalism, any more than it's an objection to Rationalism that it doesn't try to explain how we know our own sensations: it's neither necessary nor possible to account for all self-knowledge in one fell swoop, and it would be a good start to at least have a successful account of how we know our own beliefs, desires, etc. This brings us to the main question I want to address in this chapter: is Rationalism any good at least as an account of intentional self-knowledge?

In Chapter 1, I mentioned several worries about Rationalism, one of which is that it runs into trouble with the Disparity: maybe *homo philosophicus* can work out whether he believes that P by asking whether he ought rationally to believe that P but it's not clear that that's going to cut it for *homo sapiens*. This led to a discussion of the extent of the Disparity but in this chapter I want to leave that discussion behind. My question here is whether Rationalism can live with the Disparity, that is, whether you can accept that there is an extensive Disparity and still maintain that TM is for us a basic source of intentional self-knowledge. I have referred to this combination of views as 'compatibilism', and one way of starting to make the case for compatibilism is to question my understanding of Rationalism. It might be argued, in particular, is that what I've been calling 'Rationalism' is a rather crude and simple-minded version of that doctrine— call it Simple Rationalism—and that there is a more subtle form of Rationalism which can deal with the Disparity much better than Simple Rationalism. For reasons which will become clearer in a while I will refer to this more subtle form of Rationalism as Activism.

Whichever kind of Rationalist you are, one thing you are quite likely to think is that intentional self-knowledge is epistemically privileged. One idea is that intentional self-knowledge is infallible or at least authoritative: your beliefs about you own beliefs and other attitudes can't be mistaken or, even if they can be, there's a presumption that they aren't mistaken. Other Rationalists emphasize what they think of as the 'immediacy' of intentional self-knowledge, the fact that this kind of knowledge is normally non-inferential and not based on evidence.[1] So there are two questions for Rationalism, whether Simple or Activist: one is whether, bearing in mind the Disparity and the other difficulties I mentioned in Chapter 1, it explains how we can *know* our own beliefs, desires, and other attitudes. The other is whether, on a Rationalist construal, intentional self-knowledge comes out as *epistemically privileged* in the relevant sense. Rationalism is in trouble if the answer to either question is 'no'.

This brings me to the position I want to defend in this chapter: although I think that it *is* possible for us to know some of our attitudes by using TM, I doubt that the self-knowledge we gain by using TM has all the epistemic privileges Rationalism is after, or that this kind of self-knowledge is especially basic or fundamental. In fact, TM is one of a range of pathways to intentional self-knowledge, all of which can only deliver indirect and evidence-based self-knowledge. There is also a connection with what I was saying in Chapter 3. There I drew a distinction between 'substantial' and 'trivial' self-knowledge and pointed out that knowledge of your own attitudes—say your belief that all races are equal, or that you want another child—can be substantial. Interestingly, the intentional self-knowledge which Rationalism does by far the best job of accounting for is the trivial variety; the more substantial your intentional self-knowledge, the less convincingly TM accounts for it. So the more strongly you believe that the philosophy of self-knowledge should focus on substantial self-knowledge, the less satisfied you should be with Rationalism about self-knowledge. Even when it comes to trivial self-knowledge, Rationalism runs into a variety of problems, not all of which are connected to the Disparity. In the end I think that the right thing to say about TM is that it is a minor player in the true story about intentional self-knowledge, but that it's not an objection to TM that it only delivers evidence-based self-knowledge: pretty much any self-knowledge that is worth having is going to be evidence-based.

In getting to this conclusion I want to begin by reminding you of the main tenets of Rationalism, and then introducing the distinction between two versions of Rationalism as a response to some of the problems I mentioned in Chapter 1. The way I introduced Rationalism in that chapter was by quoting Gareth Evans as saying that he gets himself in a position to answer the question whether he

---

[1] The immediacy of intentional self-knowledge is an important theme in Moran 2001.

believes that P by putting into operation whatever procedure he has for answering the question whether P. In making a self-ascription of belief, Evans says, 'one's eyes are, so to speak, or occasionally literally, directed outward- upon the world' (1982: 225). This idea is taken up by Richard Moran in his book *Authority and Estrangement*. In Moran's terminology, the question 'Do I believe that P?' is an inward-directed question, whereas the question 'Is P true?' is outward-directed. These questions have different subject-matters, but Moran argues that the inward-directed question is, as he puts it, 'transparent' to the corresponding outward-directed question. Furthermore:

[I]f the person were entitled to assume, or in some way even obligated to assume, that his considerations for and against believing P (the outward-directed question) actually determined in this case what his belief concerning P actually is (the inward-directed question), then he would be entitled to answer the question concerning his believing P or not by consideration of the reasons in favour of P. (Moran 2004: 457)

In brief:

(a) To say that the question whether you believe that P is transparent to the question whether P is true is to say that you can answer the former question by answering the latter question.

(b) What makes it possible for you to answer the inward-directed question by answering the corresponding outward-directed question is your assumption that your belief concerning P is determined by your reasons for and against believing P.

What makes this a *Rationalist* account of self-knowledge is that it takes your belief concerning P to be determined by your reasons and so to be knowable by reflecting on your reasons.

Both Evans and Moran reckon that the transparency account can explain the epistemic privileges of self-knowledge. Evans talks about his procedure not allowing 'even the most determined sceptic' to 'insert his knife', which suggests that he thinks that his version of the Transparency Method delivers a kind of infallible self-knowledge.[2] For Moran, the key issue isn't infallibility but immediacy. Sometimes what he means by immediate self-knowledge is knowledge not based on *behavioural* evidence.[3] At other times he means knowledge not based on *any* evidence.[4] Then there is the idea that immediate self-knowledge is non-inferential, which may or may not be equivalent to saying that is not based on evidence. There's also the point that non-inferential knowledge can be either

---

[2] Evans 1982: 225.   [3] Moran 2001: xxix.   [4] Moran 2001: 11.

psychologically or epistemically immediate, and it's not clear what kind of non-inferential self-knowledge TM is supposed to deliver. I'll come back to this.

One question about TM which came up in Chapter 1 was: how can it account of self-knowledge of attitudes other than belief? Even if the question 'Do I believe that P?' is transparent to the question 'Is it true that P?', the same can't be said for 'Do I desire that P?' or 'Do I fear that P?' I'm going to call this the Generality Problem for Rationalism: the problem is that the version of TM you get from Evans and Moran can only account for a sub-class of intentional self-knowledge. It isn't just knowledge of your own sensations and lots of substantial self-knowledge that it can't account for; it can't even account for your knowledge of your own desires and fears.

Finkelstein's solution to the Generality Problem on behalf of Rationalism is to read TM as proposing that the question whether you believe that P is transparent to the question whether you *ought rationally* to believe that P.[5] You can answer the first of these questions by answering the second, and the same method can be used to account for knowledge of your fears and desires: you can determine whether you desire that P by determining whether you *ought rationally* to desire that P, just as you can determine whether you fear that P by determining whether you ought rationally to fear that P. Determining whether you ought rationally to believe (or desire or fear) that P is a matter of asking yourself whether what Finkelstein calls 'the reasons' require you to believe (or desire or fear) that P. Suppose that you ask yourself this question and you judge that the reasons do require you to have the attitude in question. How can judging that you *ought* rationally to have a given attitude enable you to know that you actually have that attitude? Because, and only insofar as, you assume that the attitude you have is one that, by your lights, the reasons require you to have. Finkelstein calls this the Rationality Assumption, and it's tempting to see this assumption as mediating the transition from a claim about what your attitude ought to be to a claim about what your attitude is.

This way of putting things is a little problematic if you want your knowledge that you believe that P to come out as immediate. If your knowledge is mediated by the Rationality Assumption doesn't that make it, by definition, mediate rather than immediate knowledge? In response it might be argued that the role of the Rationality Assumption isn't to *mediate* but to *enable* TM-based self-knowledge, and that in any case the fact that a piece of knowledge is 'mediated' by highly general assumptions such as the Rationality Assumption doesn't mean that it isn't, in the relevant sense, 'immediate'. But this is all a bit mysterious. For a start,

[5] Finkelstein 2012: 103.

it's not at all clear how to distinguish between the idea that the Rationality Assumption mediates self-knowledge and the notion that it merely enables it. Also, why does the fact that an assumption is 'highly general' not threaten the immediacy of any knowledge that is 'mediated' by it? Maybe we shouldn't be bothered by the fact that self-knowledge acquired by using TM isn't immediate, but insisting that it *is* immediate is an entirely different matter.

The next problem with TM is that it represents us as substituting what is often a more difficult question ('Do the reasons require me to believe that P?') for an easier question ('Do I believe that P?'). This is the Substitution Problem for Rationalism. The idea of substituting one question for another is borrowed from Daniel Kahneman, but substitution in Kahneman's sense is the exact opposite of the substitution involved in applying TM.[6] Substitution in Kahneman's sense happens when you answer a difficult question by answering an easier one. For example, you might find yourself answering the question 'How happy are you with your life these days?' by answering 'What is your mood right now?' Or faced with 'How popular will the President be six months from now?' the question you answer is, 'How popular is the President now?' The motto is: if you can't answer a hard question, find an easier one you can answer. But when it comes to TM the motto seems to be: even if there is an easier question you can answer, find a harder question you can't easily answer.

Why think that the question 'Do the reasons require me to believe/ want/ fear that P?' is any harder than the question 'Do I believe/desire/fear that P?' The point here is that there are many occasions when it's more obvious to you that you have a given attitude than that you ought rationally to have it, or that 'the reasons' require you to have it. As I sit down for dinner it's perfectly obvious to me that I want to start with a vodka martini but I would be flummoxed if someone asked 'Do the reasons require you to want a vodka martini?' I have no idea what I ought rationally to want to drink, and if that is the case then why would I think that figuring out whether I ought to want to have a vodka martini is a good way of figuring out whether a vodka martini is what I want? I know without reflecting on my reasons that I want a vodka martini, just as I know without reflecting on my reasons that I'm scared of the spider in my bathtub.

In fact, the problem for TM is even deeper than this way of putting things suggests. It's not just that it can be very hard to *know* which attitude one ought rationally to have but that in many cases there is no such thing as *the* attitude 'the reasons' require one to have. As Finkelstein notes, that are many attitudes that are

---

[6] See Kahneman 2011: 97–9 for an account of what he calls 'substitution'.

neither required nor prohibited by one's reasons. Examples include disdain, adoration, jealousy, regret, revulsion, and hatred:

What these are other attitudes have in common is that, even though we sometimes deliberate about their appropriateness, they are rarely thought to be *required* by practical reasons. A friend might try to convince me that it's unreasonable for me to adore a dog who is continually leaving teeth-marks on my furniture. But when a dog behaves well, I'm under no rational obligation to adore him. (Finkelstein 2003: 163)

If I'm under no rational obligation to adore my dog then the problem with asking 'Do the reasons require me to adore my dog?' is not just that it's a *harder* question to answer than 'Do I adore my dog?' but that it's the *wrong* question. It implies that there is a uniquely correct attitude to have in such cases but there isn't.[7] The answer to the question 'Do the reasons require me to adore my dog?' is plainly *no* even though the answer to the question 'Do I adore my dog?' is plainly *yes*. In trying to answer the latter question by answering the former question I would be barking up the wrong tree.

An especially interesting attitude to think about in relation to these difficulties is the attitude of hoping that P. Suppose you have been single for a long time and that all your previous relationships ended badly. Still, you live in hope. You hope the next person you date will end up as your significant other even though your close friends think that your hopes will almost certainly be dashed. Their sage advice is: don't hope for too much and you won't be disappointed. So what do the reasons require you to hope? As you head for your next date would it be right to think that you ought rationally to hope that things will work out, even though they almost certainly won't? From the standpoint of reason, is it better to be a hopeful romantic than a hope-less one? The problem with these questions is not just that they are hard to answer but that it's difficult to know how to even go about answering them. Presumably it's permissible for you to hope for the best, but what would it be for hoping for the best in this case to be a rational requirement? Figuring out what the reasons require you to hope for looks like a distinctly unpromising way of figuring out what you actually hope for.

Obviously, all this talk of questions like 'Do I believe that P?' being easier to answer in many cases than questions like 'Do the reasons require me to believe

---

[7] Someone else who makes this point is Jonathan Way. If I'm driving and there are two equally good routes to where I'm going, I can know which one I want or intend to take even though there is no sense in which I ought rationally to take that route rather than the equally good alternative. Equally, my evidence might be good enough to permit belief in some proposition P, without being so good as to require belief in P. As Way puts it, 'the claim that there is always a uniquely correct attitude to take towards P, when one is considering whether P, remains a strikingly strong claim' (2007: 228). Not just strikingly strong but strikingly implausible.

that P?' begs an obvious question: how is the inward-directed question to be answered if *not* by answering the corresponding outward-directed question? What's needed to make any progress with this is a positive theory of self-knowledge, and I will outline my own theory in Chapter 11. However, to avoid any confusion, it would be worth noting the following now: when I say that the answer to an inward-directed question is easier to come up with than an answer to an outward-directed question I'm not saying that it doesn't require cognitive effort to answer an inward-directed question or that it is never appropriate to use TM. A more sensible view is that there are different pathways to knowledge of one's own attitudes, and that it's much easier in some cases than in others to know what your attitude is. Equally, it's much easier in some cases than in others to know what your attitude ought rationally to be. The fact remains, however, that figuring out what our attitudes ought to be is often harder than knowing what they are, and this suggests that there has to be something wrong with the idea that using TM is a fundamental way for us to acquire knowledge of our own attitudes; the fact is that we often know what we want or fear or even believe without having to reflect on our reasons, and reflecting on our reasons might actually make it harder to know our own attitudes because our reasons are often opaque.

The next problem for TM is what I'm going to call the Matching Problem. Here is a crude statement of this problem: what you believe isn't always what you ought rationally to believe, what you want may not be what you ought rationally to want, and what you fear may not be what you ought rationally to fear. In each of these cases, there is the possibility of a mismatch between your actual attitude and what your attitude ought to be (assuming now that it's clear what your attitude ought to be). But if there is always the possibility of this kind of mismatch how can you determine what your attitude is by determining what it ought to be? If you judge that you ought to have a certain attitude A that doesn't guarantee that you have A, so how can you know that you have A on the basis that you ought to have it?

A popular way of illustrating the Matching Problem is to start talking about belief-perseverance. Brie Gertler characterizes belief-perseverance as a 'common psychological phenomenon that threatens the method of transparency' (2011b: 138). She says that it 'occurs whenever a dispositional belief that P endures despite the discovery that one has no evidence for P, or that one's evidence favours not-P' (2011b: 137). For example, people hold fast to the conviction that 'their spouses are faithful, and their children innocent, despite abundant evidence to the contrary' (2011b: 137). These are all cases in which people believe things that, as rational beings, they shouldn't believe, and in which they will therefore go wrong if they try to figure out what they believe by reflecting on what they should believe.

One response to this which Gertler considers says that belief-perseverance is after all a relatively rare phenomenon, that one's evidence will generally match one's beliefs, and that 'the method of transparency may achieve a degree of reliability that is high enough to qualify its results as knowledge' (2011b: 138). Gertler isn't convinced because she thinks that belief-perseverance isn't all that rare. However, there is a question about how Gertler characterizes belief-perseverance. As we saw in the case of KAREN, after the total discrediting of the sole evidence for her belief that she is especially good at science and music she has no evidence for this belief but she doesn't realize that her sole evidence has been discredited. That is why her belief persists. Although in this case there is 'the discovery' that she has no evidence for her belief, this is not something that *Karen* has discovered. The whole point of the example is that the subject herself doesn't know that she has no evidence for P, or that her evidence favours not-P.

The phenomenon Gertler has in mind is what I've been calling recalcitrance rather than belief-perseverance. This is significant because while Gertler might be right that belief-perseverance is relatively commonplace, recalcitrance is a different matter; how is it even possible, let alone commonplace, for someone to continue to believe that P despite knowing that her evidence for P has been totally discredited? Presumably, the wife who continues to believe her husband is faithful despite overwhelming evidence to the contrary doesn't accept that there is overwhelming evidence to the contrary and so isn't irrational in the sense that her attitudes fail to conform to her own judgements about what she is warranted in believing. So there is nothing to stop her from answering the question whether she believes her husband is faithful by answering the question whether this is something she ought rationally to believe.

In Chapter 2, I tried to make sense of the possibility of belief-recalcitrance by drawing on Harman's idea that once a belief has become established a great deal of effort might be needed to get rid of it, even if the believer comes to see that he or she ought to get rid of it because all the evidence for the belief has been undermined. For example, I envisaged Karen as realizing that her evidence for the belief that she has an aptitude for science and music has been undermined but as still being disposed to think that she has an aptitude for science and music when the question arises and as using the thought that she has an aptitude for science and music as a premise in reasoning about what to do. She therefore still believes something she knows she oughtn't to believe, which makes this a case of recalcitrance rather than belief-perseverance.

One reaction to this attempt to make sense of belief-recalcitrance might be to suggest that after the discovery of the mix-up over the test results Karen no longer *believes* that she has an aptitude for science and music but *alieves* it. In Tamar Gendler's terminology, an alief is a 'habitual propensity to respond to an apparent stimulus is a particular way' (2008: 557). What Harman sees as Karen's 'habits of thought' are in fact belief-discordant aliefs. Unlike beliefs, aliefs are arational, and the fact that Karen realizes that she no longer has grounds for believing that she has an aptitude for science and music doesn't mean that she doesn't alieve that she has an aptitude for science and music, though it does mean that this is something she no longer believes.

The belief/alief distinction helps TM deal with the Matching Problem. The worry for TM is that what you yourself think you ought rationally to believe might not match what you do believe, and that this stops you from determining what you believe by determining what you ought rationally to believe. This assumes that your beliefs can be irrational, but Gendler is suggesting that supposed examples of irrational belief are in reality examples of arational *alief.* Unlike your aliefs, your beliefs line up with what you take yourself to have reason to believe, and this allows you to use TM to discover your own beliefs. What we have here is a combination of Rationalism about belief with Rationalism about self-knowledge; the idea is that Karen is a problem for Rationalism about self-knowledge if it's an example of evidence-discordant belief but not if it's an example of belief-discordant alief. Of course, what you believe can be out of sync with what there *is* reason to believe, or with what the evidence actually shows, but not with what you think there is reason to believe or what you take the evidence to show.

The idea that Gendler's alief/belief distinction can be used to deal with the Matching Problem is, though superficially appealing, no good at all. Obviously quite a lot depends on what you think belief is, but I'm inclined to agree with Scanlon that it's sufficient for you to believe that P if you are disposed to think that P when the question arises and use the thought that P as a premise in practical reasoning.[8] Since Karen satisfies these conditions with respect to the thought that she has an aptitude for science and music it follows that she believes (and doesn't merely alieve) that she has an aptitude for science and music. It's also worth pointing out that when it comes to attitudes other than belief, a Gendler-type response to the Mismatch Problem isn't even superficially plausible. Suppose you have a liver problem and have been warned of the disastrous consequences for your health of continuing to drink vodka martinis. Should you

---

[8] Scanlon 1998: 21.

still want a vodka martini before dinner this evening? No. Do you want a vodka martini before dinner this evening? Yes. Your desire for a vodka martini is recalcitrant, and it would be absurd to suggest that you don't really desire a vodka martini, you only arationally 'asire' one. You can't introduce new categories of mental state by linguistic fiat in order to keep your desires rational, and the same goes for your beliefs: what look like irrational beliefs that can't be uncovered by using TM really are irrational beliefs. They aren't mere 'aliefs' the positing of which allows your beliefs to be discovered by using TM.

Another superficially appealing but equally unconvincing way of dealing with attitude-recalcitrance is to argue that recalcitrant attitudes are ones with respect to which we are in some way alienated, and that they aren't a problem for Rationalism because Rationalism is only interested in accounting for unalienated self-knowledge, that is, knowledge of those of one's attitudes that are responsive to how they ought rationally to be by one's own lights. It's not clear where this restriction came from. There was certainly no sign of it in the initial set-up of Rationalism, and saying that Rationalism doesn't deal with alienated self-knowledge is a significant concession given the range of attitudes that are, to varying degrees, recalcitrant. Anyway, the idea that an attitude is alienated just in virtue of being recalcitrant has very little going for it. Alienated attitudes are ones that one can't identify with, but in reality it is the attitudes that a person identifies with most wholeheartedly that are most likely to be recalcitrant.[9] If a particular belief is fundamental to your self-conception or *weltanschauung* it's hardly surprising that you find it very hard to give up despite realizing that it has been undermined.

So Rationalism is stuck with the Matching Problem, and can't get itself off the hook by talking about aliefs or alienation. There remains the option of arguing that the kind of mismatch between what your attitudes are and what they ought to be that is a problem for TM is, though not impossible, nevertheless rare. As I've emphasized, the mismatches that are a problem for TM are mismatches between what your attitudes actually are and how they ought rationally to be *by your own lights*. This is the sort of mismatch that casts doubt on the possibility of determining what your attitudes are by reflecting on your reasons. But is there any

---

[9] Harry Frankfurt has some very helpful things to say about all of this. Focusing on desires, he points out that the fact that a person's desires are susceptible to rational justification doesn't entail that a person can identify with his desires only insofar as he supports them with reasons or believes that it is possible to do so. Here is a nice illustration of the point: 'Suppose I were to conclude for some reason that it is not desirable for me to seek the well-being of my children. I suspect that I would continue to love them and to care about their well-being anyhow. This discrepancy between my judgement and my desire would not show that I had become alienated from my desire. On the contrary, it would show at most that my love for my children is nonrational and that it is "stronger than I am"' (Frankfurt 2002: 223).

reason for thinking that such mismatches are rare? And if mismatches are rare, does that get TM off the hook, or is there still a Matching Problem for TM? For example, you could think that no more than the *possibility* of recalcitrance is required to put pressure on the idea that TM can be a pathway to epistemically privileged self-knowledge.

When it comes attitudes other than belief it's not clear how to defend the suggestion that attitude-recalcitrance is rare or unusual. After all, there is nothing particularly unusual about fearing a spider you know you have no reason to fear, or wanting a martini you know you have strong and decisive reasons not to want. In such cases, what you take yourself to have reason to want or fear isn't a sufficiently reliable guide to what you want or fear to give you *knowledge*, let alone epistemically privileged knowledge, of your actual wants or fears. In contrast, it is surely much more unusual for you to believe that P despite realizing that the evidence shows that not-P. This suggests a hybrid view according to which you can acquire knowledge of your own beliefs by using TM but not knowledge of your desires, fears, hopes, or other attitudes. You can know your own beliefs by using TM because what you believe is reliably related to what you take yourself to have reason to believe.

One problem with the hybrid view is that it severely limits the scope of Rationalism and reintroduces the Generality Problem. I've said that there are two key questions for Rationalism: does it explain how we can know our own beliefs, desires, and other attitudes, and does it vindicate the idea that our intentional self-knowledge is epistemically privileged? If we go for the hybrid approach then what we are saying is that Rationalism can explain our knowledge of our own beliefs but not self-knowledge of other attitudes. That leaves Rationalism with a large explanatory hole that will need to be filled in in some other way. In fact, Rationalism is in one way even more limited in scope than the hybrid view implies. Even when it comes to explaining self-knowledge of beliefs TM has its limitations. Suppose you believe that it's raining, then look out of the window and see that it's not raining. You now no longer regard yourself as having a warrant to believe that it's raining, and it's hard to think of circumstances in which you would continue to believe that it's raining. But in the case of beliefs which tangle with your self-conception, or beliefs you have been wedded to for years, it's not hard to imagine how you might hang on to them despite now knowing or believing that they are unwarranted. You judge that they are unwarranted but fail to take your judgement to heart.[10] These are cases in which

---

[10] Taking it to heart is an interesting and important topic in its own right. In an illuminating discussion Jennifer Church points out that we can assent to a proposition without ever taking it to

knowledge of what you believe would be a form of substantial self-knowledge, and the issue is whether TM is sufficiently reliable to be a source of such self-knowledge given the genuine, and not just theoretical, possibility of a mismatch. The answer to this question depends in part on how reliable is 'sufficiently reliable' but it seems a bit optimistic to suppose that you can always use TM to know what you believe about a given topic regardless of the topic.

This leads to another question: suppose that recalcitrance is sufficiently rare for TM to be capable of delivering knowledge of what you believe, at least in cases in which the subject-matter is trivial. It's then a further question whether it can deliver infallible or immediate knowledge of what you believe. The answer to this further question is almost certainly 'no'. Whatever the subject-matter, concluding that you ought rationally to believe that P doesn't *guarantee* that you believe that P, so your beliefs about your own beliefs formed by using TM are still fallible even if they are unlikely to be wrong. Your self-knowledge in such cases isn't immediate either. I've already commented on the way in which, when you come to know what you believe by using TM, your knowledge is mediated by the Rationality Assumption. Another way of putting pressure on the idea that TM can deliver immediate self-knowledge is this: suppose you judge you ought rationally to believe that P and know that this is your judge-ment (another piece of self-knowledge that needs accounting for). Judging that you ought rationally to believe that P doesn't entail that you believe that P but it *indicates* that you believe that P; to put it another way, the fact that you judge that you ought to believe that P looks like pretty good evidence that you *do* believe that P, at least on the assumption that what you believe in trivial matters is generally in line with what you think you ought rationally to believe. But your knowledge on the basis of 'pretty good evidence' that you believe that P can't be regarded as immediate if immediate knowledge is knowledge that isn't based on any evidence; in effect, you *infer* that you believe that P from your judgement about what you ought rationally to believe, and inferential knowledge clearly isn't immediate knowledge.

Perhaps it's worth adding that immediacy can be understood either epistem-ically or psychologically, and that Rationalism is in trouble either way. If you believe that you ought to believe that P and infer that you do believe that P, then your knowledge that you believe that P (assuming that you do know this) isn't psychologically immediate because it is the product of conscious reasoning or

---

heart. Members of a jury may deliver a 'guilty' verdict and yet remain unconvinced on a deeper level. Conversely, people may dismiss their prejudices as mere prejudices while continuing to hold on to them. In such cases there is a certain lack of what Church calls '*depth*' to one's beliefs (2002: 361).

inference. And it isn't epistemically immediate either because your justification for believing that you believe that P comes in part from your having justification to believe other supporting propositions, such as the proposition that you ought rationally to believe that P, and that what you believe about P is determined by what you think you ought rationally to believe.

None of this is good news for Rationalism. It suggests that it fails to explain quite a lot of what it sets out to explain, and that it lacks a wholly convincing response to the Generality and Matching Problems, as well as the Substitution Problem. However, we are not quite in a position to declare 'game over' for Rationalism. Indeed, many Rationalists would argue that the real game hasn't even started because I have so far neglected to mention a key dimension of their view, namely, the fact that we are active rather passive in relation to our own beliefs and other attitudes. For Rationalism, intentional self-knowledge is a form of what might be called 'agent's knowledge', and this is the key to understanding Rationalism. So what I want to do next is to explain this aspect of Rationalism and argue that it doesn't get Rationalism off the hook: the agential version of Rationalism—what I call Activism—runs into versions of the same problems I have just been discussing.

So far I've been taking it that believing that P is one thing, while judging that you ought rationally to believe that P is a different matter. I've taken it that if you judge that you ought rationally to believe that P, that is evidence that you believe that P, and that that is how it enables you to know (though not infallibly or immediately) that you believe that P. Now consider a different view of the matter: suppose that the question arises whether you believe that P. The first thing you do in response is to deliberate, that is, consider whether there is reason to believe that P. You conclude that there is, and your conclusion is expressed in the form of a judgement: you judge that you ought rationally to believe that P. Put more simply, your deliberation leads you to judge that P. Now comes the crucial Rationalist move: the relationship between judging that P and believing that P isn't evidential; rather, your judging that P *constitutes* your believing that P.[11] To judge that P, or that you ought rationally to believe that P, is to take P to be true, and that can only mean you believe that P. By deliberating about whether you ought rationally to believe that P you make up your mind about P. By acknowledging that you ought rationally to believe that P you *make it the case* that you believe that P, and *thereby* know that you believe that P.

---

[11] Something along these lines is suggested by the discussion of the relationship between judging and believing in Boyle 2011a.

The key to this version of Rationalism is the idea that we have 'an ability to know our minds by actively shaping their contents' (Boyle 2009: 134). We aren't just passive observers of our own attitudes, and it's because we actively shape them that we have a special insight into what they are. That is why I call this version of Rationalism Activism. Activism makes self-knowledge a species of what is sometimes called *maker's knowledge*, the knowledge you have of what you yourself make.[12] Idealists like Kant think that we know what the world is like because it is the mind's construction, and now it turns out according to Rationalism that we know our own attitudes because they are also the mind's own construction. We can see what the Rationalist is getting at by noting an ambiguity in the word 'determine'. I've said that according to TM you determine what your attitudes are by determining what they ought rationally to be. Here, both occurrences of 'determine' are epistemic: in the case of belief, the view is that you come to know that you believe that P by coming to know that you ought to believe that P. However, there is also a constitutive sense of determine, according to which what you do when you determine that you believe that P is you *make it the case* that you believe that P. The epistemic sense of determine is 'determine$_e$' and the constitutive sense is 'determine$_c$'. In these terms, the Activist's proposal is this: by determining$_e$ that you ought rationally to believe that P you determine$_c$ that you believe that P, and can thereby determine$_e$ that you believe that P.

Does Activism give a plausible account of how we relate to our own attitudes, and does it solve the Generality, Substitution, and Matching Problems in a way that allows TM to count as a source of epistemically privileged self-knowledge? On the one hand, there is something right about the idea that we are sometimes active rather than passive in relation to our attitudes. There is such a thing as reasoning yourself into believing or wanting something, and it certainly isn't correct in these cases to say that you are a mere passive observer of your attitudes. On the other hand, as Moran concedes, 'we'd end up with many fewer beliefs for coping with the world than we actually have if we could only acquire them through explicit reasoning or deliberation' (2004: 458). Perceptual beliefs are a case in point; I see that there is a computer screen in front of me and believe on this basis that there is a computer screen in front of me. I know I believe there is a computer screen in front of me but I don't know this because I have reasoned my way to this belief. Neither the belief itself nor my knowledge of it is the product of explicit deliberation. Indeed, even in the case of beliefs originally acquired by

---

[12] There is more on the idea of maker's knowledge in Hintikka 1974, Mackie 1974, and Craig 1987.

deliberation I don't need to keep deliberating in order to know that I have them. If I have the stored belief that P, and the question arises whether I believe that P, what I need to do is not to *form* the belief (I already have it) but *retrieve* it from storage.[13]

The question whether Activism can account for our knowledge of our stored beliefs comes to the fore in an exchange between Moran and Nishi Shah and David Velleman. Shah and Velleman argue that the question 'Do I believe that P?' can either mean 'Do I already believe that P?' or 'Do I now believe that P?' If the question is whether I already believe that P, the way to answer it is to pose the question whether P and see what one says, or is spontaneously inclined to answer. However, this procedure 'requires one to refrain from any reasoning as to whether P, since that reasoning might alter the state of mind one is trying to assay' (2005: 506). In reply, Moran objects that my stored beliefs only count as *beliefs* insofar as I take them to be true, and that if I relate to a stored belief as something I take to be true 'it will be hard to see how I can see my relation to it, however spontaneous, as insulated from the engagement of my rational capacities for determining what is true or false' (2012: 221). I am, in this sense, 'active' in relation to my stored beliefs. Something similar can be said about one's perceptual beliefs; the fact that they are passively acquired doesn't mean that they are insulated from the engagement of one's rational capacities. Even passively acquired perceptual beliefs must be sensitive to our grasp of how they fit into the rest of our network of beliefs. Perceptual beliefs are, to this extent, 'active' but the relevant sense of 'activity' is 'the ordinary adjustment of belief to the total evidence' (Moran 2004: 460).

What is right about this is that nothing that is recognizable as a belief can be totally insulated from the engagement of one's rational capacities, but the question is whether the sense in which we are 'active' in relation to our stored or perceptual beliefs casts any light on how we *know* them. Let's suppose that I have the stored or perceptual belief that P, and that I stand prepared to revise this belief if I encounter good grounds for revising it. For example, P might be the perceptual belief that there is a computer screen in front of me, and the grounds for revising it might include the discovery that I am the subject of an experiment in which what I seem to see will be deceptive. But how is the fact that I stand prepared to revise my belief, or that I would revise it in certain circumstances, supposed to explain my knowledge that I believe that P? There are two scenarios

---

[13] That is why, as Baron Reed points out, recognizing that one already believes P may count not merely as a reason to believe that P but as the answer to the question whether one *does* believe that P. See Reed 2010: 177.

to consider: in the first scenario, my belief that P is automatically extinguished by evidence against P regardless of whether I realize that I have until now believed that P, or that P needs to be revised; we can imagine that all the necessary adjustments are made sub-personally rather than by me, the subject of the belief. In this case, talk of the ordinary adjustment of belief to the total evidence neither explains nor presupposes the knowledge that I believe that P. In the second scenario, I revise my belief that P because I realize that it needs to be revised, but how can I realize that a given belief of mine needs to be revised if I'm not even aware that I have it? In this scenario, my knowledge that I believe that P is presupposed but not explained. It's not an explanation of my knowledge that I believe that P to point out that my belief is subject to revision. The explanans and explanandum just don't connect in the right way.

The underlying problem here is that Activism operates with two very different senses of activity. In one sense, we are active in relation to our attitudes to the extent that they are *formed* through acts of deliberation. In another sense we are active in relation to our attitudes insofar as that they are *sensitive* to one's reasoning or deliberation. Activism's master thought is that we are able to know our own attitudes by forming or determining$_c$ them through acts of deliberation, and the challenge is to explain how this casts any light on our self-knowledge of attitudes that aren't formed by deliberation. Activism responds to this challenge by bringing in the idea of a *readiness* to deliberate and revise in the light of deliberation but it's just not clear how this helps. Deliberating is something you actually do, and it's one thing to say that when you form the belief that P by deliberating you can thereby determine$_e$ that you believe that P. The 'thereby' in this formulation needs explaining but at least isn't totally opaque. What does seem opaque is the suggestion that being *prepared* to deliberate and revise your belief that P is what puts you in a position to know that you believe that P.

Let's agree, then, that Activism has trouble accounting for self-knowledge of stored beliefs or beliefs not formed by deliberating. This is a version of the Generality Problem for Activism, and attitudes other than belief bring this issue even more sharply into focus; if your desire for exercise is the result of deliberating then maybe the reasoning that is responsible for the formation of the desire also enables you to know that you have it. But many desires aren't like that; they come over you without any activity on your part but this doesn't mean that you don't know that you have them. Again, your knowledge in these cases can't be accounted for along Activist lines. How can you have agential knowledge of desires that have nothing to do with your agency? Saying that desires that come over you are still responsive to reasoning or deliberation doesn't cast any light on your ability to determine$_e$ what you desire; if you know that you want a martini but can be reasoned out of wanting one, saying that your desire is in this sense responsive to reason doesn't explain how you know you have it.

Even when it comes to attitudes that *are* formed through explicit deliberation there are questions about the epistemology of Activism. Suppose that by deliberating you make it the case that you believe that P. How does making it the case that you believe that P enable you to know that you believe that P? To put it another way, when Activism says that you make it the case that you believe that P and *thereby* know that you believe that P, what is the force of the 'thereby'? After all, it's not a necessary truth that if you make it the case that P then you know that P; Boyle has the nice example of someone making it the case that his hair is on fire by standing too close to the fire but not realizing that his hair is on fire.[14] This raises a more general question about Activism: it sees intentional self-knowledge as a product of our rational agency with respect to our attitudes, but how is rational agency supposed to give us self-knowledge?[15]

Here is what an Activist might say in reply: suppose I am considering the reasons in favour of thinking that it is raining, and that these reasons are convincing enough to lead me to judge that I ought rationally to believe that it is raining. To judge that I ought rationally to believe that it is raining is, in effect, to judge that it is raining. This latter judgement is the conclusion of my reflection of the reasons in favour of rain. The next question is: how do I get from judging that it is raining to knowing that I believe that it is raining? Moran writes:

I *would* have a right to assume that my reflection on the reasons in favour of rain provided an answer to the question of what my belief about rain is, if I could assume that *what* my belief here is was something determined by the conclusion of my reflection on those reasons. (2003: 405)

The 'conclusion of my reflection on those reasons' is the judgement that it is raining. If I understand what it is to judge and what it is to believe then I will understand that judging that it is raining makes it the case that I believe that it is raining. So if I know that I judge that it is raining, then I 'thereby' know that I believe it is raining.

As we have seen, this approach doesn't get round the Generality Problem; there are many attitudes our knowledge of which can't be explained in this way because judging that you ought to have such attitudes doesn't, even in the normal case, constitute your judging or believing that you have them. The Substitution

---

[14] Boyle 2009: 138 footnote.
[15] Someone else who presses this question is Lucy O'Brien. See O'Brien 2003: 375–82.

Problem is also still an issue for Activism; it's still the case that when you answer the question whether you have a given attitude by asking whether you ought rationally to have that attitude you are answering what is typically a much easier question by answering a much harder one. Intuitively, the cognitive effort required to reflect on the reasons in favour of P is often much greater than the cognitive effort needed to determine whether you believe that P; your reasons may well be opaque even if your beliefs are not. That leaves the Matching Problem, and I want to end this chapter by seeing whether Activism has a response to this problem.

Here is a version of the Matching Problem for Activism: suppose that reflection on the reasons in favour of some proposition P leads you to judge that P. However, judging that P is not the same as believing that P. Even if you know that you *judge* that P this leaves it open that you still don't *believe* that P, and so don't know that you believe that P. Here is how what you judge and what you believe can come apart:

Someone can make a judgement, and for good reasons, but it not have the effects that judgements normally do—in particular, it may not result in a stored belief which has the proper influence on other judgements and on action. Someone may judge that under-graduate degrees from countries other than her own are of an equal standard to her own, and excellent reasons may be operative in her assertions to that effect. All the same, it may be quite clear, in decisions she makes on hiring, or in making recommendations, that she does not really have this belief at all. (Peacocke 2000: 90)

Obviously, if judging that P *normally* results in the stored belief that P you can still infer from the fact that you judge that P that you believe that P but this clearly isn't what Activists have in mind when they talk about a person's reasoned judgements *constituting* his beliefs, and thereby providing direct access to them.

Not everyone finds Peacocke's example convincing or even coherent.[16] One thought I have already mentioned is that to judge that P is to take P to be true, and that you can't take P to be true without believing that P. So there can be no gap between believing that P and judging that P. But then what is going on in Peacocke's example? Here is one possibility: you recognize that you have excellent reasons to judge that undergraduate degrees from other countries are as good as undergraduate degrees from your own country, and that this is what you ought rationally to judge, but you fail to make the judgement. You might say the words 'undergraduate degrees from other countries are of an equal standard' but you don't actually take this to be true, and therefore neither judge nor believe that

---

[16] See Boyle 2011a: 6.

undergraduate degrees from other countries are of an equal standard; the very considerations which show that you don't really believe that undergraduate degrees from other countries are of an equal standard also show that you don't judge that undergraduate degrees from other countries are of an equal standard.

This doesn't really help because it closes one gap while opening up another. It closes the gap between judging that P and believing that P while opening a gap between judging that you ought rationally to judge or believe that P and actually judging or believing that P. This is the mismatch I've been talking about for most of this chapter, and Activism doesn't show that there can't be this kind of mismatch. Even if judging that P amounts to believing that P, at least at the moment that you judge that P, Activism still owes us an account of how you know your own conclusions or judgements. The point is that just because you take yourself to have good reason to judge that P it does not follow that you actually judge that P. As O'Brien points out, 'a subject can have warrant for thinking that she has judged that P when she has in fact only concluded that she has good reason to judge that P and then drawn back in a fit of risk aversion' (2003: 379). Obviously, there is still the option of arguing that what you take yourself to have reason to judge is a good enough guide to what you actually judge (and believe) to give you mediate knowledge of what you actually judge (and believe), but this is no different from the position that Simple Rationalism ended up in. There is certainly no indication that Activism has intentional self-knowledge come out as infallible or immediate.

It might be that what is really going on here is that Activism's conception of belief is different from mine, and that we are to some extent talking at cross purposes. My view of belief is broadly dispositional. Whether you actually believe that P depends on whether you are disposed to think that P when the question arises, act as if P is true, and use P as a premise in reasoning. On this conception of belief, it's easy to think of the relationship between what you judge, or think you ought to judge, and what you believe as evidential: judging that P is not guaranteed to result in the stored dispositional belief that P, even if this is what normally happens. Judging, unlike believing, is a mental action, and the effects of this action may vary. But Activism seems to think of at least some beliefs as occurrences, the idea being that when you judge that P you occurrently believe that P. Occurrently believing that P might not result in your believing that P in the dispositional sense—maybe this is what happens in Peacocke's example—but if you know that you judge that P then at least you thereby know immediately that at that moment you occurrently believe that P.

Setting aside any doubts one might have about the notion of an occurrent belief, this move is still of limited help to Activism. It still leaves Activism with the problem of accounting for a person's knowledge that he judges that P, and doesn't close the gap between taking yourself to be warranted in judging that P and actually judging or occurrently believing that P. There is also the worry that, at best, Activism is only equipped to account for immediate knowledge of our own occurrent attitudes. When it comes to dispositional beliefs and other attitudes, the Activist is in the same boat as the Simple Rationalist: if A is a recalcitrant (dispositional) attitude, then your judgement as to whether you ought or ought not to have A will cast little light on whether you have A. In other cases, your judgements about whether you ought to have A might tell you whether you have A, but your knowledge will still be mediated by the Rationality Assumption and your knowledge of what you ought rationally to judge. Even for Activism, unless you are *homo philosophicus* judging that you ought rationally to believe that P can only be an *indication* that you judge or believe that P.

Does this matter? That depends on why Rationalism is so keen on the notion that we have epistemically privileged access to our own attitudes. There isn't much to be said for the idea that self-knowledge of attitudes is infallible: you can think you believe that the present government will be re-elected but your lack of surprise when the election goes the other way suggests otherwise. When the waiter asks you what you would like to drink what you think you want is a gin martini but when you take your first sip you realize that what you wanted all along was a vodka martini. These are all straightforward cases in which you are fallible about your attitudes, and it's not a requirement on a theory of self-knowledge that it has our knowledge of our own attitudes come out as infallible. An account of self-knowledge that has this consequence has got to be wrong. Maybe in the cases I have described there is some kind of (defeasible) presumption that you aren't wrong about your attitudes, but whether there is such a presumption depends on the nature and content of the attitude.

For many Rationalists it isn't the infallibility but rather the immediacy of self-knowledge that is the starting-point, but is there actually a presumption that self-knowledge is immediate? On one reading, immediate self-knowledge is not based on behavioural evidence. On another reading, it is knowledge that is not based on any evidence. If judging that you ought rationally to believe that P doesn't count as a form of 'behaviour', and you know on the basis of this judgement that you believe that P, then your knowledge in this case isn't based on *behavioural* evidence but it isn't true that it's based on *no* evidence. If judging is a mental act then your 'evidence' is psychological rather than behavioural. To the extent that you have 'privileged access' to your attitude it is because the evidence at your disposal is excellent and readily available.

In other cases, you might have to rely on behavioural evidence. For example, you might need to rely on behavioural evidence broadly construed to know whether you really believe in God or that your spouse is faithful. These are among your 'deepest' attitudes, and it's not counter-intuitive to suppose that you need evidence, including behavioural evidence, to know such attitudes. Indeed, when it comes to attitudes other than belief, even relatively superficial self-knowledge might need to draw on behavioural evidence; if you order a vodka martini and the question arises how you know you want a vodka martini it wouldn't be beside the point to point out that you've just ordered one. You might know independently of placing your order that you want a vodka martini, but there again, you might not. Sometimes the best guide to what you want is what you choose; it would be nice to think that you chose a vodka martini because you already knew that that is what you wanted but it isn't always like that.

In a weird way these observations are actually helpful to Rationalism. Rationalism sets itself the target of explaining how it's possible to know our own attitudes without relying on behavioural or other evidence. It succeeds in explaining how, by using TM, you are able in at least some cases to know your own attitudes without relying on behavioural evidence but not without relying on any evidence. What I'm now questioning is whether it was ever sensible to assume that intentional self-knowledge doesn't require any evidence. Once we give up on this idea, and are prepared to think of knowledge of our own (dispositional) attitudes as evidence-based knowledge, then we will need to tell a story about the kinds of evidence that are relevant. One kind of relevant evidence is, as Rationalism suggests, judgemental. If you are lucky (or unlucky) enough to be *homo philosophicus*, and judge that you ought rationally to believe that P, that is excellent evidence that you do believe that P. If you are *homo sapiens*, and you judge that you ought rationally to believe that P, that is less than excellent, but still potentially good evidence that you believe that P, depending on the nature of the belief. If you are *homo sapiens* and judge that you ought rationally to want that P that is not very good evidence that you want that P. The evidence that you want that P might have to come from a range of other sources, including what you say and do.

We now have at least the makings of an answer to what I referred to in Chapter 1 as the sources question: what are the sources of self-knowledge for humans? The first thing to say about this is that it depends on the kind of self-knowledge that is at issue. When it comes to knowledge of our own attitudes it's tempting to look for a magic bullet, a single source that will account for all our intentional self-knowledge. Unfortunately, there just is no magic bullet; there are multiple sources of intentional self-knowledge, depending on the type and content of the attitude known.

Among the sources of some intentional self-knowledge is TM, but TM only accounts for a narrow range of intentional self-knowledge, and even in the best case the knowledge it accounts for doesn't come out as based on no evidence. So the natural next step would be to look for other sources of intentional self-knowledge which help account for the varieties of intentional self-knowledge that Rationalism doesn't handle well. I will come back to this 'multiple pathways' approach to self-knowledge in Chapters 11 and 12. But before then, there is another piece of business that needs to be taken care of.

One thing I didn't say, and probably should have said, when I introduced Rationalism via Evans' idea of gaining self-knowledge by 'looking outwards' was that this model of self-knowledge didn't just come out of thin air. It arose as a response to the historically influential idea that the way to explain self-knowledge is to appeal to the idea of *looking inwards*. Locke, Kant, and many others operated with the idea that humans have a quasi-perceptual faculty of 'inner' or 'internal' sense, and that we know our own states of mind by exercising this faculty. Evans characterizes this as the idea that knowledge of our own mental properties 'always involves an *inward* glance at the states and doings of something to which only the person himself has access' (1982: 225). This is the model to which the 'looking outwards' approach is opposed, so before going any further it would be worth pausing to ask whether the 'inward glance' model has anything going for it. This is the question for the next chapter.

10

Looking Inwards

I said at the end of the last chapter that the 'looking outwards', transparency account of self-knowledge arose as a response to the idea that we acquire self-knowledge by looking inwards. For example, Evans prefaces his defence of his version of the transparency method by quoting something obscure that Wittgenstein is once reported to have said in a discussion in Oxford and observing that Wittgenstein was 'trying to undermine the temptation to adopt a Cartesian position, by forcing us to look more closely at the nature of our knowledge of our own mental properties and, in particular, by forcing us to abandon the idea that it always involves an *inward* glance at the states and doings of something to which only the person himself has access' (1982: 225). Evans doesn't say very much about why we should abandon this idea, beyond pointing out that a person's internal state 'cannot in any sense become an *object* to him. (He is in it)' (1982: 227). So my question in this chapter is this: what exactly is wrong with the 'inward glance' model of self-knowledge?

Although this model has had a fairly bad philosophical press in recent years, even its staunchest critics accept that there is something intuitive about the idea that we acquire self-knowledge by some form of inner perception, by looking inwards. It's natural to suppose that a basic source of self-knowledge for humans is introspection, and the point of talking about knowing one's own states of mind by means of an 'inward glance' is to suggest that introspection is a form of inner observation: we know our own states of mind by perceiving or observing them. Obviously introspection isn't perception in the ordinary sense, and involves the exercise of 'inner' rather than 'outer' sense. Still, even if introspection isn't literally perception you might think that perception is, as Armstrong puts it, 'the model for introspection' (1993: 95).[1]

Saying that there is something intuitive about the idea that we acquire self-knowledge by some form of inner perception might not cut a whole lot of ice philosophically speaking. There are lots of examples of philosophy overturning

[1] Among the great, dead philosophers, Locke, Hume, and Kant all endorsed versions of this view.

our intuitions, and who is to say that the supposedly intuitive perceptual model of introspection won't turn out to be another victim of philosophical reflection? What we need is *arguments* in support of the perceptual model, not intuitions. Okay, so here's an argument: suppose you start out with the idea that knowledge of our own beliefs and other attitudes is normally direct or immediate. In this context, direct knowledge is non-inferential knowledge. As Boghossian puts it in a passage I first quoted in Chapter 4, in the case of others I have no choice but to *infer* what they think from what they do or say but in my own case 'inference is neither required nor relevant' (1998: 150-1). In my own case inference is neither required nor relevant because 'normally I know what I think—what I believe, desire, hope or expect—without appeal to supplementary evidence' (1998: 151).

Suppose we label the premise that self-knowledge is normally non-inferential the *immediacy premise*. Then the next question is: how can the immediacy premise be correct? One possibility is that inference can be neither required nor relevant when it comes to self-knowledge because knowledge of one's own thoughts is normally based on nothing. But this is hard to swallow. Maybe cognitively insubstantial self-knowledge—say the knowledge that I am here—can be based on nothing, but self-knowledge isn't cognitively insubstantial and so can't be based on nothing.[2] That leaves only one option: self-knowledge can be immediate and yet not based on nothing if and only if it is a form of perceptual knowledge. Assuming that perceptual knowledge is immediate, then modelling introspection on perception is really the only effective way of securing the immediacy of introspective self-knowledge. I'll refer to this as the Immediacy Argument for the 'inner perception' model of introspection.

Some proponents of TM won't agree that thinking of self-knowledge as perceptual or as based on nothing are the only two ways of securing its immediacy. Rationalists like Moran think that TM is a source of immediate self-knowledge but I have argued that they are wrong about that; self-knowledge acquired by using TM is notably indirect, so if you want self-knowledge to come out as immediate then TM doesn't look like a good way of getting what you want. Given the immediacy premise, it would appear that all roads lead to the perceptual model, and that's the point of the Immediacy Argument.

I don't much care for the Immediacy Argument, though it does at least have the merit of being an argument. There are basically two things wrong with it.

---

[2] See Finkelstein 2003 for a contrary view. I'm not proposing to go into this here but do need to acknowledge that Finkelstein's book can be read as a defence of the idea that substantial self-knowledge is very often based on nothing. In a fuller discussion I would also spend time on Bar-On 2004.

Firstly, the immediacy premise is no good, despite its popularity with philo-sophers of self-knowledge. Secondly, it's far from obvious that perceptual know-ledge is non-inferential and, in this sense, immediate. If perceptual knowledge is based on inference then modelling introspection on perception won't provide much of an explanation of the immediacy of self-knowledge. It's good that the Immediacy Argument is no good because it so happens that there are also other, independent objections to the perceptual model. As we will see, this model is more robust than it is usually given credit for being, but is ultimately unacceptable.

If you accept the immediacy premise but reject both the perceptual model and the view that self-knowledge is based on nothing then, as Boghossian points out, you really are in trouble. When it comes to explaining knowledge of our own thoughts the only three options are that this knowledge is:

1. Based on inference or reasoning.
2. Based on inner observation.
3. Based on nothing.

If, like Boghossian, you end up rejecting all three options then all you're left with is the sceptical thesis that we can't know our own minds. The sensible response to Boghossian's trilemma is to question the immediacy premise and argue instead in favour of *inferentialism*, the view that knowledge of our own attitudes can be, and indeed is, a form of inferential knowledge. I will defend inferentialism in the next chapter. What I want to do in the rest of this chapter is to discuss some arguments against the inner observation model. Specifically, I want to take a look at what I'm going to call the *neo-Humean* argument against this model. This argument, versions of which can be found in Boghossian's paper 'Content and Self-Knowledge' and in Sydney Shoemaker's Royce Lectures, leads naturally to the inferentialism I ultimately want to defend.[3]

This is my plan: I'll start by setting out the orthodox way of representing introspection as perceptual, which Shoemaker labels the 'object perception model of introspection'. Then I will look at various arguments against the object perception model, including the neo-Human argument. Although I'm sympa-thetic to some aspects of this argument, there is one element of it which is fishy but nevertheless common ground between some proponents and some oppon-ents of the object perception model. This is the assumption that genuinely perceptual knowledge is non-inferential. As we have seen, proponents of the object perception model rely on this assumption in defence of the idea that the perceptual model of introspection has introspective self-knowledge come out as

---

[3] 'Content and Self-Knowledge' is Boghossian 1998. The Royce Lectures are Shoemaker 1996.

non-inferential. And as we will see, opponents rely on it when they argue that introspection can't be perceptual because it is inferential. They are both wrong because 'perceptual' and 'inferential' aren't contradictories. However, in the end I don't think that we should accept the object perception model. Nor, as I will argue at the end of this chapter, should we accept the alternative perceptual model which Armstrong defends in *A Materialist Theory of the Mind*.[4] The right view is that knowledge of our own beliefs and other standing attitudes *is* inferential and is *not* perceptual. In this chapter I will defend the second conjunct of this conjunction. I will defend the first conjunct in the next chapter.

The basic idea of the object perception model is that being introspectively aware of one's own states of mind (beliefs, sensations, or experiences) is like being perceptually aware of a non-mental object: just as sense perception acquaints us with non-mental objects, so introspection acquaints us with mental objects. Introspection, on this view, is a kind of internal searchlight that illuminates, and provides us with, knowledge of our own states of mind in the way that ordinary sense perception illuminates, and provides us with, knowledge of bits of non-mental reality. Of course there are differences between introspection and ordinary sense perception of objects but the claim is that they are sufficiently alike for it to make sense to think of introspection as a kind of perception.

How alike is 'sufficiently alike'? It's hard to answer this question in the abstract but consider these apparent differences between introspection and ordinary perception: when you perceive a non-mental object such as a tree or a table you use your sense organs—your eyes, for example—but there is no organ of introspection. Sense perception involves the occurrence of impressions that are distinct from the object of perception but 'no one thinks that one is aware of beliefs and thoughts by having sensations or quasi-experiences of them' (Shoemaker 1996: 207). The objects of ordinary sense perception exist whether or not they are perceived but introspectable mental states do not exist whether or not we are introspectively aware of them. These are all respects in which introspection and ordinary perception are *not* alike, so how can the object perception model possibly be correct?

The object perception model has at its disposal two ways of dealing with such points. One is to argue that the alleged differences between introspection and perception aren't genuine. The other is to argue that though the differences are genuine they aren't significant enough to undermine the model. For example, it's true that there is no organ of introspection but there can also be perception without an organ of perception; bodily perception (proprioception) is what tells

---

[4] Armstrong 1993.

you whether you are sitting or standing but there is no organ of bodily perception. It's also false that the proper objects of introspective awareness aren't independent of our introspective awareness of them: you can have a belief or desire or hope you aren't introspectively aware of. Since our beliefs and other standing attitudes are not self-intimating, this leaves it open that our introspective awareness of them is quasi-perceptual. It's true that we aren't introspectively aware of our beliefs by having sensations of them, but this difference between introspection and perception isn't important enough to undermine the object perception model.

No doubt there is more to be said about these issues but the discussion so far suggests that many of the standard objections to the object perception model aren't decisive. There is, however, another objection to this model which looks much more threatening. What I have in mind is an objection implied by the neo-Humean argument, and it's now time to say what this argument is. Boghossian's version of the argument turns on what he calls an 'apparently inevitable thesis about content', the thesis that 'the content of a thought is determined by its relational properties' (1998: 149). Given this apparently inevitable thesis, 'we could not know what we think merely by looking inwards' because 'what we would need to see, if we are to know by mere looking, is not there to be seen' (1998: 149). Hume gets into the picture on the assumption that the relational properties of a thought which determines its content are causal properties. This assumption causes a problem for the object perception model because it's not possible to know a thought's causal role directly: 'the point derives from Hume's observation that it is not possible to ascertain an item's causal properties non-inferentially... discovering them requires observation of the item's behaviour over time' (1998: 162).

An example might help: suppose that what makes a thought a thought about vodka as opposed to a thought about gin is the thought's causal properties: thoughts with causal role R_1 are thoughts about vodka whereas thoughts with causal role R_2 are about gin.[5] So to know that my present thought is about vodka thought I would need to know that it has causal role R_1 as opposed to causal role R_2 but I couldn't possibly know non-inferentially, by mere inspection, a thought's causal role. A thought's causal role is what is 'not there to be seen', and that's why

---

[5] The causal role of thoughts of a given type consists of the typical causes and effects of thoughts of that type. Functionalists think that mental states generally are individuated by their causal roles. There are also non-functionalist conceptions of how a thought's content is determined by its relational properties. See below for more on this. Either way, the neo-Humean argument goes from a broadly relationalist conception of thought to the unacceptability of the object perception model.

we could not know what we think by looking inwards. Shoemaker is making essentially the same point when he argues against the object perception model on the grounds that our mental concepts are concepts of states that occupy certain causal or functional roles: 'we have been "taught by Hume" (I do not say that we have been *correctly* taught this) that any report that carries causal implications goes beyond what we can, strictly speaking, perceive to be the case' (1996: 221).

Is the neo-Humean argument any good? The two key questions here are:

(a) Is the content of a thought is determined by its causal or relational properties?
(b) Is it possible to ascertain an item's causal or relational properties perceptually?

The neo-Humean argument goes through only if the answer to the first question is 'yes' and the answer to the second question is 'no'. In fact, the answer to both questions is 'yes'. Even if you can't ascertain an item's relational properties *non-inferentially* it doesn't follow that you can't ascertain an item's relational properties *perceptually*. The point is not that the object perception model is okay after all but rather that the neo-Human argument isn't decisive as it stands. What actually undermines this model is a variation on the neo-Humean argument which doesn't require acceptance of 'what Hume taught us'.

Let's start with (a). The functionalist thesis that the content of a thought or belief is determined by its causal role is one way, but not the only way, of expressing the idea that its content is fixed by its relational properties. There are 'externalist' or 'anti-individualistic' accounts of content on which the answer to (a) is also 'yes'. For example, the answer to (a) is 'yes' if a person's thought contents are determined by the relations he bears to the physical or social environment. I haven't committed myself to either externalism or functionalism but I have endorsed a dispositionalist view of belief and other attitudes. For example, in Chapter 2, I described beliefs as 'habits of thought' and I said in the last chapter that whether you believe that P depends on whether you are disposed to think that P when the question arises, act as if P is true, and use P as a premise in reasoning. The dispositions that go with believing that P are multi-track and include what Schwitzgebel calls 'phenomenal' dispositions—dispositions to have certain sorts of conscious experiences—as well as cognitive and behavioural dispositions.[6] Now the question is: what is the impact of this view of belief on (a)?

The answer to this question is 'very little'. For a start, dispositional properties are still broadly relational, in which case thinking that the content of a belief or

---

[6] See Schwitzgebel 2002.

thought is determined by its dispositional properties about belief is not at odds with thinking that it is determined by its relational properties. The sense in which dispositional properties are relational is that they can't be described without describing other things.[7] In the case of beliefs, the other things include certain sorts of behaviour and conscious experiences. Functionalism and the dispositionalism I've been presupposing are different forms of Boghossian's 'apparently inevitable thesis about content', and it might seem that the neo-Humean argument works fine either way: surely it isn't possible to detect an item's dispositional properties perceptually any more than it is possible to detect an item's causal properties perceptually.[8] So the answer to (b) is still 'no'.

When a philosopher says 'surely P' it's generally a good idea to watch out, and what I have just said is no exception. It's actually far from obvious that functional or dispositional properties can't be ascertained perceptually. For example, you might think that colour and shape are causal or dispositional properties of objects but this doesn't imply that you can't know by seeing that an object is square or red. Reports of shape and colour certainly carry causal implications but such reports don't go beyond what we can, strictly speaking, perceive to be the case. This is one reason for thinking that 'what Hume taught us' isn't right; just because the content of a thought is determined by its relational properties it doesn't follow that we couldn't know what we think merely by looking inwards, or that what we would need to see, if we are to know by mere looking, is not there to be seen.

Here's an even better example that also suggests that the correct answer to (b) is in fact 'yes':

> Being a dime is not an intrinsic property of an object. For something to be a dime it must bear a number of complicated relations to its economic and social environment. And yet we seem often able to tell that something is a dime purely observationally, by mere inspection of its intrinsic properties. (Boghossian 1998: 162–3)

Here is how Boghossian thinks that the neo-Humean argument should deal with this potential counterexample:

> The reason an extrinsic property seems, in this case, ascertainable by mere inspection, is due to the fact that possession of that property is correlated with possession of an intrinsic property that is ascertainable by mere inspection. The reason the coin's dimehood seems detectable by mere inspection derives from the fact that it having the value in question is neatly encoded in several of its purely intrinsic properties: in the phrase "ten cents" that is

---

[7] Langton 2006 has more on this conception of 'relational'.
[8] There is a helpful discussion of all this in Goldman 2006: 248.

inscribed on it, and in several properties of its size, shape, and design characteristics. (1998: 163)

What this means, Boghossian concludes, is that 'the process by which we know the coin's value is not really inspection, it's inference: you have to deduce that the coin is worth ten cents from your knowledge of its intrinsic properties plus your knowledge of how those intrinsic properties are correlated with possession of monetary value' (1998: 163-4).

Let's just grant that the process by which we know the coin's value is inference. In talking about 'inference' in this context we obviously aren't talking about something we are conscious of doing. The inferences in question require no attention; they are automatic and effortless. How it is supposed to follow that the process by which we know the coin's value is 'not really inspection'? It follows only on the assumption that genuine perception is non-inferential but why should we accept that assumption? It's no good arguing that perception can't be inferential because we aren't conscious of inferring when we perceive; that would also be a reason for questioning the idea that we know a coin's value by inference. The issue is whether, apart from whether it *feels* like perception involves inference (it doesn't), there are nevertheless good explanatory reasons for supposing that genuinely perceptual knowledge is, or can be, inferential. The natural view here is that while there might be a sense in which knowledge of a dime's monetary value is inferential, there is also a perfectly straightforward and intuitive sense in which you can *see* that it's a dime.

There is a whole lot to be said about the role of inference in perception, certainly far more than I can possibly say here. To save time, I'm just going to state dogmatically that I'm pretty much in agreement with the view that perception involves inference. As Harman argues in his book *Thought*, one indication that this is so is that the inferential approach provides the best explanation of perceptual 'Gettier cases' such as the following: you come to believe by looking that there is a candle directly in front of you. There is a candle there but it's obscured by a mirror which is showing you the reflection of a candle off to one side. Your belief that there is a candle directly in front of you is true and justified but not knowledge. Why not? Because you infer that it looks to you as if there is a candle there because there is a candle there, but this explanation is false; it only looks to you as if there is a candle there because you can see the reflection in the mirror of a candle that is not directly in front of you.[9]

---

[9] Harman 1973: 174.

In addition to explaining perceptual Gettier cases, the inferential approach also seems to accord with the best scientific understanding of perception. For example, you determine how far away a perceived object is by means of visual cues from which you infer the location of the object: 'given those cues the perceiver infers that objects are in those places' (Harman 1973: 175). It's true that we sometimes say things like 'I don't infer that P, I can see that P' but this can be read as shorthand for 'I don't just infer that P, I can see that P'. As it happens, the justification for reading the first statement this way is itself inferential: given that the best total explanatory account of perception implies that it involves inference, the basis for saying that perception involves inference is inference to the best explanation.

Suppose this is all correct. This spells trouble for the neo-Humean argument because it deprives it of one of its key premises. The argument goes: the content of a thought is fixed by its relational properties; we can only know our own thoughts perceptually if we can know them non-inferentially; our knowledge of our own thoughts can't be non-inferential if the content of a thought is determined by its relational properties; therefore our knowledge of our own thoughts can't be perceptual or modelled on perception. It's the second premise of this argument which now seems dubious. For all that the neo-Humean argument proves, it would be open to someone who wants to hang on to the object perception model to insist that we can know our own thoughts by 'looking' even if it's not possible to ascertain a thought's content-determining relational properties non-inferentially.

This might strike someone like Boghossian as a pretty hollow victory for the object perception model. After all, this model was first introduced as an *alternative* to an inferential conception of self-knowledge, as a way of explaining how inference can be neither required nor relevant when it comes to knowledge of one's own thoughts. If it turns out that the object perception model is itself committed to regarding self-knowledge as inferential then it is in no position to accommodate the immediacy premise, but without this premise the Immediacy Argument for the 'inner perception' model of introspection also lapses. This is what I meant when I said that both proponents and opponents of the object perception model rely on the same dubious assumption that 'perceptual' and 'inferential' are contradictories; neither the Immediacy Argument nor the neo-Humean argument can do without the assumption.

Given that this is where we have ended up the obvious next step would be to question the immediacy premise. What causes all the trouble is the assumption that inference is neither required nor relevant for knowledge of one's own thoughts. I'm going to argue in the next chapter that the immediacy premise has much less going for it than is generally assumed, and is only as popular as it is because critics of inferentialism are usually attacking a straw man. Going back to Boghossian's trilemma, this means that I'm going for a version of option 1: knowledge of our own thoughts is based on inference or reasoning. What I've been arguing in this chapter is that this doesn't rule out option 2: knowledge of our own thoughts is based on inner observation. Be that as it may, I think that we should still reject option 2, if not for the exact reasons given by the neo-Humean argument then for closely related reasons.

The point is this: suppose that you know that you believe your socks are stripy, and we're trying to model the introspective awareness on which this knowledge is based on object perception. When you *perceive* that your socks are stripy you do so *by* perceiving your socks but you aren't introspectively aware that you believe your socks are stripy *by* being aware of the belief that your socks are stripy. In perception you are normally aware of a multiplicity of objects, and there is such a thing as singling out an object and distinguishing it from others by its perceived properties and spatial location. In contrast, even if you are introspectively aware that you believe that your socks are stripy, this isn't a matter of singling this belief out and distinguishing it from other beliefs you are also introspectively aware of. Propositional attitudes aren't 'objects' waiting to be 'singled out' on the basis of introspectively available information about their relational and non-relational properties.

This points to another difference between introspection and perception: as Shoemaker notes, 'perception of objects standardly involves perception of their intrinsic, nonrelational properties' (1996: 205). When it comes to beliefs and other attitudes, it isn't clear what their 'intrinsic, nonrelational properties' are, let alone what it would be for introspection to involve awareness of such properties. Suppose you are some kind of physicalist and think that the 'intrinsic properties' of mental states are physico-chemical. Then you can hardly fail to notice that you aren't introspectively aware of such properties. Perception yields detailed awareness of the intrinsic properties of objects whereas introspection provides us with little information about what physicalism regards as the intrinsic nature of mental events.

These objections to the object perception model are in the same general ballpark as the neo-Humean argument, though the emphasis is somewhat different. That argument starts with the idea that the content of a thought is determined by its relational properties and then objects to the object perception model on the basis that it's not possible to ascertain an item's causal properties non-inferentially and hence perceptually. But even if perceptual knowledge can be inferential this is of no help to the 'inner perception' model of introspection unless in introspective awareness of a belief there is an 'item' whose intrinsic properties you are aware of and from which you can infer that it has certain relational properties. The problem is that there is no such 'item' or 'object' of awareness, and this is the point at which the analogy with Boghossian's dime breaks down completely. When you see that the coin in your hand is a dime you are implicitly inferring its monetary value from its intrinsic properties because its monetary value is correlated with its intrinsic properties. In the case of a thought or belief, you aren't aware of the intrinsic properties of a mental 'item', and even if you were that wouldn't get you anywhere because, 'facts about a thought token's content are not correlated with any of that token's purely intrinsic properties' (Boghossian 1998: 163).

Let's see where we've got to: I've argued that as far as knowledge of our own beliefs and thoughts is concerned the object perception model is no good, even if it has turned out to be a tougher nut to crack than one might have expected. However, before giving up on the idea that introspection is a form of inner perception it's worth pointing out that the object perception model is only one version of the perceptual model and that there are others which avoid quite a few of the difficulties the object perception gets into. As I've already indicated, what I have in mind is Armstrong's 'broad' perceptual model of introspection. This is by far the best bet for someone who is really serious about the immediacy premise so I'd like to end this chapter by briefly explaining why, in the end, the broad perceptual model isn't the way to go.

Armstrong's basic idea is really very simple, and depends on his background conception of knowledge and perception more generally. Here's the basic story: perception is the acquiring of beliefs or information about the current state of the organism's body and environment. A belief is a dispositional state and, like other mental concepts, the concept of a belief is the 'concept of *a state of a person apt for bringing about a certain sort of behaviour*' (1993: 82). Perceptions are events rather than dispositional states; they are *acquirings* of beliefs, and the major source of our non-inferential knowledge. Non-inferential knowledge is in turn a matter of reliability. You know that P non-inferentially just if, in the absence of reasons for believing that P, you do believe that P and your belief is empirically sufficient for the truth of P.[10] For example, if by using your eyes you acquire the belief that you are wearing stripy socks then your belief is knowledge just if it is an empirical truth that your wearing socks is a necessary condition of your acquiring that belief. If your belief is reliable in this sense then you have acquired knowledge.[11]

---

[10] Armstrong 1993: 189.   [11] Armstrong 1993: 237–8.

The idea that mental states are dispositional might seem difficult to reconcile with the claim that our introspective awareness of them is quasi-perceptual. If dispositional properties are relational then introspective awareness of a mental state would be direct awareness of an 'abstract, relational state of affairs'; in effect, it would be 'direct awareness of counter-factual truths' (Armstrong 1993: 96), and the worry is that this isn't possible. However, on an information-flow view of perception there is no difficulty. Just as perception is the acquiring of information or misinformation about our environment, so introspection is 'the getting of information or misinformation about the current state of our mind' (1993: 326). Introspectively acquired beliefs about your own states of mind are self-knowledge as long as they are reliable. It's the picture of introspection as an internal searchlight that lights up the mind that causes all the trouble for the perceptual model. If introspection is simply the getting of beliefs, there is no reason to deny that these beliefs can be about one's current states of mind, dispositional or otherwise.

Among the apparent advantages of Armstrong's picture, one is that it seems to explain how introspective awareness of one's mental states can be perceptual in a way that bypasses many of the objections to the object perception model. The issue of whether inferential knowledge can be perceptual doesn't arise because for Armstrong one's knowledge that one believes that P can be non-inferential even if the content of one's belief is determined by its dispositional properties. On the issue of whether introspection tells us anything about the intrinsic nature of the mental, Armstrong is happy to accept that it does not. He thinks that mental states are in fact 'physico-chemical states of the brain' (1993: 90) but that there are perfectly good biological reasons why 'introspection should give us such meagre information about the intrinsic nature of mental events' (1993: 99). The main reason is that having such information is of little value in the conduct of life. So we are not in the position of having to infer a belief's dispositional properties from our introspective awareness of its intrinsic properties; there is no such awareness and no such inference. We are directly aware of the dispositional properties of our beliefs and that is why Armstrong's model appears to be in a much better position than the object perception model to regard self-knowledge as genuinely 'immediate'.

Still, there are good reasons not to settle for Armstrong's view. The first point is *ad hominem*: comparing introspection with perception only makes it plausible that introspective knowledge is non-inferential if perceptual knowledge is non-inferential, but Armstrong himself ends up arguing that a lot of ordinary perceptual knowledge is inferential. Even when it comes to something as simple as seeing a cat's head or a sheet of paper 'there is a concealed element of inference' from 'a certain group of properties of objects that may be called *visual* properties', including colour, shape and size (1993: 234). What we see 'immediately' is that there is a thing with certain visual properties before us. This, 'by an automatic and instantaneous inference, produces the further belief that there is a cat's head or a sheet of paper before us' (1993: 235). However, if only a special sub-class of perceptual knowledge is non-inferential, then what exactly is the argument for modelling introspective knowledge on non-inferential rather than on inferential perceptual knowledge? This is just the view I've been exploring, and Armstrong doesn't show that there isn't a concealed element of inference in introspection, just as there is perception. The fact that we aren't aware of any inference in introspection is of little significance because Armstrong is perfectly happy with the idea that inference can be unconscious.[12] This isn't an argument against thinking of introspection as perceptual but it is an argument against thinking of introspective knowledge as immediate.

A more substantive worry about Armstrong's view is that it makes intro-spection out to be fundamentally no different, epistemologically or phenom-enologically, from clairvoyance. What I mean by clairvoyance is the kind of thing Laurence BonJour has talked about over the years.[13] For example, there is the case of Norman who, for no apparent reason, finds himself with beliefs about the President's whereabouts; Norman has neither seen nor heard that the President is in New York but believes that the President is in New York, and his belief is reliable. Even if it's right to describe Norman as 'knowing' that the President is in New York his knowledge is very different from ordinary perceptual knowledge. When you know that the President is in New York by seeing him in New York you are *aware* of the President, and your knowing requires a degree of cognitive effort, even if it's only the minimal effort of looking and paying attention to where the President is. In contrast, Norman is not aware of the President and his belief is not the result of any cognitive effort on his part. The belief that the President is in New York simply comes to him; he has no justification for believing that the President is in New York and no idea why he believes this or how he could possibly know where the President is. That's why some critics have concluded that what Norman has is not really *knowledge*, properly so-called, or that it is only knowledge in a secondary or derivative sense.[14]

---

[12] Armstrong 1993: 194–8.   [13] See, for example, BonJour 2001.

[14] One such critic is Michael Ayers. See Ayers 1991, especially chapter 15, for a defence of the view that what Norman lacks is knowledge in the primary sense. In primary knowledge, you not only know but also know *how* you know.

In what sense is introspection, as Armstrong thinks of it, like clairvoyance? Suppose that, in addition to believing that the President is in New York, Norman also has the second-order belief that he believes that the President is in New York. If introspection is simply the 'getting of beliefs' by means of a reliable mechanism then the way that Norman 'gets' his second-order belief is similar to the way he 'gets' his first-order belief about the President's whereabouts. No effort is required and he just finds himself believing things about his beliefs. Could this be how we know our own beliefs? Aaron Zimmerman thinks not:

> We are not in the position of the infallible psychic who just finds herself believing things about the future for no good reason; we simply do not find ourselves believing that we believe some things and not others. (2006: 349)

Zimmerman's point here is primarily phenomenological rather than epistemological but there is also an underlying epistemological worry about Armstrong's model of self-knowledge. Just as Norman has no justification for believing the President is in New York, and no idea why he believes this, so he has no justification for believing that he believes the President is in New York and no idea why he believes that he believes the President is in New York. If there is anything to this comparison then the upshot is that what Norman gets from introspection is not self-knowledge properly so-called or only self-knowledge in a secondary or derivative sense.

If you are drawn to the broad perceptual model of introspection could you just bite the bullet in response to such objections and argue that self-knowledge *is* in the relevant respects like clairvoyance? After all, if you ask Norman whether he believes that the President is in New York he has no trouble answering your question but he would be hard pushed to say how he knows what he believes. The belief that he believes the President is in New York just comes to him when the question arises but he has no reason for believing that he believes the President is in New York. Doesn't this mean that Norman is in the position of finding himself believing that he believes some things and not others? He doesn't know how he knows that he believes the President is in New York, any more than he knows how he knows that the President is in New York. Yet, at least on an externalist understanding of knowledge, he still knows that the President is in New York and knows that he believes that the President is in New York. His knowledge in both cases in non-inferential, and externalism denies that in order to know non-inferentially that P you have to have a reason for believing that P.

The problem with this line of thinking, apart from its reliance on a pretty full-on form of externalism, is that it ends up undermining the idea that introspection should be modelled on perception. As I've argued, perceptual knowledge is strikingly different from clairvoyant 'knowledge' so it doesn't exactly help the perceptual model to say that self-knowledge is like clairvoyance. If perceptual knowledge that P requires you to be conscious that P as well as a degree of cognitive effort then the net effect of admitting that Norman's knowledge that he believes the President is in New York is epistemologically and phenomenologically on a par with his knowledge that the President is in New York is to suggest that his self-knowledge is *not* perceptual. It lacks some key features of ordinary perceptual knowledge and only comes out as 'perceptual' on an impoverished view of perceptual knowledge which has very little going for it.

It's also worth pointing out that there are significant chunks of self-knowledge which clearly don't fit the broad perceptual model, on the assumption that this model is prepared to live with the accusation that it treats introspection as akin to clairvoyance. For example, if the question arises whether you truly believe that all races are equal or whether you want another child you may know that the answer is 'yes' because you have thought about these things before. But if you haven't thought about them before then knowing what you believe or want in such cases isn't a matter of finding yourself with the yen to believe that you believe that all races are equal or that you want another child. To take such questions seriously is to be prepared to do some *thinking*; it isn't like putting money into a slot machine and waiting to see what comes out. Self-knowledge can be a hard-won cognitive achievement, and the broad perceptual model doesn't have anything to say about this.

Cases in which self-knowledge is a hard-won cognitive achievement are cases of what I have called substantial self-knowledge. From the fact that the broad perceptual model is ill-equipped to account for substantial self-knowledge it doesn't follow that it is ill-equipped to account for trivial self-knowledge. There is always the possibility of a hybrid approach which sees self-knowledge, even knowledge of one's own attitudes, as being sometimes perceptual and sometimes inferential. However, given all the objections to the broad perceptual model I have been discussing it would be worth considering another possibility: what I have in mind is the possibility that even supposedly 'trivial' self-knowledge is *not* perceptual but *is* at least implicitly inferential. I've emphasized that your knowledge that P can be inferential even if you aren't conscious of inferring that P. Could it not be, then, that when it comes to knowing what you want or believe or hope inference is always involved, even in straightforward cases, and that various attempts to account for the immediacy of self-knowledge are doomed at the outset because self-knowledge is not in fact immediate? This is the inferentialist approach to self-knowledge which I'm going to discuss in the next chapter.

11

Self-Knowledge and Inference

It's time to cut to the chase. So far in this book I've spent a lot of time criticizing a range of standard approaches to self-knowledge but the question raised by these criticisms is: do you have any better ideas? Beating up on other views is easy but the real challenge is to replace them with something better. In this chapter I'm going to defend what I've been calling inferentialism about intentional self-knowledge, the view that knowledge of our own beliefs, desires, hopes, and other 'intentional' states is first and foremost a form of inferential knowledge. In Chapter 1, I identified the following sources question about self-knowledge:

(SQ) What are the sources of self-knowledge for humans?

Inferentialism says that inference is a key source of intentional self-knowledge for humans. Whether inferentialism regards any of our intentional self-knowledge as *non*-inferential is a question I will come back to later in this chapter. In the next chapter, I'll answer the sources question in relation to substantial self-knowledge. Again, inference will turn out to play a key role.

I think it's fair to say that inferentialism hasn't exactly been a popular approach to self-knowledge is recent years. Many currently influential discussions of self-knowledge start out with a statement to the effect that intentional self-knowledge is normally 'immediate', that is, non-inferential.[1] Philosophers who defend inferentialism—Ryle is usually mentioned in this context—are then berated for defending a patently absurd view.[2] The assumption that intentional self-knowledge is normally immediate—this is the immediacy premise that came up in the last chapter—is rarely defended; it's just seen as obviously correct. In contrast, I think that the immediacy premise is not obviously correct, and that inferentialism is a live option. So I need to do two things in this chapter: make a positive case for inferentialism and show why the usual objections to this view don't work.

---

[1] Moran 2001 makes much of this.
[2] See the damning discussion of Ryle in Boghossian 1998.

Here's a simple statement of inferentialism: suppose you know that you have a certain attitude A and the question arises how you know that you have A. In the most straightforward case you know that you have A insofar as you have access to evidence that you have A and you infer from your evidence that you have A. As long as your evidence is good enough and your inference is sound you thereby come to know that you have A. On this account, the idea that self-knowledge is inferential is closely related to the idea that it is based on evidence. Moran writes that 'the basic concept of first-person awareness we are trying to capture is that of awareness that is not based on evidence, behavioural or otherwise' (2001: 11). The concept of first-person awareness—or self-knowledge—which inferentialism is trying to capture is that of awareness or knowledge that *is* based on evidence, behavioural or otherwise.

It will save time and help to prevent various kind of misunderstanding if I make a few things clear at the outset:

(a) The attitudes I'm talking about are 'standing' rather than 'occurrent'. Standing attitudes remain in existence when you are asleep; they aren't mental events like judging or deciding. It's controversial whether a belief can ever be occurrent but when I talk about belief I'm talking about beliefs understood as standing states. Ditto for desires, hopes, and so on.

(b) I take it that if E is evidence for some proposition P then E makes it more likely or probable that P is true. Evidence can be, but needn't be, conclusive. When inferentialism says that self-knowledge is based on, or inferred from, evidence it remains to be seen what kind or kinds or evidence are at issue. One kind of evidence is behavioural but there are other possibilities; you can discover your own standing attitudes on the basis of your judgements, inner speech, dreams, passing thoughts and feelings.[3] These are all potentially varieties of evidence but they aren't behavioural evidence.

(c) Inference can be, but needn't be, conscious. This came up in the last chapter, in connection with the idea that perception involves inference. To repeat what I said there: it isn't a knockdown argument against representing perception as inferential to point out that we aren't normally conscious of inferring when we perceive. There might be strong theoretical grounds for seeing perceptual knowledge or self-knowledge as inferential regardless of whether they involve any conscious inference. It is also worth adding that sometimes the claim that a particular type of knowledge is

---

[3] Lawlor 2009 is good on the variety of 'internal' sources of self-knowledge.

inferential is a claim about the various conscious or unconscious psychological processes that underpin it. At other times the claim is primarily epistemological rather than psychological; assuming that you can't know that P unless you are justified in believing that P, saying that your knowledge that P is inferential might be a way of making a point about its justificational structure: your knowledge that P is inferential if your justification for believing that P comes in part from your having justification to believe other, supporting propositions.[4]

(d) If E is your evidence that you have a particular attitude A, and you know that you have A by inference from E, then you need access to E. What kind of access to E? That depends on the nature of your evidence. If your evidence is behavioural then your access to E might have to be perceptual, but this won't be true if your evidence consists of your passing thoughts or inner speech. Inferentialism is not committed to regarding our access to these things as inferential. I will more to say about this later in this chapter.

(e) The inferences that lead to self-knowledge are normally mediated by the subject's implicit grasp of what is sometimes called a 'theory of mind'.[5] You only infer from E that you have A because you take E to be evidence (at least in your own case) for A. Taking E to be evidence for A is an implicit theoretical commitment of yours. Here's an example: suppose that you judge that you ought rationally to believe that P and infer from this that you do in fact believe that P. You can only get from a claim about what you ought rationally to believe to a claim about what you actually believe on the assumption that you actually believe what you ought rationally to believe. The role of this assumption about how your mind works—Finkelstein calls it the Rationality Assumption—is to mediate the transition from 'ought' to 'is'.

In view of what I've been arguing so far in this book inferentialism might seem a surprising position for me to be defending. I've criticized Rationalism for operating with an over-optimistic and unrealistic conception of how humans think; in effect, the charge is that Rationalists over-intellectualize human beings and regard us as far more intellectually virtuous and capable than we are. For example, humans often believe things on the basis of little or no actual evidence; and even when they have evidence for their beliefs they frequently don't consult it. Doesn't this make it unlikely that self-attributions of propositional attitudes

---

[4] In giving this account of inferential justification I'm basically following Pryor 2005.
[5] I guess this makes me a 'theory theory' theorist of self-knowledge. Gopnik 1993 and Carruthers 1996 both defend versions of the view that self-knowledge is theory involving.

are evidence-based? Insofar as inferentialism represents humans as coming to know their own attitudes by theory-mediated inference from evidence isn't it just as guilty as Rationalism of over-intellectualizing human self-knowledge?

Well, it all depends on how notions like 'theory' and 'inference' are understood. Inferentialism is only in danger of over-intellectualizing self-knowledge on what is itself an over-intellectualized understanding of these notions. Take inference as an example: there is the case in which inferring something from something else is a careful and reflective piece of 'slow' rather than 'fast' thinking. The inferences that give us self-knowledge can be like this but needn't be. They can be, and often are, automatic, effortless, and barely conscious. They are 'fast' rather than 'slow', and the assumptions that underpin them are usually implicit rather than explicit. Describing these assumptions as amounting to a 'theory' of mind is misleading if the implication is that in order to know your own attitudes you need to be able to do the philosophy of your own situation. Nothing beyond the intellectual reach of normal human adults is required.[6] It's also worth pointing out that our inferences, even our inferences about our own states of mind, aren't always good, and these are cases in which we will end up making mistakes about our own attitudes. Such mistakes are possible and inferentialism explains how they are possible. It also explains how, when we do know our own attitudes, we know them: we know them by inference.

Another worry about inferentialism might be that it goes against my insistence that when it comes to explaining human self-knowledge there is no magic bullet, no one source that is capable of accounting for all our intentional self-knowledge. Isn't inference a single source? There are two things to say about this: first, saying that inference is a key source of intentional self-knowledge for humans doesn't mean that there aren't other sources. Later I'll consider the possibility that memory is a source of intentional self-knowledge, and that when you know what you think about something by remembering what you think about it your self-knowledge isn't inferential. The second point is that 'inference' as I understand it is such a broad category and covers so many different things that inferentialism hardly amounts to a 'magic bullet' explanation of human self-knowledge. For example, if you come to know your own attitudes by using the Transparency Method your self-knowledge is inferential but your self-knowledge is also inferential if it is based on awareness of your behaviour or passing thoughts. Inferentialism is an inclusive doctrine that keeps many doors open. What it does is to help structure our thinking about self-knowledge, and puts paid

---

[6] Or, indeed, beyond the intellectual reach of children. See Gopnik 1993.

to various myths about self-knowledge that have grown up in recent years, the primary myth being that intentional self-knowledge is normally 'immediate'.

What is the case for inferentialism? I'm going to outline three arguments in favour. Then I'll discuss and respond to a range of more or less standard objections to inferentialism. The first argument for inferentialism, which I call the argument by elimination, goes back to Boghossian's trilemma which came up in Chapter 10. Here's the trilemma again: knowledge of our own attitudes can only be:

1. Based on inference.
2. Based on inner observation.
3. Based on nothing.

I've already rejected 2 and 3 so that leaves 1 as the only remaining option. It had better be the case that we can know our own attitudes by inference because there is no viable alternative to inferentialism. We can argue about what self-knowledge is an inference *from* but rejecting 1 would leave us in the unhappy position of having to say that we do not know our own minds. If you are convinced that there are decisive objections to 2 and 3, and that scepticism about self-knowledge isn't a serious option, then by default 1 has to be right: inferentialism is the only game in town.

Like all arguments of this form, the argument by elimination for inferentialism is only as strong as the case for thinking that:

(i) All the alternatives have genuinely been eliminated.
(ii) There aren't problems with the remaining option that are just as serious as the problems with all the other options.

With regard to (i), I have already argued at length against 2 and won't repeat these arguments here. The basic objection to 3 is this: self-knowledge can't be based on nothing unless it is cognitively insubstantial, like knowing that I am here now.[7] However, as Boghossian points out, there are plenty of indications that self-knowledge is not cognitively insubstantial: one can decide how much attention to pay to one's thoughts, some adults are better than others at reporting on their inner states, and self-knowledge is fallible and incomplete. It's natural to understand the difference between getting it right and failing to do so with regard to our own attitudes as 'the difference between being in an epistemically favourable position with the relevant evidence—and not' (Boghossian 1998: 167). On this account of the fallibility and incompleteness of self-knowledge

---

[7] But see footnote 2 in Chapter 10 for a possible caveat.

the door is wide open to viewing self-knowledge not just as cognitively substantial but as inferential. That leaves (ii). If, as I'll be arguing below, there aren't decisive objections to inferentialism then the argument by elimination is in good shape. The position, then, is this: there aren't decisive objections to inferentialism, there are decisive objections to the alternatives, so let's all be inferentialists.

It's one thing to think that inferentialism must be right but we also need to understand *how* knowledge of our own attitudes can be inferential. This brings me to my next argument for inferentialism, which I'll call the argument by example. This argument builds on the idea that self-knowledge is cognitively substantial by giving examples of how human beings come to know their own attitudes by inference. Having an abstract guarantee that self-knowledge must be inferential is one thing but inferentialism will be much more concrete and secure if it is possible to come up with realistic examples of inferential self-knowledge. Such examples will serve to demystify inferentialism by showing it to be grounded in how we actually seek and acquire knowledge of our attitudes.

I've already mentioned one somewhat surprising example of inferentialism in action. If you come to know that you have an attitude A on the basis that you ought rationally to have A then your self-knowledge is by inference: with the help of the Rationality Assumption you infer what your attitude is from what it ought to be. I say that this is a surprising example because influential proponents of the Transparency Method, such as Richard Moran, represent it as a way of acquiring 'immediate' self-knowledge. I suggested at the end of Chapter 9 that TM is quite consistent with inferentialism, though it's a further question to what extent humans actually rely on TM to know their own attitudes. Given all the problems with TM I've been discussing in this book it seems likely that TM is a relatively peripheral source of inferential intentional self-knowledge, at least when it comes to knowledge of such things as our hopes, desires, and fears.

For a more compelling example of humans acquiring self-knowledge by inference we need look no further than Krista Lawlor's paper 'Knowing What One Wants'.[8] I want to spend some time on this paper because I'm very much is sympathy with Lawlor's approach. Lawlor rightly observes that 'too little atten-tion has been paid to the experience of getting (and trying to get) self-knowledge, especially of one's desires' (2009: 56). She focuses on desires that are not easy to know about, such as the desire for another child. She gives the detailed example of Katherine who feels there is a fact of the matter about her desire for another child but struggles to know the answer to the question 'Do I want another child?' Notice how odd it would be for Katherine to answer this question by asking

---

[8] Lawlor 2009.

herself whether she ought rationally to want another child. She might ask herself this question if she conceives of herself as *homo philosophicus* but if she is a well-adjusted human being there are lots of other things she can and will do to answer her question:

Katherine starts noticing her experiences and thoughts. She catches herself imagining, remembering, and feeling a range of things. Putting away her son's now-too-small clothes, she finds herself lingering over the memory of how a newborn feels in one's arms. She notes an emotion that could be envy when an acquaintance reveals her pregnancy. Such experiences may be enough to prompt Katherine to make a self-attribution that sticks. Saying "I want another child", she may feel a sense of ease or settledness. (Lawlor 2009: 57)

If her self-attribution sticks, if she experiences a sense of ease when she says 'I want another child', then she has an answer to her question. She has evidence that she wants another child. If her self-attribution doesn't stick then there are further things she can do in pursuit of self-knowledge. She can concentrate on her imaginings and try to replay imaginings about having another child. Her imaginings and fantasies are further data from which she can infer that she does, or does not, want another child.

If Katherine concludes on the basis of her feeling, imaginings and emotions that she wants another child it would be reasonable to describe her self-knowledge as inferential. What tells her what she wants is what Lawlor calls '*inference from internal promptings*', which is in turn a form of 'causal self-interpretation' (2009: 48-9). Inference from internal promptings is, as Lawlor points out, a 'routine means by which we know what we want' (2009: 60) and the resulting self-knowledge is a cognitive accomplishment. Clearly, there's a lot at stake for Katherine when she asks whether she wants another child, but more prosaic examples can be dealt with in much the same way. The waiter asks you if you would like a pre-dinner cocktail and you ask for a glass of champagne. The minute you say the words 'I'd like a glass of champagne' you realize that what you actually want is a vodka martini. It's possible that you have changed your mind but it's also possible that your reaction to placing your order tells you something about what you really wanted all along. This might be called the 'suck it and see' route to self-knowledge: if you can't work out what you want, go through the motions of committing to an option and it might become apparent what you want. In principle you could run the same line for cases of belief: you say you believe the present government will be re-elected but the minute you say the words you realize they don't ring true. To say that something does or doesn't feel right or ring true is to draw attention to the way that conscious experience or phenomenology can have an evidential role in relation to one's attitudes. Beliefs and desires aren't feelings but what you feel can sometimes tell you what you believe or desire.

A worry you might have about cases like Katherine is that they aren't representative. The thought would be that although you can on occasion figure out your desires by inference from internal promptings you normally 'just know' what you want without any inference. Lawlor feels the force of this in her discussion. She contrasts her view with the view that our desires are self-intimating and concedes that sometimes our desires are so 'simple' that 'the idea that the desire is self-intimating is very plausible' (2009: 56). To the extent that our desires are self-intimating our knowledge of them is neither inferential nor a cognitive accomplishment. Lawlor is relaxed about the existence of self-intimating desires because she is happy to concede that 'there are many ways to discover one's wants' (2009: 60). However, the issue isn't whether inference from internal promptings is *a* way to know one's desires but whether it is the *normal* way. This is what Lawlor's opponents will deny, and the existence of Katherine-type cases is neither here nor there as far as this issue is concerned.

In fact, the inferentialist's position is far stronger that Lawlor's discussion suggests. The objection to inferentialism is that 'in normal cases' one's desires are self-intimating because 'knowing one's desire is not a matter of successfully finding out about or discovering desires that one has through cognitive effort' (2009: 55). There are several things the inferentialist can say in response. Here are three:

(a) Just because a desire is self-intimating it doesn't follow that you (the subject of the desire) don't know of its existence by inference. To say that a desire or other attitude A is self-intimating is to say that if you have the relevant concepts then you can't have A without knowing that you have it. This doesn't explain *how* you know you have A and leaves the epistemological issues wide open; on the face of it you could think that you can't fail to know that you have A but that inference from internal promptings is the *means* by which you know you have A. Anyway, it's not clear why we should view simple desires, such as the desire for something cool to drink, as self-intimating in the first place. Just because 'many times, knowing what one wants is easy' (Lawlor 2009: 56) it doesn't follow that it's in the nature of such desires that you can't have them without knowing that you have them.

(b) In 'normal' cases in which we seemingly know our own desires without conscious inference it is open to the inferentialist to maintain that we know our desires by unconscious inference. This goes along with the idea, which

I've already mentioned, that 'the cognitive processes of inference can be very swift, barely rising to consciousness' (Lawlor 2009: 65). What is good about the idea that inference is always involved is that you then don't have to think that different desires have different epistemologies. The difference between easily and not so easily known desires is a difference in degree, and it would be in keeping with this to suppose that knowledge of our own desires is always inferential. The difference between having to work out what you want and 'just knowing' what you want isn't the difference between desires your knowledge of which is inferential and desires your knowledge of which is non-inferential. It is the difference between obviously and unobviously inferential knowledge.

(c) Many of the supposed examples of 'immediate', non-inferential self-knowledge actually have little to do with self-knowledge. Saying to the waiter that you would like something cool to drink is in the first instance a way of ordering something cool to drink and not a statement about your state of mind. The question whether your knowledge of what you want is inferential or non-inferential doesn't arise because your statement isn't expressive of self-knowledge. By the same token, many statements of the form 'I believe that P' are, according to what Moran calls the Presentational View, nothing more than 'the speaker's way of presenting the embedded proposition P' (2001: 70-1). If you say 'I believe that P', the way to contradict you is to deny P, not to deny that you believe that P. Where 'I believe that P' *is* genuinely a statement about your state of mind, and the question arises whether you do in fact believe that P, inferentialism claims that you know that you believe that P by conscious or unconscious inference. Exceptions would be cases where your statement doesn't fall within the scope of the Presentational View and your knowledge of your state of mind is in no sense inferential. Later I will argue that there are such cases but that they put no pressure on the idea that inference is a key source of intentional self-knowledge for humans.

That's just about as much as I want to say about the argument by example. If you are the kind of philosopher who takes it for granted that intentional self-knowledge is normally immediate or that, as Boghossian claims, 'knowledge of one's own mental states *has* to be non-inferential' (1998: 153) then this argument should help you. It's telling that Katherine is recognizably a human being addressing a humanly important question in a human way. Given the extent to which the philosophical literature has been dominated by examples of allegedly immediate intentional self-knowledge it's good to be reminded that a lot of perfectly ordinary intentional self-knowledge is *manifestly* inferential, and that intentional self-knowledge that isn't manifestly inferential could still be inferential. Whatever the merits of arguing that cases like Katherine aren't 'normal', the very least they do is raise questions about the tendency to take the immediacy of intentional self-knowledge as a datum.

The final argument for inferentialism points in the same general direction and is really just an extension of the argument by example. I call it the argument by experiment. This draws attention to the experimental evidence for inferentialism. Needless to say, the evidence isn't conclusive, but should certainly give pause to people who think that inferentialism is a crazy view. As an illustration of the craziness of inferentialism philosophers often quote the following passage from Ryle's *The Concept of Mind*:

The sorts of things that I can find out about myself are the same as the sorts of things that I can find out about other people, and the methods of finding them out are much the same. (1949: 149)

Since I find out what other people think by observing what they say and do Ryle seems to be saying that I find out what I think by observing what I say and do. Byrne says that this view 'can appear obviously absurd' (2012: 1) and defends Ryle on the grounds that it isn't what he really thought. In contrast, Davidson doesn't accuse Ryle of defending an apparently or even actually absurd view but he does insist that 'Ryle was wrong' because 'it is seldom the case that I need or appeal to evidence or observation in order to find out what I believe' (1998: 87). The clear implication is that while it's not ruled out that you might rely on behavioural evidence to find out what you believe such cases are far-fetched and unusual.

As I've emphasized, inferentialism isn't committed to the view that the evidence from which you infer your own attitudes is behavioural rather than, say, psychological. Still, it's worth considering the role of behavioural evidence in intentional self-knowledge in the light of the work of social psychologists such as Daryl Bem. Bem is a proponent of what he calls 'self-perception theory' (SPT), which he describes as follows:

Self-perception theory was initially formulated, in part, to address empirically certain questions in the "philosophy of mind" ... When an individual asserts, "I am hungry", how does he know? Is it an observation? An inference? Direct knowledge? Can he be in error or is that impossible by definition? How does the evidential basis for such a first-person statement (or self-attribution) differ from the evidential basis for the third-person attribution, "He is hungry"? (1972: 2)

This passage is in one respect misleading because it suggests that SPT is concerned with self-attributions of sensation, whereas in fact its focus is the self-attribution of attitudes, including beliefs. Bem mentions Ryle's view as a philosophical precursor of SPT, and it's clear why he does so given the two 'postulates' of SPT. The first states that: 'individuals come to "know" their own attitudes, emotions, and other internal states partially by inferring them from observations of their own overt behaviour and/or the circumstances in which this behaviour occurs' (1972: 5). The second states: 'to the extent that internal cues are weak, ambiguous, or uninterpretable, the individual is functionally in the same position as an outside observer, an observer who must necessarily rely upon those same external cues to infer the individual's inner state' (1972: 5). These postulates are distinctly Rylean but Bem, unlike Ryle, appeals to experimental evidence rather than conceptual analysis to support his theory. Could it be, then, that Ryle's 'behavioural' inferentialism can be defended on the basis of such evidence?

The experimental evidence to which Bem refers includes the experiment described by Festinger and Carlsmith in their famous 1959 paper on 'Cognitive Consequences of Forced Compliance'. In the classic Festinger–Carlsmith experiment, 60 students were randomly assigned to one of three conditions: in the $1 condition, the subject was first required to perform long, repetitive laboratory tasks and then paid $1 to tell a waiting fellow student that the tasks were enjoyable and interesting. In the $20 condition subjects were paid $20 to do the same thing. Control subjects simply engaged in the repetitive tasks. The results showed that the subjects paid $1 evaluated the tasks as significantly more enjoyable than subjects who had been paid $20. The latter subjects didn't express attitudes significantly different from those expressed by the control subjects. What is going on here? Bem writes:

[S]elf-perception theory considers the subject in such an experiment as simply an observer of his own behaviour. Just as an outside observer might ask himself, "What must this man's attitude be if he is willing to behave in this fashion in this situation?" so too, the subject implicitly asks himself, "What must my attitude be if I am willing to behave in this fashion in this situation?" Thus the subject who receives $1 discards the monetary inducement as the major motivating factor for his behaviour and infers that it must reflect his actual attitude; he infers that he must have actually enjoyed the tasks. The subject who receives $20 notes that his behaviour is adequately accounted for by the monetary inducement, and hence he cannot extract from the behaviour any information relevant to his actual opinions; he is in the same situation as a control subject insofar as information about his attitude is concerned. (1972: 16-17)

There are many other experiments that point in the same general direction: in every case you have a subject who, in keeping with the postulates of SPT, knows his own opinion or attitude by inference from his own behaviour. The subject doesn't 'just know'.

Clearly, none of this amounts to a proof of inferentialism, not least because SPT is itself a controversial view among social psychologists.[9] However, Bem's discussion does call into question some of the bolder pronouncements of philosophers about the Rylean view. It is neither absurd nor far-fetched to suppose that subjects in forced compliance scenarios come to know their own attitudes by inference from their behaviour. Nor can it be assumed without further argument that it is very rare or unusual for us to self-attribute attitudes on the basis of behavioural evidence. According to Bem's second postulate we rely on such evidence when internal cues are weak, ambiguous, or uninterpretable. If we take such internal cues to include internal promptings in Lawlor's sense then it looks like an empirical question whether it is or is not unusual for such cues to be deficient in one way or another. However, whether we rely on internal promptings or behavioural evidence to determine our own attitudes, the resulting self-knowledge remains inferential and based on evidence. Bem's work is helpful because it provides empirical support for the view that, while the evidence for self-attributions needn't be behavioural, it certainly can be.

To sum up, I have described inferentialism as the view that inference from evidence is a key source of intentional self-knowledge for humans. One kind of evidence is behavioural, and the argument by experiment supplies experimental evidence that we sometimes come to know our own attitudes on the basis of our own behaviour. Inferentialists should obviously refrain from saying that we can *only* know our own attitudes on the basis of behavioural cues but they can plausibly insist that the evidence we rely on in self-attributing attitudes *includes* behavioural evidence. There is experimental evidence for this, just as there is more informal but equally compelling evidence of our reliance on internal promptings for intentional self-knowledge. Combining the argument by elimination, by example, and by experiment it's hard to avoid the conclusion that inferentialism, in the moderate and inclusive form I've set out, is not only not a non-starter but a coherent, intuitively plausible, and well-supported alternative to the view that intentional self-knowledge is, if not impossible, then based on inner observation or based on nothing.

Why, then, has inferentialism had so few takers until recently? Because although it's true that some critics have been far too quick to dismiss it, there are serious challenges and objections to inferentialism that still persuade many philosophers that it is not the way to go even if, as I've tried to show, it's a position that deserves to at least be taken seriously. So it's now time to deal with

---

[9] For further discussion, see Fazio, Zanna, and Cooper 1977.

these objections and show that they don't refute inferentialism. Here's a quick summary of the objections I am going to take on:

A. Inferentialism can't account for the epistemic asymmetry ('the Asymmetry') between knowledge of oneself and knowledge of others.

B. On an 'internalist' conception of epistemic justification inferentialism generates a vicious regress.

C. There are obvious counterexamples to inferentialism, cases which make it clear that inference is neither required nor relevant for self-knowledge.

D. Although inferentialism accounts for a certain form of self-knowledge, it doesn't account for ordinary self-knowledge; inferential self-knowledge is alienated self-knowledge.

These are all potentially serious objections and some of them have some merit. Still, if we are careful about what inferentialism is and is not committed to then there is no need to lose any sleep over any of them.

Here's a nice, clear statement of the Asymmetry from the preface to Moran's *Authority and Estrangement*:

[F]or a range of central cases, whatever knowledge of *oneself* may be, it is a very different thing from knowledge of others, categorically different in kind and manner...It is not necessary to say that the mind of another person is "essentially" hidden from me, in order to acknowledge that this person knows, and comes to know, his own thoughts and experiences in ways that are categorically different from how I may come to know them. (2001: xxxi)

If I know the mind of another person by inference, and how I know my own mind is different in 'kind and manner' from how I know the mind of another person, the obvious conclusion is that in unexceptional cases I don't know my own mind by inference.

The idea that inferentialism is no good because it is at odds with the Asymmetry is the most serious and certainly the most influential objection to this view. The options available to inferentialism are *accommodation, denial,* or some mixture of the two. The best bet is some mixture of the two, but with a greater emphasis on denying the existence of the Asymmetry than on attempting to accommodate it. Inferentialism can accept that there is *an* asymmetry between knowledge of oneself and knowledge of others but not the difference that Moran is talking about. In Alex Byrne's terminology, our access to our own attitudes is 'peculiar', but not as peculiar as is commonly supposed.[10]

---

[10] To say that we have what Byrne calls 'peculiar' access to our own mental states is to say that we know about them in a way that is available to no one else. This account of peculiar access in Byrne 2011 follows McKinsey 1991.

To see how far inferentialism can accommodate the Asymmetry let's go back to the case of Katherine. She wants to know whether she wants another child, and we can suppose that her best friend Melissa also has an interest in the question 'Does Katherine want another child?' Katherine answers this question by inference from internal promptings but Melissa is in no position to work out what Katherine wants on the same basis. Melissa can only find out what Katherine wants on the basis of what Katherine says and does rather than on the basis of what she feels and imagines. In this sense their methods of finding out are not the same even by the inferentialist's lights; if you are an inferentialist you don't have to think that, with respect to the question whether Katherine wants another child, Katherine and Melissa are in exactly the same boat epistemologically speaking, since they have access to different types of evidence.

On this account, the 'asymmetry' between knowledge of oneself and knowledge of others boils down to a difference in the kinds of evidence that are available in the two cases.

Although this is a significant difference, it's not a difference in 'kind and manner'. Even if Katherine and Melissa have access to different kinds of evidence, their 'ways of knowing' are the same to the extent that they both know what Katherine wants by drawing inferences from the evidence available to them. The difference in evidence (if there is one) isn't the kind of difference that justifies talk of an epistemic Asymmetry. As for whether Katherine's access to her own desires is 'peculiar', that depends on whether she knows about her desires in a way that is available to no one else. Suppose she discovers her desire for another child on the basis of her passing thoughts, feelings, inner speech, and dreams. In one sense her way of knowing is peculiar, since no one else has direct access to her passing thoughts, feelings, inner speech, and dreams. But in another sense there is nothing peculiar about Katherine's way of knowing since Melissa can also infer what Katherine wants, and Katherine can make her 'internal' evidence available to Melissa simply by telling her about it.

The clear implication of this discussion is that inferentialism fails to accommodate the Asymmetry; even if Katherine and Melissa aren't in exactly the same boat epistemologically speaking, their boats aren't sufficiently different to give Moran the kind of Asymmetry he is looking for. This is therefore the point at which inferentialism needs to shift from half-baked accommodation to full-blown denial: instead of pretending to accommodate the Asymmetry it should question its existence. The issue isn't whether there is *an* asymmetry between self-knowledge and knowledge of others—even inferentialism can accept this— but the kind of Asymmetry that rules out inferentialism. It's no use saying that the Asymmetry is a primitive datum which doesn't need to be argued for because it's so obvious. As far as inferentialism is concerned it's *not* obvious that there is an Asymmetry, and there is nothing more boring than two philosophers reiterating that their opposing views are 'obvious'. Nor is it much of an improvement for proponents of the Asymmetry to go on about how a 'categorical' difference between self-knowledge and knowledge of others is built into the naïve conception of self-knowledge. Even if this is so, so what? Couldn't the naïve conception be mistaken, especially in view of the trouble we get into when we deny that self-knowledge is inferential? Anyway, it's doubtful whether we are naïvely committed to the existence of the Asymmetry, as distinct from the existence of an asymmetry.

The alternative to claiming that the Asymmetry is obvious is to argue for its existence, and the most promising argument is what might be called the *argument from authorship*. This says that we are the authors of our own attitudes, and that that is why our access to them must be non-inferential (as well as non-observational). Now we have two questions: in what sense are we the authors of our own attitudes, and why does being the 'author' of an attitude imply non-inferential knowledge of its existence? On the first question, the idea is that your beliefs, desires, and other attitudes don't come over you in the way that a headache might come over you. When all goes well your attitudes are the product of rational deliberation and a reflection of your judgements or decisions. Stuart Hampshire gives the example of a man who does not know whether he wants to go to Italy and who has to stop and think whether he does. If, from his initial state of uncertainty, 'he moves to a conclusion which amounts to his now knowing what he wants, or to his now knowing what his attitude is, his process of thought is properly characterized as deliberation' (1979: 289). It is *his business* whether he wants to go to Italy and it is for him to decide. When he decides after thinking about it that he wants to go, he is the author of his own desire in the sense that he has formed the desire 'as the conclusion of a process of thought' rather than come across it as a 'fact of his consciousness'. In this respect, he is unlike Katherine, who merely 'finds herself' wanting or not wanting another child rather than taking control of her desire.

When you form a desire as the conclusion of a process of thought what you are doing is making up your mind, and in making up your mind you *know* your mind.[11] Since you are the author of your own attitude you don't need to rely on evidence to know it. Your knowledge is epistemically and practically immediate: you are able to know what you think without relying on any evidence, observation,

---

[11] Moran seems to equate making up your mind with coming to know your mind. Moran 2001: 95 is revealing.

or inference because *your* attitude is *your* responsibility. In contrast, I have to rely on evidence in order to know what you think because my relationship to your attitude isn't authorial. This is the sense in which there is a difference in kind and manner between self-knowledge and knowledge of others. In brief: we have non-inferential access to our own minds because we make them up. We don't have non-inferential access to other minds because we don't control them in the same way. This is the asymmetry (and, indeed, the Asymmetry) that inferentialism does not and cannot account for.

The argument from authorship trades on what I referred to in Chapter 9 as Activism. Activism says that we know own minds by actively shaping their contents, and that 'making something puts one in a special cognitive relation to what one has made' (Gaukroger 1986: 29). The argument from authorship adds that this special cognitive relation is such that, where you are the author a particular attitude A, you can know without inference or observation that you have A. Obviously this does nothing to show that we have non-inferential access to those of our attitudes which we *haven't* authored. With respect to such attitudes, the argument from authorship leaves it open that there is no difference in kind and manner between first-person and third-person access. Even more problematically, it isn't even clear that making something means that you know of its existence and nature without inference or observation. Consider this example: you work in a souvenir factory where your job is to make miniature replicas of a famous building, say Buckingham Palace. Your replicas are supposed to have a specific number of windows—say 27—and you set about producing replicas with the requisite number of windows. Do you know that the replicas you have made, or are making, have 27 windows? Clearly, the fact that you have made or 'shaped' the replicas doesn't make you infallible about the actual number of windows they have—you might have miscounted. You might still know without looking that they have 27 windows each, but only insofar as you know how many windows they are supposed to have, and also have general grounds for thinking that by and large when you try to make something with 27 windows it turns out to have 27 windows. This enables you to infer that your replicas have 27 windows but your knowledge that they have 27 windows is broadly inferential; it's certainly not 'based on nothing'.

No doubt there are all sorts of disanalogies between the sense in which we 'shape' our own attitudes and the sense in which we make things in factories but the question remains whether and how it is possible to get from 'we shape our own attitudes' to 'we know our own attitudes non-inferentially'. It's certainly not obvious that this is a legitimate move, and the epistemology of maker's knowledge is in any case pretty obscure. Given the choice between saying that 'maker's knowledge' is based on inference, observation, or nothing, the best bet is the first option; at any rate, nothing has so far been said to rule this option out. Activists will no doubt want to say that the knowledge they have in mind is *sui generis* and doesn't fall into any of Boghossian's categories but it's hard to know what to make of this without a positive account of the supposedly unique epistemology of maker's knowledge. It's worth adding also that we are now a very long way from the idea of the Asymmetry as a premise or datum from which philosophical reflection on self-knowledge is to start. A better approach is to avoid making contentious assumptions at the outset about the relationship between self-know-ledge and knowledge of others, and focus instead on how we actually come to know our own minds and other minds. When we do that it becomes apparent that there is no knockdown argument against inferentialism from the Asym-metry. If anything, it's the other way round: since a lot of ordinary self-knowledge is clearly inferential, and so is a lot of our knowledge of others' minds, it would seem to follow that the Asymmetry is yet another philosophical myth.

What about the objection that inferentialism about self-knowledge generates a vicious regress, at least on an internalist view of justification? Boghossian writes: 'on the assumption that all self-knowledge is inferential, it could have been acquired only by inference from yet other known beliefs. And now we are off on a vicious regress' (1998: 155). Suppose you believe you are wearing socks and believe that you believe you are wearing socks. On an internalist view of justifi-cation the latter belief is epistemically justified only if you grasp the fact that it bears some appropriate relation to your other beliefs. However, these other beliefs must also be ones you are justified in believing you have, and this is what threatens a regress. The only way to avoid a vicious regress is to suppose that it's possible to know the content of some mental states non-inferentially. Specifically, it follows from the regress argument that 'not all knowledge of one's beliefs can be inferential' (Boghossian 1998: 156).

It's easy to see where the regress argument goes wrong. The assumption is that if self-knowledge is inferential it must have been acquired from inference from other known *beliefs*, but there is no reason to accept that assumption even if you are an internalist about epistemic justification. For example, Katherine infers her desire for another child not from other beliefs but from internal promptings that aren't standing attitudes. The passing thoughts, emotions, and imaginings from which her infers her desire aren't beliefs, and there is no reason why she couldn't infer (some of) her beliefs on the same basis. There's no question that her intentional self-knowledge is inferential but it isn't inferred from other known beliefs. This isn't to say that you *can't* infer one belief or standing attitude from another, only that this isn't how it has to go. Notice also that there is no conflict with internalism in either of its two standard forms. One kind of internalism ('Accessibilism') says that the epistemic justification of your beliefs is determined by things to which you have some sort of special access. Another kind of internalism ('Mentalism') says that your beliefs are only justified by things that are internal to your mental life.[12] None of this is a problem for Katherine, on the assumption that she has 'special access' to her own inner speech, passing thoughts, and imaginings. Such 'internal promptings' are about as internal to her mental life as anything could be.

It might seem that this only pushes the problem a stage further back. Inferentialism's response to the regress is to say that you can infer your standing attitudes from your internal promptings, but what's the story about access to internal promptings? Doesn't inferentialism have to think that this is also inferential, in which case there is still a regress? Well, no. As I have emphasized, inferentialism is specifically a view about knowledge of our own standing attitudes. Just because knowledge of standing attitudes is inferential that doesn't mean that all other self-knowledge is also inferential. So inferentialism doesn't *have* to claim that we only have inferential knowledge of our internal promptings. The alternative is to say that we have non-inferential access to our own inner speech, fantasies, judgements, etc., and that, given the appropriate theory of mind, we are then able to infer our own standing attitudes on this basis. Clearly, even if it is *open* to inferentialism to adopt such a hybrid approach to self-knowledge it's a further question whether it *should* adopt it. That depends, in part, on whether the hybrid approach can account for our supposedly non-inferential access to the internal promptings from which we infer our standing attitudes. I will have more to say about this in Chapter 12.

The next objection to inferentialism says that there are obvious counterexamples that make it clear that inference is neither required nor relevant for self-knowledge. Some of the supposed counterexamples clearly don't work. Here's one from Boghossian:

You think: even lousy composers sometimes write great arias. And you know, immediately on thinking it, that this is what you thought. What explanation can the Rylean offer of this? The difficulty is not merely that, contrary to appearance and the canons of epistemic practice, he has to construe this knowledge as inferential. The difficulty is that he has to construe it as involving inference from premises about behaviour that you could not possibly possess. (1998: 152)

---

[12] See Conee and Feldman 2001: 233 for the distinction between 'Accessibilist' and 'Mentalist' versions of internalism.

Boghossian's target here is the view that knowledge of our occurrent thoughts is inferred from premises about behaviour. This is not inferentialism about self-knowledge as I interpret it, and is also not Ryle's view. You don't have to think that knowledge of our own occurrent thoughts is inferential in order to think that knowledge of our standing attitudes is inferential. When it comes to self-know-ledge of standing attitudes, it is not 'contrary to the canons of epistemic practice' to construe this knowledge as inferential, whether the inferences in question are from behaviour or from other evidence.

Another potential counterexample to inferentialism turns on the role of mem-ory in self-knowledge. Consider Katherine again. She wonders whether she wants another child and infers from various internal promptings that she does. Days later someone asks her whether she wants another child and she already knows the answer to this question. The answer, let's suppose, is 'yes'. She doesn't have to rethink the question, since she already knows she wants another child. In order to answer the question all she has to do is to retrieve from memory what she already knows. This is significant because remembering that she wants another child does not require her to infer that she wants another child; the source of her self-knowledge in this case is not inference but memory, and she knows what she wants because of the role of memory in the preservation of her self-knowledge.[13]

If in turns out that memory is a source of non-inferential intentional self-knowledge this wouldn't be a disaster for inferentialism. Inferentialism says that inference is a basic source of intentional self-knowledge for humans. This could be true even if some of our self-knowledge, including intentional self-knowledge, is non-inferential. It's worth pointing out, however, that it's not obvious that Katherine's memory-based knowledge of her desire for another child is non-inferential. Suppose someone were to object that Katherine only knows that she wanted another child when she last thought about it, and that it doesn't follow from this that she *now* wants another child or that she now knows that she wants another child. The obvious thing to say in response to such sceptical doubts is that while it's quite true that these things don't *follow*—she could have changed her mind—it's reasonable for Katherine to take it, in the absence of any evidence to the contrary, that her desires haven't changed. In effect, she infers that what she wanted when the question last arose is what she still wants, and this is how she knows that she (still) wants another child. Her self-knowledge is inferential, even though based on memory.

The lesson is this: if you are sympathetic to inferentialism about self-know-ledge, and are presented with a supposedly obvious counterexample to this view,

---

[13] Reed 2010 gives some other examples which point in the same general direction.

you have quite a range of options at your disposal. One is to show that the counterexample isn't relevant because it is attacking something to which inferentialism isn't actually committed; this is the way to take care of counterexamples such as Boghossian's. If that doesn't work, then another option to show that the example is one in which the subject's self-knowledge is inferential. It's always possible that what seems to be an example of non-inferential self-knowledge is in reality an example of unobviously inferential knowledge, unobvious because the inferential element might be unconscious or only implicit. In such cases, the justification for regarding the subject's self-knowledge as inferential might itself be inferential, a case of inference to the best explanation. Finally, there remains the option of conceding that the counterexample is genuine but arguing that inferentialism can make space for it because saying that inference is a basic or key source of intentional self-knowledge for humans doesn't require you to say that there is *no* non-inferential intentional self-knowledge. Inferentialism is only in trouble if there are counterexamples which can't be dealt with in any of these three ways, and there is no reason to think that such counterexamples exist.

The final objection to inferentialism says that inferential self-knowledge is alienated rather than ordinary self-knowledge, and that inferentialism doesn't account for ordinary, 'unalienated' self-knowledge. This is Moran's objection to inferentialism. He argues that a person lacks ordinary self-knowledge 'if he can only learn of his belief through assessment of the evidence about himself' (2001: 67). Even if the evidence from which you infer your attitudes is highly reliable, and includes 'internal' as well as behavioural evidence, you will still only end up with 'theoretical' or 'attributional' self-knowledge. Whereas self-knowledge in the ordinary sense is a 'specifically first-person phenomenon' (2001: 2), attributional self-knowledge is 'the expression of an essentially *third-personal* stance towards oneself' (2001: 106). Ordinary self-knowledge is knowledge of attitudes you can identify with and rationally endorse, but attributional self-knowledge can be of attitudes you don't identify with, and whose reasons are opaque to you. In such cases, you only have alienated self-knowledge, and the reason it is alienated is that it is third-personal.

An example might help. Suppose you have evidence that our old friend Oliver has a particular attitude A. You can infer that A is Oliver's attitude even if you find A repellent or incomprehensible. Suppose A is the belief that the 9/11 attacks were the work of government agents rather than al Qaeda terrorists. You find it impossible to identify with, or endorse, this belief; indeed, you find Oliver's belief absurd, but you still recognize that it is what Oliver believes. The belief you are justified in attributing to him is not the one that is supported by overwhelming evidence of al Qaeda's responsibility for the 9/11 attacks but rather the one supported by psychological and behavioural evidence relating to Oliver. But if inferentialism is correct then you could find yourself with evidence that *you* have a belief or other attitude that is as difficult for you to identify with as Oliver's belief. You will then find yourself in the absurd position of having to admit that you have an attitude which you can't make any sense of. Your relation to your own attitude in this case will be no different from your relation to Oliver's attitude; you will be as deeply alienated with respect to your own attitude as you are with respect to Oliver's attitude.

The reply to this objection to inferentialism is straightforward: just because inferential or attributional self-knowledge *can* be of attitudes you don't identify with and can't endorse, it doesn't follow that this kind of self-knowledge *has* to be alienated in these ways. The mere fact that you self-ascribe an attitude on inferential grounds doesn't make the attitude alienated or impervious to reason. You can infer on behavioural or psychological grounds that you have a particular belief or desire and yet have no difficulty endorsing or identifying with that belief or desire. It's also worth pointing out that the rationalist alternative to inferentialism can itself result in a form of alienation. Depending on the kind of person you are, you might find it hard to identify with attitudes you only take yourself to have because you assume that they are the attitudes you ought rationally to have.

Katherine is a good illustration of all this. Suppose she infers from the internal and behavioural evidence available to her that she wants another child. Just because this is how she knows that she wants another child, that needn't prevent her from recognizing the desire as fully her own. Indeed, the fact that the desire is manifested in her emotions, dreams, and fantasies might actually *enhance* her sense of the desire as fully her own, an expression of who she is at this point in her life. If this is the case, then the fact that she comes to know her desire on the basis of these same emotions, dreams, and fantasies can hardly make her self-knowledge alienated. It's true, of course, that inferring from her internal promptings that she wants another child might not be the end of the matter for Katherine. There is a further question she can ask, namely, is there *good reason* to have, or to want to have, another child? Acquiring her self-knowledge by inference doesn't make it impossible for her to ask this further question, or for her to change her mind in response to the arguments for and against having another child. If she does change her mind at this point then she will need evidence to know that this is what has happened. On the other hand, suppose her desire for another child survives her recognition that there are good practical reasons for her not to have one. That still doesn't make her desire alienated; it might instead be viewed as an indication of the strength of her identification with the desire. As Harry Frankfurt points out, 'some of the desires with which a person is most deeply and significantly identified, and from which it is nearly impossible for him to become alienated, are not based on any thought about what is good to be pursued' (2002: 223). There is no tension or conflict in such cases between being committed to the attitude and knowing inferentially, on the basis of evidence, that you have it.

The point about rationalism and alienation is this: Rationalists are keen on the idea that unalienated attitudes are ones that are answerable, and knowable by reference to, to rational considerations. For example, Moran suggests that a person's unalienated desires are those that are 'guided by the direction of his thought about what is desirable', so that 'he takes the general question of what he wants ... to be the expression of his sense of what he has best reason to pursue in this context' (2001: 117-18). Now consider the following variation on the case of Katherine: suppose that she has no children and asks herself whether she now wants a child. She has never thought of herself as interested in having children and has always been comfortable with the idea of not having any; she has never been envious of her female friends with children and doesn't see herself as cut out for motherhood. However, she worries that she will one day regret not having children, and convinces herself on a variety of grounds that she ought to have a child. Suppose that she now attributes to herself the desire for a child on the basis that it is what she ought rationally to want. One possibility is, of course, that it's just false that she wants a child, however convinced she is that she ought to want one. It might turn out, however, that at some level she does now want a child; maybe this is the effect of her rehearsing to herself the reasons in favour. Still, there remains a sense in which this new desire, even though a genuine expression of her sense of what she has best reason to pursue in this context, *isn't* a genuine expression of *her*. It doesn't fit her self-conception and might take a lot of getting used to. It feels to her like an alien or alienated desire precisely *because* it is grounded in reason rather than in her sense of who she is.

If this is right then rationalism is on shaky grounds when it accuses inferentialism of only explaining alienated self-knowledge: inferential self-knowledge needn't be alienated, and Rationalism about self-knowledge isn't immune to worries about alienation. This should come as no surprise since, as I've argued in previous chapters, Rationalism in any case only delivers inferential self-knowledge. For the purposes of this chapter the key point is that inferential self-knowledge needn't be alienated. That more or less takes care of the 'objection from alienation' to inferentialism, and shows that this objection is no more effective in undermining inferentialism about self-knowledge than all the other objections I've discussed. Inferentialism is alive and kicking, and remains the only game in town.

12

Knowing Your Evidence

So far in this book I've concentrated on just one type of self-knowledge: knowledge of our own standing attitudes. The sense in which standing attitudes are 'standing' is that they are ones you have even when you aren't entertaining them. For example, you still believe that Sacramento is the capital of California even when you are asleep or thinking about something else. Standing attitudes aren't mental events; they aren't datable occurrences even if the onset or acquisition of a standing attitude is a datable event. I've been defending an inferentialist account of our knowledge of our standing attitudes but we have attitudes that aren't standing, and some of our states of mind aren't attitudes, that is, 'propositional' attitudes. Judging that the government will be re-elected, or deciding to spend the summer in Italy are examples of 'occurrent' mental events rather than standing attitudes, and feelings like pain or nausea aren't attitudes to propositions. The obvious question, then, is: what does inferentialism have to say about knowledge of occurrent attitudes and feelings?

If you are a lazy inferentialist you might try dodging this question by pointing out that inferentialism is specifically an account of self-knowledge of standing attitudes and so does not have to say anything about other kinds of self-knowledge. As argued in the last chapter, an inferentialist about self-knowledge of standing attitudes doesn't have to be an inferentialist about self-knowledge of occurrent attitudes. You can have a hybrid view according to which self-knowledge of standing attitudes is inferred from non-inferential knowledge of occurrent attitudes and feelings. Alternatively, you might think that knowledge of one's feelings and occurrent attitudes is itself inferential. This would raise the question what *this* knowledge is inferred from, but the lazy inferentialist doesn't see why he has to answer this question. The question he was supposed to be answering is whether self-knowledge of standing attitudes is inferential, and this question has been answered: the answer is 'yes'.

It would certainly make life easier if one could get away with this, but in reality no one is going to be terribly impressed by an account of self-knowledge which only talks about how we know our standing attitudes, and has nothing to say about any other self-knowledge. It's not just that such an account is disappointingly limited in scope. It's also incomplete in its own terms. Suppose you infer from evidence E that you have a particular attitude A. You can't infer A from E unless you have access to E, and you haven't fully explained your knowledge that you have A without also explaining how you have access to E. Suppose that you judge you are wearing socks, and infer from this that you believe that you are wearing socks. Merely judging that you are wearing socks won't enable you to infer and thereby know that you believe you are wearing socks unless you *know* that you judge that you are wearing socks, and that your so judging is good evidence that you believe you are wearing socks. If you have nothing to say about your knowledge that you judge that you are wearing socks, then you haven't fully explained your knowledge that you believe that you are wearing socks. Your account is incomplete.

It's possible to imagine some inferentialists objecting that in order to know on the basis of evidence E that you have standing attitude A you don't have to know that you have E. Consider this analogy: you know there is a pig in front of you because you can see a pig in front of you. Your evidence of porcine presence is your visual experience of the pig, but in order to know on the basis of this evidence that there is a pig in front of you you don't need know or believe that you are having the visual experience of a pig. You certainly don't know or believe that you are having the visual experience of a pig if you lack the concept of visual experience, but not having this concept needn't prevent you from knowing on the basis of your visual experience that there is a pig in front of you. You have evidence that there is a pig in front of you but you don't need to know your evidence. It's enough that you *have* evidence and use it appropriately. In that case, why can't you know that you believe you are wearing socks on the basis of your judgement that you are wearing socks even if you don't know your judgement? Why isn't it enough that you make the judgement and use it in the appropriate manner to arrive at the conclusion that you believe you are wearing socks?

The reason is that the two cases are quite different. You knowledge that there is a pig in front of you is based on your experience but you don't infer it from your experience. In contrast, the inferentialist's proposal is that you infer, and thereby know, your standing attitude from the corresponding judgement or other evidence. In the case of knowledge that is not only based on evidence but inferred from evidence it's more plausible that you need to have knowledge of your evidence, at least on the assumption that your inference is conscious. Another porcine example makes the point: imagine knowing there is a pig in the vicinity not because you can see a pig but because there are pig droppings on the ground and buckets of half-eaten pig food. You infer from this evidence that there is a pig in the vicinity but you only come to know on this basis that there is a pig in the vicinity because you know that there are pig droppings on the ground and that this is evidence that there is a pig in the vicinity. Unless, by whatever means, you actually know your evidence and grasp its significance you can't infer anything from it.

Suppose the lazy inferentialist is convinced by this and accepts that he has to account for our knowledge of the psychological and other evidence from which we infer our standing attitudes. There are many different kinds of evidence that bear on our standing attitudes. I've talked in this chapter about occurrent judgements as evidence of our standing beliefs. In the last chapter, I talked about the possibility of inferring our standing attitudes from behavioural evidence and from internal promptings, including inner speech, emotions, feelings, and mental images. What should inferentialism say about our knowledge of these things? Should it go for the 'hybrid' view that self-knowledge of internal promptings is non-inferential, or should it insist that it's inference all the way? Inference all the way means that, in addition to inferring your standing attitudes, you also know by inference the internal promptings from which you infer your standing attitudes. The question which can no longer be avoided is: which way should the inferentialist about self-knowledge of standing attitudes go?

It's easy to see why the 'inference all the way' option looks unattractive since it threatens a regress. The epistemological buck has to stop somewhere and this means that self-knowledge can't be inferential all the way—or so you might think. On this view, the question is not *whether* any self-knowledge is non-inferential but *which* self-knowledge is non-inferential. If knowledge of our own judgements, feelings, and mental images turns out to be inferential one would face the challenge of identifying their evidential base, but this seems like a lost cause; presumably we don't know our own feelings and mental images by inferring them. Better to accept that self-knowledge of internal promptings is non-inferential. This deals with the regress because inferential self-knowledge of standing attitudes is now seen to be based on non-inferential self-knowledge.

This amounts to a kind of 'foundationalism' about self-knowledge, motivated by just the kind of regress argument which motivates other, more familiar forms of foundationalism. The basic thought of the regress argument is that no knowledge or epistemic justification can be inferential unless some knowledge or epistemic justification is non-inferential. This claim raises a whole lot of questions that are well beyond the scope of this book but the point I want to make here is that foundationalism about self-knowledge has less going for it than you might think. Specifically, I'd like to suggest that:

(a) There are in fact excellent positive reasons for thinking self-knowledge of internal promptings is inferential.
(b) The fact that self-knowledge of internal promptings is inferential doesn't generate a problematic regress.

You can say that self-knowledge of internal promptings is inferential without saying that it's inference *all* the way but it's certainly inference much more of the way than foundationalism implies.

A good way of seeing the force of these claims is to look at Carruthers' account of self-knowledge in his 2011 book *The Opacity of Mind* and 2009 paper on the same subject. Carruthers focuses on knowledge of our (oc)current thoughts and thought processes. He doesn't spend much time on self-knowledge of standing attitudes because he—mistakenly in my view—takes it as uncontroversial that 'knowledge of our own standing attitudes depends upon knowledge of the corresponding (or otherwise suitably related) current mental events' (2011: xi). He calls his positive account the Interpretive Sensory Access (ISA) theory of self-knowledge. ISA holds that 'our only mode of access to our own thinking is through the same sensory channels that we use when figuring out the mental states of others' (2011: xii). On this account, access to our propositional attitudes is 'almost always interpretive (and often confabulatory), utilizing the same kinds of inferences (and many of the same sorts of data) that are employed when attributing attitudes to other people' (2011: 1).

What would it be for access to our occurrent propositional attitudes to be interpretive? Carruthers describes a self-interpretive process as 'one that accesses information about the subject's current circumstances, or the subject's current or recent behaviour, as well as any other information about the subject's current or recent mental life' (2009: 3). It's in this sense that 'self-attributions of propositional attitude events like judging and deciding are always the result of a swift (and unconscious) process of self-interpretation' (2009: 4). When you interpret propositional attitude events in the light of information about your circumstances, behaviour, and mental life the resulting self-knowledge is not just interpretive but inferential. It's inferential because it's interpretive, but being inferential in this sense doesn't produce an unacceptable regress. That's the point of (a) and (b).

We can start to flesh all of this out by going back to the example of Katherine figuring out whether she wants another child. Her desire for another child is a standing attitude, and she knows that she has this attitude by inference from internal promptings: she is aware of a range of feelings, emotions, and mental images from which she correctly infers that she wants another child. Her internal promptings are her evidence, and what they are evidence *of* is a particular standing desire. How, then, does Katherine know her evidence? Suppose that her internal promptings include a feeling of wistfulness or the yearning for another child as she puts away her son's clothes. What tells Katherine that this is what she is feeling? The hybrid view says that what tells Katherine what she feels is—what could be more obvious?—the feeling itself: it has a raw feel or phenomenal character which enables Katherine to identify it as the yearning for another child as long as she attends to it. All she has to do to know her evidence is to 'notice' her feelings, emotions, and images. Noticing that you have a particular feeling F is a way of knowing that you have that feeling, and is different from inferring that you have F. So Katherine discovers her standing desire for another child by inference from internal promptings which she knows about by means other than inference.

What's wrong with this account? One thing that is wrong with it is that it's barely an 'account' of Katherine's self-knowledge. Saying that Katherine 'notices' her feelings doesn't casts much light on the nature of her knowledge of her feelings. Noticing that P, where P is a proposition about your mental life, might be your way of knowing that P, at least in the sense that it entails that you know that P, but it's a further question *how* you notice that P. For all that the hybrid view says, noticing that you have a particular feeling could itself be the result of an inference. More to the point, it's also implausible that there is such a thing as the 'raw feel' of a yearning for another child. The feelings we classify as such are subtle and complex. Given a collection of mental images, bodily changes, memories, and inner speech, it takes cognitive effort to identify them as amounting to the yearning for another child, and the effort required isn't just the effort of paying attention. You can't just 'read off' from the way you feel that your yearning is for another child. You can yearn for any number of things, and it would be odd to think that each yearning has its own a distinctive phenomenology. When you identify your feeling as the yearning for another child what you are doing is *interpreting* it, and your cognitive effort is the effort of interpretation. Crucially, when you interpret your feeling you don't just go on 'how it feels'. You also take account of contextual factors, such as the fact that you have recently been thinking about whether to have another child. More often than not, at least in the case of complex feelings and emotions, it is your knowledge of the context which makes it possible for you to determine its nature, which means that you are to some extent *inferring* what you feel from your background knowledge. Your inference is an inference to the best explanation rather than inductive or deductive.

It's an interesting question how far this view can be pressed. I've talked about the role of interpretation as a source of self-knowledge of complex feelings and emotions but what about knowledge of simple feelings or sensations like nausea and pain? When you are in pain isn't it just the pain itself, without any interpretive effort on your part, that tells you that you are in pain? Surely you don't interpret what you feel as pain on the basis of background knowledge of your circumstances and behaviour. If this is right then here we have a case of non-interpretive and non-inferential access to an 'internal prompting'. However, this is a possibility that inferentialism about self-knowledge of standing attitudes and more complex feelings and emotions can allow, as long as self-knowledge of simple sensations isn't seen as the basis of all other self-knowledge. Knowledge of sensations like pain contributes little to self-knowledge of standing attitudes, and even the true extent to which our access to so-called 'simple' sensations is non-interpretive can be questioned. The answer to the question 'Are you in pain?' isn't always obvious, and it's not unusual for people to report being conscious of sensations which they are unsure whether to classify as pain. In such cases, it can happen that discovering the cause of the sensation can help you to make sense of it, to classify it one way rather than another. Here, your access to the sensation look genuinely interpretive.

What about the role of interpretation in relation to inner speech? As Carruthers notes, 'we sometimes learn of our own beliefs and desires by first becoming aware of their formulation into speech (whether inner or outer)' (2009: 5). However, 'all speech—whether the speech of oneself or someone else—needs to be interpreted before it can be understood' (2009: 5). It might seem that this can't be right because our own utterances aren't ambiguous to us in the way that other people's utterances can be. But consider Katherine saying to herself 'I want another one' as she folds her son's clothes. Another what? It's obvious to Katherine that the force of her utterance is that she wants another child but this is only obvious to her because her circumstances, memories, and mental images leave her in no doubt as to the topic of her utterance. She doesn't find what she says ambiguous or unclear, but not because she has non-interpretive access to her utterance. It is because it is *obvious* to her how to interpret her utterance. Viewed in isolation, her utterance 'I want another one' would mean very little to her; it's her knowledge of the context of the utterance that makes it possible for her to interpret it.

We can put all this together in the form of a two-step argument in support of the view that self-knowledge of internal promptings is inferential:

1. Access to internal promptings is interpretive.
2. Interpretive access is inferential.

The point of 1 is that what enables you to make sense of your internal promptings and attach a specific significance to them is your background knowledge of your current circumstances, current or recent behaviour, and current or recent mental life. Carruthers defines interpretive access as access that depends on such background knowledge, and this is the background knowledge on which self-knowledge of internal promptings is dependent. But couldn't self-knowledge of internal promptings depend on background knowledge without being inferred from it? In other words, 1 couldn't be true without 2 also being true? This raises the question whether you can be a Carruthers-style *interpretationist* without also being an *inferentialist* about self-knowledge of internal promptings.

This isn't just a theoretical possibility because it's not true in general that knowledge of one proposition P can depend on knowledge of another proposition Q only if P is inferred from Q. Suppose you see and thereby know there is a pig in front of you.[1] You can only know this if you have the concept of a pig, and (let's suppose) you only have this concept if you know something about pigs, for example, that pigs are animals. Although your knowledge that there is a pig in front of you depends in this way on your background knowledge of pigs this doesn't mean that your knowledge that there is a pig in front of you is inferred from your knowledge that pigs are animals. The role of such background knowledge is to sustain your grasp of the concept of a pig and thereby to enable you to know, by seeing, that there is a pig in front of you. In that case, why can't knowledge of your internal promptings be 'enabled by', rather than 'inferred from', knowledge of your circumstances and current or recent mental life?

To make any progress with this we need to get clearer about the notion of inferential knowledge. One understanding of this notion is purely epistemic rather than psychological. The idea is that your knowledge that P is inferential just if your justification for believing P is inferential, and your justification is inferential as long as it comes in part from your having justification to believe other, supporting propositions. This is an epistemic conception of inferential knowledge and justification because it says nothing about how you arrived at your belief that P. If you also arrived at your belief that P by inferring it from other, supporting propositions then your knowledge/justification is inferential in a psychological as well as an epistemic sense.

We can now see why interpretive access to one's internal promptings is inferential, both epistemically and psychologically. The epistemic point is easier

---

[1] This example is borrowed from Austin 1962.

to see. In the porcine example your justification for believing that there is a pig in front of you doesn't come even in part from your justification to believe pigs are animals. The two propositions just aren't related in the right way. There might be other propositions from which your justification for believing that there is a pig in front of your derives, but the propositions that pigs are animals isn't one of them. The role of your background belief that pigs are animals is purely enabling; what it makes available to you is the concept of a pig, not the knowledge that there is a pig in front of you. Now compare the justification Katherine has for believing that what she feels is a yearning for another child. If we imagine that her background knowledge includes the knowledge that the question whether to have another child has been on her mind recently it's reasonable to suppose that her justification for believing that her yearning is for another child comes in part from her justification to believe that the topic of another child has been on her mind recently. This is a case in which the subject's background knowledge is playing a supporting and not just enabling role, and Katherine's knowledge of her feeling is inferential in the epistemic sense.

It doesn't straightforwardly follow that her knowledge is inferential in the other sense. You could accept that Katherine's self-knowledge is inferential in the epistemic sense while remaining silent regarding the psychological processes which result in her coming to know her own feelings or other internal promptings. But having got as far as agreeing that her self-knowledge is inferential in the epistemic sense it's not clear why one would want to deny that it's also inferential in the psychological sense. If we imagine Katherine making the transition from not knowing to knowing it's natural to ask how, from a psychological standpoint, she makes this transition. This question is easy to answer if we think of her inferring (consciously or not) the nature of her feeling from how it feels, together with her background knowledge. Positing such a psychological transition isn't strictly unavoidable but is a case of inference to the best explanation: the best explanation of Katherine's psychological transition from not knowing to knowing is one that represents her as inferring what she feels from, among other things, her background knowledge. Again, the contrast with the pig example could hardly be clearer: you plainly don't come to know that there is a pig in front of you by consciously or unconsciously inferring that there is a pig in front of you from your background knowledge that pigs are animals.

To sum up: once you accept that access to your internal promptings is interpretive, there is no reason to deny that it is also inferential, both epistemically and psychologically. The next question is whether this generates a problematic regress. The worry is this: if you are an inferentialist then you think that knowledge of your standing attitudes is inferred from knowledge of your internal promptings, but now it's being claimed that the knowledge of your internal promptings is also inferential. In that case, inferentialism also needs to account for the background knowledge from which knowledge of internal promptings is inferred. Is this knowledge inferential? If it is, then where does *it* come from? And so on. This is just the regress that foundationalism tries to avoid, and it's not clear how inferentialism can avoid it.

This 'regress objection' to inferentialism sounds threatening but isn't. Here are a few things that can be said in response to it: to begin with, inferentialism doesn't say that internal promptings are the only evidence from which our standing attitudes can be inferred. There is also behavioural evidence, our access to which is presumably very different from our access to internal promptings. If, as in the Festinger-Carlsmith experiment, you are doing something boring and repetitive for little financial reward, the question why you are doing it only arises for you if you *know* you are doing something boring and repetitive for little financial reward. If you conclude that you must be enjoying the task (otherwise you wouldn't be doing it), one can imagine someone asking how you know you are doing something boring and repetitive. The reason this now doesn't seem a terribly pertinent or threatening question is that we don't normally have much difficulty with the idea that when explaining knowledge of one thing it's legitim-ate to take knowledge of other things for granted. If knowledge of what you are doing is partly interpretive, and takes other knowledge for granted, that isn't necessarily a problem. Again, it's simply an example of the need to take some knowledge for granted in explaining other knowledge. The myth that drives the regress argument is the myth of an explanation of a particular piece of knowledge which assumes no other knowledge.[2] Once we give up on that idea, we are then free to explain some of our standing attitudes on the basis of behavioural evidence.

Even if we just focus on self-attributions of standing attitudes on the basis of internal promptings the regress argument isn't much of a threat. Let's say that, as I've been arguing, you infer your standing attitudes from internal promptings your knowledge of which is also inferential in the sense that it derives in part from your background knowledge. Again, this is not a problem if we are prepared to take your background knowledge for granted. But what if we aren't? What if someone insists on an account of your background knowledge? So, for example, Katherine infers that what she feels is the yearning for another child in part

---

[2] To put it another way, what the regress argument is looking for is an understanding or explanation of what Barry Stroud calls 'human knowledge in general'. The question I am raising is whether this is a sensible aim. For further discussion, see Stroud 2000.

because she knows that this subject has been on her mind over the last few weeks, but how does she know *that*? It's hard to feel threatened by this question because it has an obvious answer: she knows what has been on her mind because she can *remember*. It doesn't matter if you think that memory knowledge is inferential. As long as the presupposed memory knowledge isn't the knowledge you are trying to explain there is no problem: there is no need for anyone to try to explain all our knowledge at once.

This last observation brings us to the heart of the matter. When people worry about the regress problem they aren't necessarily assuming that genuine explanations of knowledge can presuppose no other knowledge. Rather, their objection is to explanations of knowledge which presuppose the very knowledge they are trying to explain. Going back to Katherine, it doesn't matter that knowledge of her internal promptings is inferred in part from background knowledge of her behaviour and circumstances but it does matter if it presupposes knowledge of her current or recent mental life. Her current or recent mental life is presumably made up of different elements, including internal promptings. So now we have not just a regress but a vicious regress: it's not just that inferentialism's explanation of self-knowledge of internal promptings presupposes *some* other knowledge, or even that it presupposes some other self-knowledge. What it presupposes is, specifically, self-knowledge of internal promptings, and that makes the account viciously circular.

It's also now possible to see more clearly the significance of the discussion, at the start of this chapter, of the discussion of what I called *lazy inferentialism*. A lazy inferentialist is someone who sees no reason why, in the course of defending the view that knowledge of our standing attitudes is inferential, he also has to account for self-knowledge of the occurrent attitudes and various other internal promptings on which self-knowledge of standing attitudes is based. I objected that lazy inferentialism's account is incomplete but there is more than one way of taking this. If the charge is that lazy inferentialism is incomplete because its account of self-knowledge presupposes *some* other knowledge which it doesn't seek to explain then it is possible to defend lazy inferentialism against this by again pointing out that explanations of knowledge can legitimately take other knowledge for granted. A much more serious charge is that lazy inferentialism is incomplete because it presupposes other *self-knowledge* which it doesn't seek to explain. It is in the course of closing this gap, and trying to account for self-knowledge of internal promptings, that we run into the problem of circularity: knowledge of our standing attitudes can be inferred from knowledge of internal promptings, but in order to infer our internal promptings we need to have background knowledge which already includes knowledge of other internal promptings. How can this be legitimate?

The answer to this question is the same answer that so-called 'coherentists' have given over the years to the regress argument: self-knowledge is holistic rather than linear, and the circularity its holism implies is genuine but not vicious. You interpret your standing attitudes in the light of justified beliefs about your feelings and emotions, you interpret your feelings and emotions in the light of further justified beliefs about your recent mental life, but your recent mental life includes standing attitudes your access to which was and is interpretive. So the picture is one in which there is a kind of interpretive circle, in which each element depends for its significance on other elements of the circle. The various interlocking elements are intelligible to us as a collectivity, and there is nothing wrong with this as long as the interpretive circle is wide enough. Making sense of your own mental life is like solving a complex simultaneous equation, and circularity per se isn't a problem. What would be a problem is if in order to know that you have a particular attitude A you already need to know that you have A, or in order to know that your feeling is F you already need to know that you feel F. However, this isn't how it is with Katherine. She doesn't already need to know she yearns for another child in order to know that she yearns for another child. There are other things about her mental life she needs to know in order to interpret her feelings but this is a benign rather than a vicious circle.

To get a sense of what a more problematic circularity might look like we should look again the role of occurrent attitudes, as distinct from other internal promptings, as evidence for standing attitudes. The example I have used is the example of someone judging that P and inferring from this that he believes that P. On the view that you have to know your evidence this only works if you know that you judge, or are judging, that P, and the question this raises is: how do you know your own judgements? That depends on what it is to judge that P, and it is harder to know the answer to this question than one might think. Schwitzgebel gives the example of a philosophy student saying some obscure words from Kant in inner speech, with a feeling of assent, but failing to reach a judgement with the appropriate content. In this case part of the problem is that the student doesn't fully grasp what the obscure Kantian sentence means, but the problem can arise even when there is no problem of meaning. You can think or say to yourself that P but fail to judge that P if 'judging that P is partly defined in terms of having the right sorts of functional connections to other P-related thoughts and behaviours' (Schwitzgebel 2011: 58). You think or say the right words in inner speech but your mental action doesn't have the right connections for it to constitute your judging that P.

What are the 'right connections'? Back in Chapter 9, I mentioned the view that to judge that P is to take P to be true, and that to take P to be true is to believe that P. If taking P to be true is believing that P then you don't count as judging that P unless you believe that P. If, in addition, you only *know* that you judge that P if you *know* that you believe that P then it would be viciously circular to claim that you infer that you believe that P from your knowledge that you judge that P: knowledge of the conclusion of your inference (that you believe that P) would be presupposed by your knowledge of its premise (that you judge that P).

One thing this might show is that the relationship between judging that P and believing that P isn't evidential. Judging that P isn't evidence that you believe that P since it constitutes believing that P. Your evidence that you believe that P must take a different form. A different line would be to question the assumption that you can't judge that P without believing that P, or the assumption that you can't know that you judge that P without already knowing that you believe that P. Each of these moves is an attempt to deal with a potentially vicious circularity which threatens a particular conception of the evidence for standing beliefs. The worry is that the supposed evidence (an occurrent attitude) to too closely tied to what it is supposed to be evidence for (the corresponding standing attitude). But this is not a reason for thinking that an occurrent attitude can't ever be evidence for an independent standing attitude or that a feeling can't be evidence for an independent feeling. The trick is not to avoid representing any psychological self-knowledge as resting on other psychological self-knowledge but to avoid representing a given piece of psychological self-knowledge as 'inferred' from the very same, or too closely related, psychological self-knowledge. As Katherine demonstrates, there is no reason to think that this trick can't be pulled off.

Hopefully, you are now persuaded that inferentialism about self-knowledge is neither incomplete nor incoherent. The inferentialism I've been defending so far is an inferentialism about self-knowledge of standing attitudes and internal promptings. The standing attitudes I have been discussing include ones our knowledge of which is relatively 'trivial' (knowing that you believe you are wearing socks) as well as ones our knowledge of which looks more 'substantial' (knowing you want another child). However, substantial self-knowledge goes well beyond self-knowledge of a range of standing attitudes. It also includes self-knowledge of such things as our values, emotions, and character. If you are already convinced that self-knowledge of deeper standing attitudes is inferential then you are unlikely to need a whole lot of convincing that other substantial self-knowledge is also inferential. Still, it's important to understand the exact sense in which other substantial self-knowledge is inferential, and to be clear about any differences between different varieties of substantial self-knowledge. This is what the next chapter is about.

13

Knowing Yourself

What does philosophy have to say about substantial self-knowledge? A depressingly popular answer to this question among philosophers of self-knowledge is: very little. When I talked about substantial self-knowledge in Chapter 3, I included knowledge of such things as one's character, values, emotions, and abilities. You would think that these are the kinds of knowledge that are at issue in the oracle's injunction to 'know yourself'. If you aren't a professional philosopher then substantial self-knowledge is probably what you think 'self-knowledge' is, and you might be taken aback to discover that when philosophers write books and articles about self-knowledge they often start by acknowledging both the existence and importance of substantial self-knowledge but then say that they aren't going to talk about it. Here's a typical example of this approach from the preface of an otherwise excellent book on self-knowledge by Peter Carruthers:

Disappointingly for some readers, this book *isn't* about the sort of self-knowledge that has traditionally been thought to be part of wisdom. This includes knowledge of one's abilities and limitations, one's enduring personality characteristics, one's strengths and weaknesses, and the mode of living that will ultimately make one happy. Everyone allows that knowledge of this kind is hard to come by, and that having more of it rather than less of it can make all the difference to the overall success of one's life. Moreover, it is part of common sense that those close to us may have a better idea of these things than we do ourselves. Instead, this book is about a kind of self-knowledge that nearly everyone thinks is *easy* to come by, almost to the point of triviality. This is the knowledge we have of our own current thoughts and thought processes, which are generally believed to be transparently available to us through some sort of introspection. (Carruthers 2011: xi)

But if substantial self-knowledge can make all the difference to the overall success of one's life, and is hard to come by then shouldn't philosophy be interested in it? Aren't philosophers usually interested knowledge that is hard to come by? Why spend so much time and energy on knowledge of our own current thoughts if this kind of knowledge is so easy to come by?

In Chapter 4, I suggested the following answer to these questions: substantial self-knowledge tends to be neglected in philosophical discussions of self-knowledge because their focus is usually the epistemology of self-knowledge, and it's widely assumed that substantial self-knowledge isn't *epistemologically* interesting, even though it might be interesting in other ways. It isn't epistemologically interesting because it isn't epistemologically distinctive. Specifically, it lacks the epistemological privileges (first-person authority, immediacy, etc.) of what I have been referring to as *trivial* self-knowledge, such as your knowledge that you believe that you are wearing socks. From the standpoint of epistemology, your knowledge that you believe that you are wearing socks is more interesting, because more distinctive, than your knowledge of your own character. Substantial self-knowledge should be of interest to moral philosophers but not to epistemologists.

One way of developing this line of thinking would be to go back to the Asymmetry which came up in Chapter 11. According to the Asymmetry, self-knowledge is different in kind and manner from knowledge of others. The way I know you believe you are wearing socks is by inference from what you say and do but that isn't how I know that *I* believe I am wearing socks. However, when it comes to knowledge of my character what I have to go on is no different from what I have to go on when drawing conclusions about your character, or what you have to go on in drawing conclusions about my character. What I know about my character is, like what I know about your character, based on evidence, and the evidence can only be behavioural evidence: I go on what I say and do in my own case, just as I go on what you say and do when it comes to figuring out your character.

Suppose we describe the view that substantial self-knowledge is based on behavioural evidence as *behaviourism about substantial self-knowledge*, or just *behaviourism* for short. If behaviourism is correct then it's understandable that philosophers like Carruthers don't find substantial self-knowledge epistemologically interesting. It's not that there are no interesting philosophical questions about knowledge based on behavioural or other evidence. If that were so there would be no problem of other minds or problem of the external world. However, the thought is that there are no *special* questions about substantial self-knowledge, questions that don't also arise about any other evidence-based knowledge. It's true that philosophers are often interested in knowledge that is hard to come by, but the sense in which knowledge of one's own character can be hard to come by is no different from the sense in which many other kinds of empirical knowledge can be hard to come by.

Needless to say, I haven't laid all this out simply in order to agree with it. Aside from any doubts one might have about the epistemological distinctiveness of trivial self-knowledge the main problem with the approach I've just outlined is that it presupposes a simple-minded and impoverished conception of substantial self-knowledge. Behaviourism about substantial self-knowledge is, to put it mildly, a fairly crude view. As well as failing to take account of subtle and interesting differences between different kinds of substantial self-knowledge, it paints a picture of substantial self-knowledge which simply doesn't ring true. You can't lump together all substantial self-knowledge and dismiss it with the remark that it's all based on behavioural evidence. No doubt some of it is based on behavioural evidence but a lot of it isn't. There is much more to be said, and philosophers need to say it.

So what's the alternative to behaviourism? The obvious alternative is inferentialism of the sort I was discussing in the last chapter. Inferentialism says that inference is a basic source of self-knowledge for us. The inferences which give us intentional self-knowledge are, or include, theory-mediated inferences from internal promptings. Could it be that a lot of substantial self-knowledge also has its source in such inferences? Suppose it does. Wouldn't that collapse the distinction between substantial and other self-knowledge? No. Going back to my list of ten characteristics of substantial self-knowledge in Chapter 3, it could still be the case that inferential knowledge of such things as one's character and values more clearly satisfies more of these conditions than my knowledge that I believe that I'm wearing socks. For example, greater cognitive effort might be required to detect one's own character, and there may be obstacles to knowing in this case are which are unlikely to be obstacles to knowing that I believe I am wearing socks. Inferentialism about substantial self-knowledge doesn't collapse the distinction between substantial and other self-knowledge, though it does support the suggestion that the difference is only one of degree.

Should we be inferentialists rather about substantial self-knowledge, and are there any forms of substantial self-knowledge that inferentialism can't handle? These are the questions I want to address in this chapter, and the way I propose to address them is to take a close look at three examples of substantial self-knowledge. These relate, respectively, to knowledge of one's character, knowledge of one's values and knowledge of one's emotions. After making the case for inferentialism in connection with each of these forms of self-knowledge I will then examine the following objections to this approach:

1. Inferentialism makes substantial self-knowledge out to be more of an *intellectual* achievement than it really is. Especially when it comes to

knowledge of one's own emotions, the worry is that inferentialism is a form of what Nussbaum refers to as 'intellectualism', and that intellectualism is no good.[1]

2. Inferentialism ignores the extent to which self-attributions of character, values, and emotions *constitute* one's character, values, and emotions. Inferentialism makes us out to be more passive in relation to such things than is actually the case.

3. There are major sources of substantial self-knowledge which inferentialism can't account for because it fails to acknowledge the role of *insight* in the acquisition of substantial self-knowledge. For example, novels and films can give you insights into your own character, values, and emotions, and the source of your substantial self-knowledge when that happens isn't inference.

All three objections have something going for them, and a defensible inferentialism needs to be able to accommodate the insights they embody. This brings me to the position I want to defend. I'd like to suggest that when it comes to accounting for substantial self-knowledge, a sophisticated and inclusive inferentialism is the best bet. There are, as I've said, interesting differences between different kinds of substantial self-knowledge but inferentialism provides the most fruitful and flexible framework for thinking about these differences, as well as about what different forms of self-knowledge have in common. But even if you aren't convinced by inferentialism I do hope by the end of this chapter to have convinced you of something else: as well as being something that humans actually care about, substantial self-knowledge, in its different forms, is much more philosophically interesting than you might have thought on the basis of the dismissive attitude of so many philosophers. If, as a philosopher and a human being, you are interested in self-knowledge then you really should be interested in substantial self-knowledge; there is no excuse for only trying to account for trivial self-knowledge and its supposed privileges.

Knowledge of one's own character is my initial test case, and the first problem we run into is that there are serious philosophers who think that there is no such thing as character or character traits.[2] If there is no such thing as character then there is no such thing as *knowledge* of one's character, in which case there is nothing to be said about how one knows one's own character. All that needs to be explained is why so many people still *believe* that there is such a thing as character. This isn't really the place for a full-blown discussion of scepticism

---

[1] I have more to say about Nussbaum later in this chapter.

[2] See, for example, Harman 1999. Ross and Nisbett 2011, originally published in 1991, is an influential source of scepticism about character.

about the existence of character traits. At the same time, the writings of character sceptics can hardly be ignored, given how much I have been making in this book about knowledge of one's character as a form of substantial self-knowledge. So before turning to the epistemological issues, something needs to be said about character scepticism. Apart from anything else, character scepticism turns on a certain view of what character is, and the nature of character is something we need to get clear about anyway.

As Harman defines them, character traits are relatively long-term, stable dispositions to act in distinctive ways. We ordinarily suppose that people differ in character and also that a person's character helps explain at least some things he or she does. Harman thinks 'there is no reason at all to believe in character traits as ordinarily conceived' (2000: 223), and that the way to explain our behaviour is in terms of situational factors rather than character. He bases this view on the work of social psychologists who argue that observers wrongly infer that actions are due to distinctive character traits of agents rather than relevant aspects of the situation.[3] For example, in the notorious Milgram experiment people were asked to administer increasingly powerful electric shocks to unseen 'victims' who gave incorrect answers to various questions, or who refused to answer. All subjects, regardless of individual character, were willing to go to at least 300 volts, and fully 65% were prepared to deliver the maximum shock of 450 volts, past the label 'Danger: Severe Shock'. Why was this? Not because of some shared character defect but because of the specifics of the situation. Harman concludes that the attribution of character is explanatorily redundant and therefore unjustified.

It's certainly plausible that in the extreme circumstances of the Milgram experiment it isn't easy to explain subjects' actions by reference to their character traits, unless destructive obedience is a character trait. But the fact that character traits don't explain *everything* we do doesn't mean that it isn't right to explain *some* of what a person does by reference to his or her character. It's also worth pointing out that character traits are not just dispositions to *act* in certain ways. Consider fastidiousness as a character trait. The dictionary definition of 'fastidious' is 'very careful about accuracy and detail' and 'concerned about cleanliness'. Synonyms include 'meticulous', 'fussy', 'pernickety', 'overcritical', and 'difficult to please'. Being concerned about accuracy and detail or difficult to please aren't just, or even primarily, dispositions to *act* a certain ways; fastidiousness is the underlying state of mind. A fastidious person is one who acts as he acts because he *thinks* in a certain ways, *cares* about certain things, and has particular desires

---

[3] See Ross and Nisbett 2011.

and emotions. If you are fastidious then you tend to be bothered by things that wouldn't bother you if you weren't fastidious. Moreover, you can be disposed to act as a fastidious person would act even you aren't fastidious; perhaps you have other motives for being disposed to act in these ways. A fastidious person is not just someone who behaves fastidiously, but one whose fastidious behaviour is a reflection of, and prompted by, a particular set of concerns, desires, and emotions.

Now consider a fictional character we can call Woody. Here are some things we know about Woody: he is meticulous in his work, and his office and desk are always tidy. When he goes to bed he folds his clothes carefully, and he is disturbed by domestic disorder. He is in perpetual conflict with his teenage children over the state of their bedrooms. They are tidy by normal teenage standards but Woody is overcritical and nit-picking about even trivial lapses. Suppose we now wonder: when Woody is at work why does he spend so much time filing and labelling documents? The obvious answer is: because he is so fastidious. This looks like a perfectly reasonable and indeed informative explan-ation of his behaviour in terms of one of his character traits. If you don't know Woody then I've just told you something which should make his behaviour intelligible to you. His behaviour would still be intelligible to you, but in a different way, if I told you that Woody files and labels because he is afraid of his boss. On a given occasion there might be situational factors that help explain his behaviour but you are unlikely to get very far if you attempt to explain *all* his complaining, tidying, and nit-picking by reference to such factors. After all, this isn't a Milgram-type scenario. We are trying to explain a *pattern* of behaviour in a range of different contexts, and we would be depriving ourselves of a valuable explanatory resource if we don't say the obvious thing about Woody's filing and labelling: he does it because he is fastidious. Reference to Woody's character isn't explanatorily redundant.

Assuming there is such a thing as character, the next question is: how do you know your own character traits? If character traits are just dispositions to act in certain ways then it's understandable that behavioural evidence should be regarded as the only basis on which it is possible for one to know one's character traits. What's more, the basis on which I'm able to discern my character traits would then be no different from the basis on which you are able to discern them. The reason that, in reality, we aren't stuck with behaviourism is that, as I have suggested, character traits aren't merely dispositions to act. If they are disposi-tions at all they are 'dispositions to have prevailing desires and emotions of particular sorts'(Velleman 2007: 243), though even this is an over-simplification. Consider Woody again. How does he know he is fastidious? Since being fastidi-ous is partly a matter of what you care about and what bothers you, for him to know that he is fastidious he would have to know, among other things, what he cares about and what bothers him. It would be strange to suppose that he only knows what he cares about or what bothers him on the basis of behavioural evidence. But it also wouldn't be right to say that he knows these things on the basis of no evidence. So the challenge is to give an account of Woody's self-knowledge which avoids both extremes.

Here is how Woody might come to know that he cares about such things as tidiness and attention to detail, and that he is bothered by their absence: when he imagines the state of his teenagers' bedrooms he is conscious of feeling a mixture of dismay and irritation. The same mixture of dismay and irritation is prompted by the recollection that he didn't have time to tidy his desk when he finished work yesterday, and he is conscious of a desire to put things right as soon as possible. When he thinks about what needs to be done tomorrow, he focuses on what he sees as the need to restore order. He knows that his work colleagues aren't nearly as meticulous as he is, and is conscious of thinking thoughts along the lines of 'if you want something done right, do it yourself'. On the basis of his thoughts, imaginings, and emotions Woody is in a position to conclude that he cares about cleanliness and attention to detail. In 'The Importance of What We Care About', Frankfurt writes that a person who cares about something '*identifies* himself with what he cares about in the sense that he makes himself vulnerable to losses and susceptible to benefits depending upon whether what he cares about is diminished or enhanced' (1998: 83). Saying that Woody identifies himself with tidiness might seem a little excessive, but he is certainly 'vulnerable' to its absence; he is vulnerable to it in the sense that he is disturbed by it.

As I have described it, Woody's knowledge that he cares about tidiness and attention is inferential. In the terminology of Chapter 11, he infers from various 'internal promptings' that he cares about these things, in a way that is not very different from the way that Lawlor represents Katherine as inferring she desires another child. This makes Woody's knowledge that he is fastidious doubly inferential. Just because he knows that he cares about tidiness and attention to detail it doesn't follow that he knows, or is even in a position to know, that he is fastidious; he might not have the concept *fastidious*, or it might never cross his mind that he is fastidious. Even if it does cross his mind, he might wonder whether he cares enough about tidiness and attention to detail to make him fastidious. Or, in his more reflective moments, he might wonder whether he is merely fastidious or has obsessive compulsive disorder. We can imagine Woody running through these possibilities and finally concluding that he is indeed a fastidious person. Assuming that this conclusion is justified on the basis of the evidence that is available to him, it counts as a piece of hard-earned self-knowledge.

He infers that he has certain psychological characteristics and infers his character from these characteristics.

It's worth emphasizing that Woody's self-knowledge is substantial in my terms; it is fallible, there may be a range of obstacles to its acquisition, it tangles with his self-conception and is open to challenge. In addition, his self-knowledge is corrigible, indirect, and requires cognitive effort. He can't acquire it by using the Transparency Method but relies instead on evidence. I have represented Woody's evidence as psychological, which isn't to say that there isn't also a role for behavioural evidence. He might appeal to behavioural evidence in support of his self-attribution of fastidiousness, but in the nature of the case his evidence isn't mainly or primarily behavioural. And that is why there remains something of an asymmetry between how Woody knows he is fastidious and how someone else knows that Woody is fastidious. His friends can only go on what he says and does but Woody also has access to his internal promptings. He still has to interpret these promptings if they are to give him self-knowledge, and he can also make them available to others by telling them about it. Nevertheless, his self-knowledge is different from the knowledge that other people have of his character.

Turning, next, to knowledge of one's values, in Chapter 3, I talked about whether and how one knows that one is not a racist. In that discussion, I emphasized the role of behaviour, on the basis that not being a racist isn't just a matter of espousing racial equality. I said that it is also a matter of whether you put your money where your mouth is, that is, a matter of how you behave with people from other races. Although this supports the idea that the evidence that bears on whether you are a racist is behavioural evidence, it ignores key questions about the values that underpin what you say and do. It's easy to imagine someone whose behaviour and dispositions to act are unimpeachable but who is still an instinctive racist. An instinctive racist is someone who, as Taylor puts it, 'only feels a sense of moral solidarity with members of his own race' (1985: 61). Figuring out whether you are an instinctive racist isn't just a matter of reflecting on your behaviour. It's also a matter of how you think and feel, so here is another case in which inference from internal promptings plays a key role in the acquisition of substantial self-knowledge. As Taylor points out, it's all too easy to imagine an instinctive racist saying he knows that race shouldn't make any difference but that 'he does not feel it' (1985: 61).

Another example: in one of his early diaries the British Labour politician Tony Benn asks 'Am I a socialist?'[4] The answer to this question might have been

---

[4] Benn 1994.

obvious to him in later years but when he asked the question the answer wasn't obvious to him. It's natural to view Benn's question as a question about his values, and not just a question about his beliefs, about whether he believed a list of propositions which express the core tenets of socialism. To be a socialist in the relevant sense is to have certain values and concerns, and to think like a socialist, that is, to be disposed to analyse and explain historical and political events along socialist lines. If, like David Lewis, we say that valuing something is desiring to desire it then someone who has socialist values is someone who desires to desire such things as equality and social justice.[5] To know that you are a socialist would be to know your relevant second-order desires, and that's no easy task. Nor is it a straightforward matter to determine whether you 'think' like a socialist. However, what does seem clear is that you aren't going to be able to determine your values just on the basis of behavioural evidence. It's more a matter of interpreting your patterns of desire and thought on the basis on an understanding of what is, and is not, relevant to having certain values rather than others.

Does this mean that behavioural evidence has no part to play in coming to know your values? That obviously depends on how we understand the notion of 'behavioural evidence'. The example of a person figuring out whether he is a socialist is trickier than the example of a person figuring out he is a racist. The difference is that we have a much clearer notion of racist behaviour than of 'socialist behaviour'. There is, of course, the way you live your life, and that might be what putting your money where your mouth is might come to in this case. But even this isn't a straightforward matter. Consider Friedrich Engels, described by one recent biographer as a 'raffish, high-living, heavy-drinking devotee of the good things in life' (Hunt 2009). It's hard to make the case that Engels lived his life in the way that a socialist might be expected to live his life but even harder to make the case that he wasn't a socialist. The whole idea of knowing your own or anyone else's values on the basis of behavioural evidence is so problematic because the relationship between a person's values and his 'behaviour' is much more complicated than behaviourism suggests. It should go without saying, however, that insofar as you do genuinely know your values, your self-knowledge is about as 'substantial' as self-knowledge can be, and that inference is still the means by which you acquire it.

My last example of substantial self-knowledge is knowledge of one's emotions. There are many different emotions, and little hope of accounting for all emotional self-knowledge in the same way. One specific form of emotional

---

[5] Lewis 1989: 116.

self-knowledge that has attracted philosophical attention is knowledge of one's own love. In 'Love's Knowledge', Nussbaum discusses what might be called Proust's epistemology of love.[6] Nussbaum interprets Proust as suggesting in *Remembrance of Things Past* that 'knowledge of the heart must come from the heart' (1990: 262). The contrary view, which she calls 'intellectualism', says that knowledge of whether one loves another person can best be attained by a 'detached, unemotional, exact intellectual scrutiny of one's condition, conducted in the way a scientist would conduct a piece of research' (1990: 262). But from an inferentialist perspective this is a false dichotomy: the sense in which knowledge of the heart comes from the heart is that it is, or can be, derived from impressions such as those which, in Proust's novel, tell Marcel that he loves Albertine. The specific means by which love's knowledge is derived from such impressions is *inference* or *self-interpretation*. These are 'intellectual' processes which only deliver emotional knowledge given the appropriate background 'theory'. If inferentialism is 'intellectualism' it isn't the pernicious intellectualism which Nussbaum caricatures. But before getting to that, let's take a closer look at the passage from Proust which Nussbaum discusses.

The passage begins with an announcement: 'Mademoiselle Albertine has gone!' Just before hearing the announcement Marcel had assumed that Albertine's departure would be a matter of indifference to him, or even what he wished for after comparing 'the mediocrity of the pleasures' she afforded him with the 'richness of the pleasures' she prevented him from realizing. The news of Albertine's departure changes everything, and Marcel observes:

How much further does anguish penetrate in psychology than psychology itself! A moment before, in the process of analysing myself, I had believed that this separation without having seen each other again was precisely what I wished.... I had...concluded that I no longer loved her. But now these words: "Mademoiselle Albertine has gone", had produced in my heart an anguish such that I felt I could not endure it much longer.... I had been mistaken in thinking that I could see clearly into my own heart. (Proust 1982, Volume 3: 425-6)

In Nussbaum's terminology, what led Marcel astray to begin with was his intellectualism, his conviction that, when it came to knowledge of his own heart, he was 'like a rigorous analyst', leaving nothing out of account. Now he knows better, and it is his anguish which reveals the truth to him. His newly acquired self-knowledge—that he loves Albertine—is self-knowledge 'through' suffering.

---

[6] Nussbaum 1990.

Nussbaum tries to make sense of what is going on here by bringing in the Stoic notion of a *cataleptic impression*. Cataleptic impressions are impressions which, by their own internal character, certify their own veracity and 'drag us to assent' (1990: 265). In these terms Marcel's anguish is a cataleptic impression. It isn't simply a *route* to knowing, it *is* knowing:

> The suffering is itself a piece of self-knowing. In responding to a loss with anguish, we are grasping our love. The love is not some separate fact about us that is signalled by the impression; the impression reveals the love by constituting it. Love is not a structure of the heart waiting to be discovered. (1990: 265-6)

Marcel's love for Albertine is *constituted* by his suffering in the sense that, 'while he was busily denying that he loved her, he simply was not loving her' (1990: 268); love denied isn't exactly love. Intellectualism tells us that our passions and feelings are 'unnecessary to the search for truth about any matter whatever' (1990: 262-3) but love's knowledge is a problem for this view. For 'to try to grasp love intellectually is a way of not suffering, not loving—a practical rival, a stratagem of flight' (1990: 268-9).

There's no denying the seductiveness of Nussbaum's account of love's knowledge but is it any good? Consider her insistence that Marcel's suffering isn't just a route to knowing. On an inferentialist reading, that is precisely what his suffering is. Marcel's anguish does not itself constitute knowledge of anything but it can be the basis of self-knowledge. For a start, love is only one possible explanation of Marcel's anguish, and there are plenty of others. For example, anguish can also be induced by the departure of a person on whom one is dependent but doesn't love. Perhaps the two kinds of anguish are different, but what is to prevent one kind of anguish from being mistaken for another? When Marcel concludes, on the basis of his suffering, that he loves Albertine it is because he interprets his suffering as signalling love for Albertine. If his interpretation is correct then he is in a position to infer, and thereby know, that he loves Albertine. The inference is mediated by an interpretation of his suffering that is grounded in his understanding of the relationship between this kind of suffering and romantic love. His *route* to self-knowledge here is inference, whereas the *basis* of his self-knowledge is suffering. Here 'basis' means 'evidence', but suffering is obviously not the only evidence of love; there is also joy. As for love not being a structure of the heart waiting to be discovered that is exactly what love can be. What Marcel discovers is a pre-existing emotional fact about himself, and it's not an objection to this view that he didn't believe he loved Albertine before he heard the announcement. It's no more plausible that love denied is not love than that jealousy denied isn't jealousy or that depression denied isn't depression.

This form of inferentialism about emotional self-knowledge doesn't have to say that feelings are redundant in the search for love, any more than it has to say that feelings have nothing to do with love itself. To love someone is, among other things, to be disposed to feel a certain way about them, and that's why actually feeling that way is such good evidence that you love them. These feelings do not give us access to truths that could in principle be grasped in other ways, for example by intellect alone, but it doesn't follow that they constitute love's knowledge or that this knowledge isn't inferential. This is the crux of inferentialism's middle way between extreme intellectualism and Proust's account: feelings of joy, anguish, or suffering provide us with access to truths about ourselves which may not be accessible in other ways, but the access is inferential, and relies on the role of feelings as *evidence* of one's underlying emotional state.

I've now examined three examples of substantial self-knowledge and interpreted each example along inferentialist lines. In Chapter 3, I gave several other examples of substantial self-knowledge, and the inferentialist's hypothesis—which admittedly can't be conclusively proved without going through all of them—is that in every case you obtain self-knowledge by means of a theory-mediated inference from internal evidence, sometimes supplemented by behavioural evidence. You have an implicit theory or background understanding of what it would be for you to have a particular attribute (character trait, value, emotion, or whatever) and infer that you have the attribute in question because you interpret the evidence available to you *as* evidence that you have it. The Asymmetry, such as it is, is an asymmetry between the *evidence* available to you and to others, not an asymmetry between inferential and non-inferential knowledge. In one sense Marcel's knowledge that he loves Albertine is different from your knowledge that he loves Albertine—your knowledge isn't derived from suffering—but neither of you knows other than on the basis of evidence. Different kinds of substantial self-knowledge are supported by, and depend on, different kinds of evidence, but in none of the examples I have considered does behaviourism look remotely plausible.

Where does this leave my insistence that there are subtle and interesting differences between different forms of substantial self-knowledge? If all substantial self-knowledge turns out to be inferential what becomes of these differences? The answer to this question is much the same as the response I gave to the earlier suggestion that inferentialism about substantial self-knowledge collapses the distinction between substantial and other self-knowledge. The answer is that there is plenty of scope for exploring differences between different varieties of self-knowledge in an inferentialist framework; indeed, inferentialism provides a fruitful and flexible framework for thinking about these differences. For example, as soon as you think of different kinds of substantial self-knowledge as supported by different kinds of evidence you need to explain in more detail which types of evidence are relevant in each case, and why. It's one thing to say that substantial self-knowledge is fallible and corrigible but it's natural to suppose that you are less fallible and more authoritative about your emotions than about your character. The obstacles and challenges are different in each case, as is the level of what I've been calling cognitive effort. There is endless scope for further reflection and analysis, and it is for philosophy to engage in this further reflection and analysis. You would have to have a wretchedly impoverished conception of philosophy to think that it has nothing of interest to say about these issues.

Before moving on to consider some potential objections to inferentialism, there is one further implication of this approach that needs to be brought out. I've suggested that, as far as inferentialism is concerned, the difference between substantial and trivial self-knowledge is a difference in degree. The difference between your knowledge that you are fastidious and your knowledge that you believe you are wearing socks is the difference between obviously and unobviously inferential knowledge rather than the difference between inferential and non-inferential knowledge. Your knowledge is manifestly and consciously inferential in the one case but not in the other. If this is what we say then we need to be careful how we bring in the notion of substantial self-knowledge. The natural way to do this is by example but examples are easily misunderstood. From the fact that love is an emotion, and that Marcel's knowledge of his love for Albertine is substantial self-knowledge, it's easy to conclude that knowledge of one's emotions is always substantial. But do we really want to say that a parent knows that she loves her child by inference or that it requires cognitive effort to determine that you love your child? These rhetorical questions open up the possibility that, in principle, knowledge of some of one's emotions might belong on the less substantial end of the spectrum. If that is the case, then it's probably best to avoid introducing the notion of substantial self-knowledge by giving examples. No doubt knowledge of one's emotions, values, and abilities is often or even typically substantial, but inferentialism can leave open the possibility that sometimes it isn't. If it turns out that something like knowledge of one's character can only ever be substantial then that's another interesting difference between varieties of self-knowledge.

To bring matters in this chapter to a close, let's go back to the three serious-sounding objections to inferentialism listed above. The first was that inferentialism makes substantial self-knowledge out to be more of an intellectual achievement than it really is. I have already talked about Nussbaum's concerns about intellectualism but there is a much simpler way of explaining what the problem is:

substantial self-knowledge is something that is available to most mature adults; it isn't only available to the educated or philosophically sophisticated. In that case, it might seem totally inappropriate to think of substantial self-knowledge as based on theory-mediated inferences from internal and other evidence, especially if the inferences are supposed to be conscious and explicit. Ordinary people don't have the 'theories' which this account requires.

There is a more and a less concessive response to this concern. The more concessive response would be to point out that it's important not to read too much into talk of theory-mediated inferences. Someone who knows, and therefore believes, he is generous or in love has to have some conception of what it would be to be generous or in love. In this sense they must have a 'theory' of generosity or romantic love but the theory doesn't have to be all that sophisticated, and their grasp of the theory may well be implicit. Perhaps they would be hard pushed to articulate their theory of romantic love but that doesn't mean that they aren't in fact relying on a 'theory' in taking themselves to be in love. To have substantial self-knowledge you must have justified beliefs about yourself, and that means understanding what is evidence for what. This leads naturally to the less concessive response. This response bites the bullet in insisting that the acquisition of substantial self-knowledge *is* an intellectual achievement, and that your level of intellectual sophistication does affect the quantity and quality of substantial self-knowledge that is available to you. Obviously no one wants to be accused of elitism but the fact is that substantial self-knowledge isn't evenly distributed across the population. For example, not every fastidious person knows that he is fastidious; you only know that you are fastidious if you know what fastidiousness is, and what counts as evidence of fastidiousness. Not knowing these things is a barrier to knowing that you are fastidious, and if you *do* know you are fastidious that is only because you have and use the necessary intellectual resources. In this case only conscious reflection of quite a sophisticated sort can deliver self-knowledge. Of course this isn't to say that a Rolls Royce intellect guarantees substantial self-knowledge. However clever or knowledgeable you are there is always the possibility of repression or self-deception. Still, the more you know, the more you are in a position to know about yourself.

The next objection to inferentialism says that it makes substantial self-knowledge out to be more passive than it really is, and underestimates our role in creating or constituting the attributes of which we have substantial self-knowledge. There are better ways of making this point than to go along with Nussbaum's view that denying that one has a particular emotion amounts to one not having that emotion. For example, in his classic paper 'Self-Interpreting Animals', Charles Taylor observes that: 'human life is never without interpreted feeling; the interpretation is constitutive of the feeling' (1985: 63). He gives the example of remorse as a feeling or emotion which involves a certain level of articulation. A feeling of remorse 'implies our sense that our act was wrong' (1985: 63), even if we can't initially articulate what is wrong about what we have done. In such cases we may try to understand further, and if we succeed our feeling may change: 'the remorse may dissipate altogether, if we come to see that our sense of wrong-doing is unfounded, or it may alter in other ways, as we come to understand what is wrong' (1985: 63). The articulation *transforms* the emotion, which means that we aren't mere passive *recorders* of our emotions. There is both an element of creation and an element of discovery, and the toughest challenge for an account of emotional self-knowledge is to do justice to both elements. Or so Taylor implies.

A lot of what Taylor says sounds right, but is that a problem for inferentialism? There would be a problem if inferentialism has to deny that interpretations or articulations play any part in constituting our emotions but that's plainly not the case. Here is how inferentialism can accommodate Taylor's insight: suppose you are trying to figure out how you feel about something you have just done, and aren't sure whether it is remorse or embarrassment. You ask yourself whether what you did was wrong and your initial thought is that it was. You see that your feeling incorporates your sense that what you did was wrong and you conclude that what you are feeling is remorse. To conclude that what you feel is remorse is to interpret your feeling as one of remorse, but you aren't making it up as you go along. You take it that what you feel is remorse because of your sense that what you did was wrong; to put it another way, you *infer* from your sense that what you did was wrong that what you feel is remorse. So far so good for inferentialism.

Next, you ask yourself whether on reflection what you did really was wrong, and the more you think about it the less convinced you are that it was. As a result, your feeling alters. The fact that you no longer have the sense that what you did was wrong implies that what you feel is no longer remorse. Maybe you don't feel anything at all, or what you feel is quite different. Again, inferentialism has no problem with any of this. Your evolving sense that what you did wasn't wrong both *makes it the case* that what you now feel isn't remorse and is *evidence* from which you can infer that what you feel isn't remorse but something else. There is no problem for inferentialism because your thoughts about the moral status of your action can play a dual role: they can both alter an emotion and reveal to you what emotion it is. Just because you interpret an emotion a certain way on the basis of your thought, it doesn't follow that those thoughts can't partially constitute your emotion. By the same token, just because a particular thought contributes to making your emotion the particular emotion it is, it doesn't follow that you having that thought isn't evidence from which you can correctly infer that you have just that emotion. Inferentialism doesn't imply that we are merely passive recorders of our emotions if what that means is that what we think can't shape what we feel. In fact, it is *because* what we think can and does shape what we feel that it is evidence of what we feel.

The last objection to inferentialism says that there are major source of substantial self-knowledge it doesn't account for because of its failure to acknowledge the role of insight in the acquisition of substantial self-knowledge. Reading a novel or seeing a movie can give you an insight into your own character and emotions but knowledge by insight isn't inferential. Here's an unflattering example: suppose that I've never thought of myself as a cold fish but I read *Anna Karenina* and can see myself in Karenin. He is unfeeling, unromantic, and cold. These are not epithets I would willingly apply to myself but now I see that temperamentally I'm not very different from him. The chances are that I will be dismayed by this realization, but perhaps I also find myself identifying with Karenin. Whatever my reaction, it is tempting to claim that this new insight into my character is a piece of substantial self-knowledge, and that the source of my self-knowledge here is the novel itself. I don't *infer* that I am like Karenin; I *see* that I am like him. The question is whether inferentialism can account for this.

There are several things to say about this. First, it's false that *Anna Karenina* is the source of my self-knowledge. It isn't the novel that tells me that I am cold but my reflection on the novel.[7] What is more, this reflection *presupposes* self-knowledge. I can only see myself in Karenin because I notice how we resemble each other, and I can only notice how much I resemble Karenin if I already know something about how I am. What reading the novel does is to make certain aspects of how I am salient to me and help me to conceptualize these aspects. If I see Karenin as cold and recognize that I am in the relevant respects like him then the inescapable conclusion is that I'm a cold person. This inescapable conclusion is the conclusion of an *inference* whose premises include statements about me and about Karenin. What the inference provides me with is still 'self-insight' but self-insight, like ordinary seeing, is inferential: I see that I'm like Karenin because I infer that I am like him.

Here's another way of reaching the same conclusion: suppose, somewhat improbably, that I am aware of identifying with Karenin as I read *Anna Karenina*. There is a lot to be said about what is involved in identifying with a literary

[7] Hetherington 2007 makes much the same point about the role of literature and film in the acquisition of self-knowledge.

character but suppose we take this notion for granted for present purposes. Just because I identify with Karenin it doesn't follow that I am like him, let alone that I know that I am like him. Still, I might wonder what the fact that I identify with him tells me about myself. It's hard to get away from the notion that identifying with a character like Karenin is somehow self-revealing but it's only self-revealing if I reflect on my identification with him and have a plausible story to tell about what my identification with Karenin reveals. If I have such a story then I can perhaps draw certain conclusions about my own character but any such conclusions are *inferred* from my reactions to the character of Karenin. Once again, what gives me self-knowledge is a theory-mediated inference.

Even if I'm wrong about this and literature turns out to be a *sui generis* source of non-inferential substantial self-knowledge it still wouldn't follow that inferentialism is no good; it wouldn't follow that inference isn't a basic source of substantial self-knowledge even if there are other sources of substantial self-knowledge. However, as I say, I don't believe that novels *are* a *sui generis* source of non-inferential substantial self-knowledge. Let's agree, then, that inferentialism is in good shape, in relation both to substantial and insubstantial self-knowledge, and proceed on that basis. None of the three objections to inferentialism I have discussed is successful, and there is no obvious alternative to inferentialism. If you still think that philosophy needn't bother with substantial self-knowledge, or that it doesn't have anything interesting or useful to say about the epistemology of substantial self-knowledge, then your conception of philosophy is very different from mine.

Where do we go from here? As well as delivering an account of the epistemology of self-knowledge one might also expect philosophy to have something to say about is value. It would hardly be worth spending so much time thinking about self-knowledge unless there are reasons for thinking that it is valuable. Whether there are such reasons will be the topic of Chapter 15. However, we aren't quite done with the epistemology of self-knowledge because it's no good having an account of self-knowledge unless you also have an account of self-ignorance. Self-ignorance is a genuine phenomenon, and something that humans go to a great deal of trouble—and expense—to overcome. In light of that fact, it would be reassuring if philosophy has answers to some obvious questions about self-ignorance: for example, how prevalent is it, what are its main sources, and to what extent can it be overcome by us? I think that these are questions to which inferentialism suggests answers, so now would be a good time to say some more about self-ignorance.

14

Self-Ignorance

Self-ignorance comes in many different varieties, some more interesting than others.[1] Suppose you have been eating too many desserts and your weight has been creeping upwards. You have put on weight but you neither know nor believe you have. This is a form of self-ignorance—physical self-ignorance—but not one that excites much philosophical interest. The natural view is that having a physical property like being overweight or weighing sixty kilos is one thing, knowing or believing that you have such properties is another. It isn't in the nature of such properties that if you have them you know or believe you have them, and there is no reason to suppose that you can't be ignorant, or plain wrong, about your weight. Neither error nor ignorance is ruled out, and neither calls for any special explanation.

When it comes to our mental properties, philosophers influenced by Descartes tell a very different story. They agree that you can be in pain without knowing that you are in pain. Maybe you don't have the concept of pain. You can believe you are wearing socks without knowing that you believe you are wearing socks. Maybe you don't have the concept of belief. However, Cartesians think if you have the necessary concepts, and there isn't anything wrong with you, then if you are in pain you must know you are in pain, and if you believe you are wearing socks then you must know that you believe you are wearing socks. On this view, core mental properties are necessarily or constitutively self-intimating: it belongs to the very nature of such properties that if you are rational and have the necessary conceptual resources you can't have them without believing and knowing that you have them.[2] If this is correct then certain forms of mental self-ignorance are ruled out; there are truths about your mental life you can't fail to know unless there is something wrong with you, whatever that means. Indeed,

---

[1] Philosophical accounts of self-ignorance are fairly thin on the ground but Schwitzgebel 2012 is a notable discussion.

[2] Shoemaker 2009 defends a version of this view.

when it comes to knowledge of your own standing attitudes, you might think that not only can you not fail to know *what* they are, you can't fail to know *why* they are as they are.

Not all mental properties are like this. Suppose you think of fastidiousness as a mental property, at least to the extent that being fastidious is a matter of what you care about or what bothers you. No one would suppose that fastidiousness is constitutively self-intimating, and it doesn't take any special effort or ingenuity to conceive of a fastidious person failing to know that, or why, he is fastidious. Nevertheless, if you are a Cartesian you might still believe you are uniquely well placed to know your own character traits, as well as your own emotions and values. Knowledge of these things might not be unavoidable in the way that knowledge of your own beliefs is unavoidable, but is still straightforwardly attainable.

What I have been describing as the Cartesian view is a form of what I'm going to call *optimism* about human self-knowledge. Consider the following three questions about self-ignorance:

1. How prevalent is it?
2. What are its sources?
3. To what extent can it be overcome?

Optimists about self-knowledge think that self-ignorance isn't and can't be prevalent, at least in relation to a designated range of mental properties: if you are rational and not conceptually impoverished then you can't fail to know your own sensations, mental actions, and standing attitudes. You normally know why your attitudes are as they are, and know much, if not all, of what there is to know about your own character, values, and emotions. Your abilities and what makes you happy are perhaps more elusive but optimists see no reason in principle why you couldn't also acquire these forms of substantial self-knowledge.

Optimists take a dim view of the sources of self-ignorance. For example, Tyler Burge contrasts knowledge of our own thoughts with perceptual knowledge. He argues that a person can be perceptually wrong without there being anything wrong with him. In this domain brute errors—ones that do not result from any carelessness, malfunction, or irrationality on our part—are possible because the objects of perception are independent of our perceptual awareness of them. In contrast 'all matters where people have special authority about themselves are errors which indicate something wrong with the thinker' (Burge 1994: 74). Optimists take such matters to include standing attitudes such as beliefs, hopes, and desires. They maintain that not knowing what you want, hope, or believe is a clear indication that there is something wrong with you, and that only irrationality or some kind of cognitive malfunction can explain your self-ignorance. Ignorance in relation to your own character traits is a different matter. This form of self-ignorance need not have its source in irrationality or cognitive malfunction but might still be an indication of lesser defects such as carelessness or laziness.

Insofar as irrationality or cognitive malfunctions are the sources of self-ignorance the only way to overcome self-ignorance is to correct or overcome these defects. But if you are irrational there may be little you can do about it, and it's also conceivable that some cognitive malfunctions can't easily be fixed. If that is how things turn out, then forms of self-ignorance that indicate something wrong with the thinker might be incurable. In this respect, optimists are pessimists. The more abnormal you regard self-ignorance as being, the more you interpret it as a sign that something is wrong with the thinker, the harder it becomes to still regard it as curable. Still, the overall picture remains optimistic in the following sense: optimists see self-knowledge in its various forms as the norm, and self-ignorance as a deviation from the norm, as an indication that something has gone wrong.

My aim in this chapter is to argue for a more pessimistic view of self-knowledge.[3] On this view some self-ignorance, even with respect to one's own standing attitudes, is inevitable and quite normal for humans. Not knowing what you want, believe, or hope doesn't indicate that you are irrational or malfunctioning, any more than not knowing your own character indicates that you are irrational or malfunctioning. All it indicates is that you are a fully paid up and normal member of the species *homo sapiens*. If Descartes is the arch optimist then Nietzsche is the arch pessimist, as indicated by this dramatic passage:

We are necessarily strangers to ourselves, we do not comprehend ourselves, we have to misunderstand ourselves, for the law "each is furthest from himself" applies to all eternity. (1997: 1)

This is a bit of an exaggeration. A sensible pessimism should refrain from claiming that self-knowledge is impossible, or that we are *necessarily* strangers to ourselves. You can think that a degree of self-ignorance is normal for humans without also thinking that self-knowledge is impossible. However, this leaves it open whether the respects in which we *are* strangers to ourselves are, as Nietzsche would no doubt say, the important ones. The trick is to strike the right balance between human self-knowledge and human self-ignorance, and to explain our self-ignorance without taking it as proof that there is something wrong with us.

---

[3] Another pessimist is Eric Schwitzgebel. See Schwitzgebel 2012.

You don't have to be irrational or mentally defective to be self-ignorant and, as we will see in the next chapter, some self-ignorance might actually be good for us.

Here is my plan for this chapter: I'll start by looking at the extent to which we can and do fail to know our attitudes, where this is a matter of failing to know *what* we want, believe, and so on. I will distinguish motivational and non-motivational explanations of self-ignorance and show how the inferentialism I've been defending in this book delivers a straightforward non-motivational explanation of self-ignorance. If you want to explain how self-ignorance is possible, you *can* hold, but don't *have* to hold, that it is motivated. It's better to think of self-ignorance as a natural by-product of the mechanisms of self-knowledge: given how we go about acquiring self-knowledge, it is entirely predictable that we don't always know our own minds, even if there is nothing wrong with us. It remains to be seen how easily, on this view, self-ignorance can be overcome.

Next, I will look at knowledge of our own attitudes in the sense of knowing *why* they are as they are. I will suggest that optimism in this domain is even less defensible than optimism about knowledge of our own attitudes in the sense of knowing what they are. Again, inferentialism has no difficulty explaining our self-ignorance in respect of why we believe what we believe, want what we want, and so on. The key is to distinguish epistemic and non-epistemic explanations of our attitudes. Going back to our friend Oliver the conspiracy theorist, an epistemic explanation of his beliefs about 9/11 will talk about his reasons or evidence. A non-epistemic explanation will concentrate on character traits such as his gullibility. Nietzsche thinks that non-epistemic explanations of our attitudes are not only the deepest explanations but also the most inaccessible. We will see if he is right about this.

Finally, I'll look at the extent to which we are self-ignorant in relation to such things as our character, values, and emotions. The more substantial a variety of self-knowledge the easier it is to accept that one can lack it. Ignorance of one's own character is straightforward, and the interesting question is not whether this form of self-ignorance is possible but rather what explains it. Ignorance in relation to one's own values and emotions is a little harder to understand but inferentialism has something to say about each case. The take-home message of this chapter is that self-ignorance is inevitable for humans and can be tough to overcome. Instead of denying that self-ignorance is possible what philosophers should be doing to trying to explain it.

How can you fail to know what you believe? If you believe the present government will be re-elected mustn't you know that this is what you believe? However, before getting too excited about the seeming inevitability of self-knowledge in this case, it would be worth asking how representative the example is. When it comes to other attitudes, it's as easy as pie to conceive of our failing to know what there is to know: you can want something without knowing that you want it, hope for something without knowing that you hope for it, fear something without knowing that you fear it, and so on. Here is a nice example of ignorance of what one hopes:

> I believe that I do not hope for a particular result to a match; I am conscious of nothing but indifference; then my disappointment at one outcome reveals my preference for another. When I had that hope I was in no position to know that I had it. (Williamson 2000: 24)

Even when it comes to one's own beliefs, it's not that difficult to imagine someone having a belief they don't realize they have: for example, perhaps it's clear from what you say and do that you do in fact believe that the present government will be re-elected, but you have never explicitly thought about the government's election prospects and do not have the belief that you believe the present government will be re-elected. Even if, in this case, you don't actually know what you believe, it might be said you are at least *in a position* to know you believe the government will be re-elected: all you have to do is think about what you believe. But even this isn't guaranteed to produce self-knowledge. Maybe the government is so odious that you are unable to admit to yourself that you believe it will be re-elected. You have a determinate belief about its election prospects you don't know you have, and aren't even in a position to know you have, since your path to knowing what you believe is blocked by a psychological obstacle. The obstacle in this case might be embarrassment or despair.

This suggests the following picture: suppose you have a particular attitude A, and the question is whether you know that you have A. Let's agree that you can't know you have A if you don't believe you have A. There is a difference between not believing that you have A and believing that you don't have A. In mild cases of self-ignorance, the sense in which you don't know that you have A is simply that you lack the second-order belief that you have A. Let's call this 'mere' self-ignorance. However, there is also the possibility that you have A but believe that you don't have A: for example, you hope for a particular outcome to a match but mistakenly believe that you don't hope for that outcome. Alternatively, you don't have A but you mistakenly believe that you have A: you don't really want another martini but believe you do. In contrast with 'mere' self-ignorance, the last two examples are ones in which you are mistaken; you don't just lack a true second-order belief about whether you have A, you have a *false* second-order belief. Let's call these cases of *self-deception*. If you mistakenly believe that you don't have an attitude which you do in fact have then this is what Shoemaker calls 'negative self-deception' (2009: 35). Positive self-deception happens where you believe you have an attitude which in reality you don't have.

In explaining mere self-ignorance and self-deception motivational approaches appeal to motivational factors. For example, if believing that you have a particular attitude A would be unpleasant or anxiety-inducing then you will be motivated not to believe that you have A. But how can you not believe you have A, or believe that you don't have A, if all the evidence points to your having A? Motivational explanations of self-deception suggest that your desire not to subject yourself to psychic discomfort motivates you to forget, misconstrue, or ignore the evidence. Looking the other way when confronted by evidence that you have A, or simply forgetting the evidence, are strategies your psyche pursues, usually unconsciously, in order to minimize its own discomfort. If successful, these strategies cause you to be self-ignorant or self-deceived and thereby maximize your psychic well-being.

One problem with this explanation of self-ignorance is that it is limited in scope. It's just not plausible that all or even most cases of self-ignorance are ones in which the unknown attitude is unpleasant or anxiety-provoking. For example, you are wrong about whether you want another martini even though recognizing that you do wouldn't cause you any psychic distress. More generally, it's not plausible that every case in which you are mistaken about what you want or hope or believe can be explained on the basis that you are trying to protect yourself from pain or anxiety. Sometimes you are ignorant or mistaken about your attitudes without any ulterior psychological motive. In such cases a different account of self-ignorance is needed, either one that refers to different motivational factors or that doesn't explain self-ignorance in motivational terms.

In addition to questions about the scope of motivational accounts of self-ignorance there are also questions about the mechanisms or processes by which what might be called 'self-protective' self-ignorance is achieved. I've talked vaguely about looking the other way when confronted by evidence that you have an anxiety-provoking attitude but perhaps the most influential account of motivated self-ignorance is associated with Freud. This says that self-ignorance is specifically the result of repression. Is there any evidence for this view? The issue here is not whether it is *always* right to explain self-ignorance by reference to repression but whether, in light of the empirical evidence, it is *ever* right. This issue has been taken up by Timothy D. Wilson and Elizabeth W. Dunn, who maintain that an empirical demonstration of repression would have to show that:

1. People are motivated to keep thought, feelings, or memories outside of awareness.
2. The attempt to keep material out of awareness is itself an unconscious process.
3. People succeed in removing the undesired material from consciousness.
4. The material, once removed from consciousness, still exists in memory and continues to influence people's thoughts, feelings, or behaviour.
5. The material is recoverable if the repressive forces are removed.[4]

Wilson and Dunn conclude that though 'a patchwork of studies depicts a mental architecture that would allow repression to occur', it's also the case that 'no single study has demonstrated all the necessary criteria to establish the existence of repression definitively' (2004: 498). At best there is suggestive evidence, and sceptics about the motivational approach will not see this as an adequate basis for constructing a theory of self-ignorance.

There is obviously much more to be said about all this but you might wonder whether it's even necessary to explain self-ignorance in motivational terms. Motivational approaches get into trouble over questions about their scope and empirical support but these questions can be avoided if it's possible to provide a non-motivational explanation of self-ignorance. A non-motivational approach needn't deny that self-ignorance is sometimes motivated, perhaps in the way that Freud describes, but insists on a core account of self-ignorance which makes no mention of motivational factors. Such factors might have a part to play but they are not the fundamental basis on which self-ignorance is to be explained. If an account along these lines can be made to work then we don't need to worry so much about the quality of the evidence for repression, or the fact that we are sometimes ignorant of attitudes which wouldn't bother us if we knew of their existence.

What would a non-motivational explanation of self-ignorance look like? Suppose that when all goes well self-knowledge comes about as a result of theory-mediated inferences from internal or other evidence. This is inferential-ism about self-knowledge, and one of the attractions of this view is that it points to a straightforward, non-motivational account of self-ignorance. If you have an attitude A then you will fail to know that you have A in any of the following circumstances:

(a) You haven't performed the necessary inference from the evidence you have.

---

[4] This list is from Wilson and Dunn 2004: 495.

(b) You lack the necessary evidence.

(c) You have all the evidence you need but draw the wrong conclusion about whether you have A because:

  (i) You reason poorly.

  (ii) You misinterpret the evidence.

  (iii) You have a defective theory about the relationship between your evidence and your attitude.

The result of (a) and (b) will be 'mere' self-ignorance. The other scenarios may result in your having a false belief about your attitude—self-deception rather than mere self-ignorance. But there is no mention of repression or of your self-ignorance being motivated by a desire not to subject yourself to psychic distress. Your failure to perform the necessary inference or your misinterpretation of the evidence *might* be motivated but needn't be.

To see how this all works in practice, let's go back to the example of Katherine from Chapter 11. In that example, Katherine wonders whether she wants another child and answers this question in the affirmative on the basis of 'internal promptings'—memories, emotions, imaginings, and so on. However, it's easy to conceive of Katherine being aware of the same internal promptings but not reflecting on their significance and not self-attributing the desire for another child. Maybe she has too much else on her mind and never gets as far as inferring that she wants another child. She wants another child but doesn't (yet) know or believe she wants another child. This is an example of mere self-ignorance. Or suppose that she does in fact want another child but has yet to encounter the internal promptings that would enable her to infer that she wants another child. This is still mere self-ignorance, but a reflection of Katherine's lack of evidence rather than her failure to perform the necessary inference.

Suppose, on the other hand, that Katherine has the evidence that she wants another child but judges that she doesn't want another child. How can she be negatively self-deceived about her desire for another child? In Lawlor's example, Katherine is described as noting an emotion that could be envy when an acquaintance reveals her pregnancy but there is always the possibility of misinterpretation or of Katherine failing to grasp the significance of her own envy on hearing of her acquaintance's pregnancy: she doesn't see that her envy is evidence of her desire for another child. Her misinterpretation of the evidence and failure to grasp its true significance explain her mistaken belief that she doesn't want another child.

Another example from Chapter 11 can be used to make the same point. In this case, a subject is paid a dollar to perform a long and boring laboratory task, and infers that he must actually have enjoyed performing the task because he discounts monetary inducement as the major motivating factor. It is completely clear in this case that the subject infers his attitude on the basis of a *theory* about why he performed the task. But of course there is no guarantee that his theory is correct. In this case he didn't enjoy the task but his defective theory leads him to infer that he did enjoy it. This is now a case a positive self-deception, that is, the self-attribution of an attitude one does not or did have. In Wilson's terminology, the theoretical route to self-knowledge can lead to 'self-revelation' but it can also result in 'self-fabrication', where you mistakenly infer the existence of an attitude that was not or is not actually present.[5] The misattribution might be motivated, but could also simply be the result of the so-called 'fundamental attribution error', whereby 'people underestimate the effects of external factors on their behaviour' and 'misattribute their actions to an internal state' (Wilson and Dunn 2004: 509–10).

The inferentialist thinks that, in principle, you can run the same kind of story to make sense of the misattribution of any attitude. You can misattribute a belief, a hope, a fear, or an emotion like jealousy because you jump to the wrong conclusion about your state of mind. This needn't be a conscious process, any more than correctly inferring your attitude needs to be a conscious process. Both self-knowledge and self-deception can be, and normally are, the result of automatic transitions rather than deliberate reflection. However, as long as you think of self-knowledge as the product of theory-mediated inferences, you are effectively building into your account the possibility of self-ignorance and self-deception. This is a strength rather than a weakness of inferentialism since self-ignorance and self-deception clearly *are* possible, and inferentialism explains with minimum fuss and without appealing to motivational factors *how* they are possible: theories can be defective, evidence can be lacking or misleading, and inferences are not guaranteed to be correct.

Do cases of positive or negative self-deception indicate that there is, as Burge puts it, 'something wrong with the thinker'? Not if the point of this is to suggest that self-deception must be the result of carelessness, malfunction, or irrationality. Of these three possibilities the easiest to deal with is irrationality. On the narrow conception of irrationality which I've been relying on in this book, irrationality in the clearest sense occurs when a person's attitudes fail to conform to her own judgements, when 'a person continues to believe something (continues to regard it with conviction and take it as a premise in subsequent reasoning) even though she judges there to be good reason for rejecting it'

---

[5] Wilson 2002: 206.

(Scanlon 1998: 25). But when the subject in the Festinger–Carlsmith experiment believes that he must have enjoyed the boring task, or if Katherine believes that she doesn't want another child, there is no irrationality in this sense; there is no conflict between their attitudes and their judgements. Carelessness isn't the issue either: the subject in the Festinger–Carlsmith experiment isn't proceeding without due care and attention when he concludes, on reflection, that he must have enjoyed the tedious task; he's just wrong. What about the idea that this kind of error indicates a malfunction? Again, that's not obvious. A malfunctioning device is one that doesn't work as it should but a person who self-attributes attitudes after due consideration of the evidence *is* in one sense operating just as he should. The fact that some of his self-attributions are misattributions doesn't indicate a malfunction unless the mere making of a mistake indicates a malfunction. If that were so then no errors would come out as 'brute'; they would all indicate something wrong with the thinker.

Burge thinks that a person can be *perceptually* wrong without there being anything wrong with him; perceptual errors can be 'brute'. What I have just been arguing is, in effect, that errors about your own attitudes can also be brute errors. When you make mistakes about your own attitudes you aren't misperceiving them but you may be misinterpreting them. Just because you occasionally misread what you believe, hope, or want, that doesn't necessarily mean that there is something wrong with you. This is a reflection of the fact that such objects of self-knowledge are independent of our knowledge of them, just as the objects of perceptual awareness are independent of our awareness of them. Inferentialism sees self-knowledge as a process of self-discovery which allows for the possibility of blameless mistakes. Gross or frequent errors about your own attitudes are a different matter. They would indicate something wrong with you, but so of course would gross or frequent perceptual errors.

It should be obvious that on this account of self-knowledge our standing attitudes are not 'constitutively' or necessarily self-intimating. There would be no question of explaining how self-ignorance is possible if you can't have a particular belief, desire, or other standing attitude without knowing that you have it. Inferentialism makes it clear *that* and *how* self-ignorance is possible, and thereby removes any basis for going along with the thesis that our standing attitudes are necessarily self-intimating. This thesis is utterly implausible quite apart from what inferentialism implies. Throughout this book I've operated with a dispositionalist account of belief and other attitudes: to believe that P is to be disposed to think that P, to act as if P is true, to use P as a premise in reasoning, and so on. Merely *having* the dispositions associated with believing that P is no guarantee that you know or believe that you have them, just as believing that you have the relevant dispositions is no guarantee that you have them. Neither ignorance nor error is ruled out, and self-ignorance is possible even if the dispositions you need in order to count as believing that P include the disposition to self-ascribe the belief that P. If you believe that P, and the question arises whether you believe that P, then other things being equal you will judge that you believe that P but it doesn't follow that you believe that you believe that P prior to the question arising. Suppose you believe that the government will be re-elected. The thought that this is what you believe might never have crossed your mind, and if it did cross your mind you might find it hard to admit to yourself. Yet your other dispositions might leave no room for doubt that this is what you believe.

In addition to the question whether you can believe that P without knowing *that* you believe that P there is the question whether you can believe that P without knowing *why* you believe that P. In addition to the question whether you can want that P without knowing *that* you want that P, there is the question whether you can want that P without knowing *why* you want that P. Pessimists see no difficulty here. They think it's obvious that self-ignorance in the 'knowing why' sense is possible, and perhaps even unavoidable. The interesting question here is not how self-ignorance is possible but how self-*knowledge* is possible, that is, how it's ever possible for you to know why you believe the things you believe, want the things you want, and so on. Inferentialism has a simple answer to this question: you can sometimes infer why your attitudes are as they are. However, your inferences can lead you astray, and at other times you may find yourself stuck for an answer. It might be obvious to you that you want to have lunch now because you are hungry but it might be far from obvious to Katherine why she wants another child. The possibilities of self-deception and confabulation are endless and self-ignorance is always on the cards.

Opposed to this form of pessimism is a form of optimism which says that insofar as our attitudes are the product of *reasoning* we are in a position to know, by reflecting on our reasons, why they are as they are. Here is Matthew Boyle's statement of this view:

> [I]f I reason "P, so Q" this must normally put me in a position, not merely to know *that* I believe that Q, but to know something about *why* I believe Q, namely, because I believe that P and that P shows that Q . . . successful deliberation normally gives us knowledge of what we believe and why we believe it. (2011a: 8)

In principle you can run the same line for any attitude that you reason yourself into. If you form the desire to go to Italy for the summer after considering the pros and cons then you are in a position to know *that* you want to go to Italy for the summer and *why* you want to do that.[6] Once again, the source of your self-knowledge is deliberation: deliberation can give you knowledge of what you want, and why you want it, to the extent that your desire is the result of deliberation.

You might wonder how much optimists and pessimists really disagree. Here is a way of splitting the difference between the two positions: some of our attitudes arise as a result of deliberation but some do not. If you reason 'P, so Q' then you are in a position to know why you believe Q but this strategy won't work if you believe that Q without having deliberated. So maybe we should say that successful deliberation gives us knowledge of what we believe and why we believe it *as long as we are talking about beliefs formed by deliberation*. If we haven't deliberated then deliberation can't be what gives us knowledge of what we believe and why we believe it, and these are the cases in which self-ignorance is genuinely on the cards.

Neither optimists nor pessimists are likely to be impressed by this attempt to split the difference between them. Optimists will argue that even if you haven't actually reasoned your way to Q you can still be asked why you believe that Q. This is a request for your reasons, and in giving your reasons you will be revealing why you have that belief. It doesn't matter whether you have actually deliberated your way to Q. What matters is that you have reasons for your belief, and that you can give them if challenged. Pessimists will insist that once you grasp what *they* mean by 'knowing why you believe that Q', it will be apparent that even if you have reasoned your way from P to Q you might *still* not be in a position to know why, in the relevant sense, you believe that Q. When it comes to knowing why your attitudes are as they are, there are different levels of explanation, some more superficial than others. In some cases, only reflection or reasoning that is external from your reasoning from P to Q can tell you why, in the deepest sense, you believe that Q. Even then, there is no guarantee of self-knowledge.

This is all too abstract and the best way of making it more concrete is to go back to the case of OLIVER from Chapter 1. You will remember that Oliver is the conspiracy theorist with a 9/11 obsession. He insists that the collapse of World Trade Center towers on 9/11 was caused by explosives planted by government agents rather than by aircraft impacts. He thinks that the 9/11 Commission Report was part of a grand conspiracy to deceive the public and that, to coin a phrase, 'the truth is out there'. He focuses on these propositions:

---

[6] This example is from Hampshire 1979.

P—Aircraft impacts couldn't have caused the collapse of the twin towers, and eye witnesses heard explosions just before the collapse of each tower, some time after the planes struck

Q—The collapse of the twin towers was caused by explosives rather than by aircraft impacts.

Oliver believes there is good evidence for P, and reasons from P to Q. P doesn't entail Q but (as Oliver sees it) strongly supports Q. So Oliver's reasoning is of the form 'P, so Q', though the 'so' is not the 'so' of entailment. Now ask Oliver why he believes that Q. He will be more than happy to tell you. He believes that Q because he believes that P and that P shows that Q.

Should we accept Oliver's explanation? Suppose we flesh out the story a little: it turns out that Oliver loves conspiracy theories. He has conspiracy theories about the assassination of JFK, alien landings in New Mexico, and all manner of other things. He is biased to believe such theories and to disbelieve official accounts. He is generally gullible and has a poor grasp of logic, statistics, and probability. He is jumps to conclusions and has little sense of his own cognitive limitations. These are all statements about what might be called Oliver's 'intellectual character'. Bearing all this in mind, let's ask again: why does Oliver believe that Q? At this point, it's hard not to think that Oliver's own explanation in terms of the logical or evidential relations between various things he believes about 9/11 is extremely superficial. The problem with Oliver is that he has a crazy view of what happened on 9/11, and the deep explanation of this fact is an explanation in terms of his intellectual character. Oliver can talk all he likes about how the various things he believes about 9/11 fit together. Perhaps, in a certain sense, they do all fit together, but that doesn't mean that what he believes is true, or that describing his conception of the relationship between P and Q is enough to explain why he believes Q. It also needs to be added that Oliver has the beliefs he has about 9/11 because he is the way he is. This explanation of Oliver's beliefs in terms of his character is based on reasoning, but reasoning that is external to Oliver's own reasoning from P to Q; rather, it is reasoning from evidence about Oliver's intellectual character to his beliefs about 9/11.

Oliver's intellectual character comes out in lots of different ways. His view of P is one example: he thinks aircraft impacts couldn't have caused the towers to collapse because he has read statements to that effect on 9/11 conspiracy websites. He attaches insufficient weight to studies which refute such statements. He doesn't consider obvious alternative explanations of the sounds witnesses are supposed to have heard on the day, and accepts that they heard explosions, in a sense that implies the presence of explosives. His interpretation of the alleged 'evidence' for P and Q manifests a range of intellectual character defects, and his beliefs about 9/11 only really make sense to us in light of these character defects. These defects, if they are genuine character defects, will affect his thinking on other topics besides 9/11 but may well be accentuated in this case by his desire for an explanation that is, as it were, proportionate in its scale and complexity to the scale of what happened on 9/11.

To explain a belief in terms of rational linkages to other beliefs or to supporting evidence is to explain it in epistemic terms. Such explanations, which Ward Jones labels 'epistemically rationalizing doxastic explanations' (2002: 220), explain by showing that the target belief was brought about by a process which should lead to a true belief. Oliver's own explanation of his beliefs is epistemically rationalizing. The suggested explanation in terms of intellectual character defects is not epistemically rationalizing. In the terminology I used in Chapter 2, it is an *undermining non-epistemic explanation*, in the sense that the belief it explains would be threatened if Oliver were to accept the explanation. As Jones puts it, 'if and when I become convinced, rightly or wrongly, that the right explanation for a belief is non-epistemic, then the grip of that belief will be loosened' (2002: 223). If this is correct then Oliver is the one person who can't believe that he only believes Q because of an intellectual character defect; he can't believe this while continuing to believe that Q.

But is it true that Oliver *only* believes that Q because of his character defects? Oliver *does*, after all, reason from P to Q, and thinks that he believes that Q because he believes that P. Who are we to say he is wrong about this? There are two issues here: one is whether, in general, we have privileged access to why we believe what we do. The other is whether, aside from any considerations of privileged access, we are entitled in this particular case to dismiss Oliver's own account of his belief that Q. Before tackling these questions head on it would be worth taking a look at the closely related discussion in a famous paper by Nisbett and Wilson.[7] First-person explanations of one's standing attitudes aren't their main concern, but pessimists will interpret what Nisbett and Wilson argue as directly applicable to such explanations, and as vindicating both pessimism and inferentialism.

One of Nisbett and Wilson's central findings is that 'people may have little ability to report accurately on their cognitive processes' (1977: 247). In particular, people are not at all good at detecting influences on their evaluations, choices, or behaviour. In one study, people were asked to evaluate four identical pairs of nylon stockings. There was a pronounced left-to-right position effect, with the

---

[7] Nisbett and Wilson 1977.

right-most pair being preferred over the left-most by a factor of almost four to one. However, 'when asked about the reasons for their choices, no subject ever mentioned spontaneously the position of the article in the array' (1977: 243–4). It is difficult not to think of this as a case of self-ignorance: people were actually being influenced in their evaluations by positional factors of which they had no knowledge. They knew *which* pair they preferred but not *why*. Another study showed that people are increasingly less likely to assist others in distress as the number of witnesses or bystanders increases. Yet the subjects seemed 'utterly unaware of the influence of other people on their behaviour' (1977: 241). In every example of this kind, there are significant influencing factors to which people are blind, even to the extent of vehemently denying that such factors could have been influential when this possibility is raised by the experimenter.

What is going on? What accounts for our self-ignorance in such cases, and how do we ever get it right when it comes to explaining our own choices and evaluations? Nisbett and Wilson's hypothesis is very much in line with inferentialism:

We propose that when people are asked to report how a particular stimulus influenced a particular response, they do so not by consulting a memory of the mediating process but by applying or generating causal theories about the effects of that type of stimulus on that type of response. They simply make judgements, in other words, about how plausible it is that the stimulus would have influenced the response. (1977: 248)

People give defective explanations when they rely on dubious assumptions about the link between stimulus and response. Even correct reports are 'due to the incidentally correct employment of *a priori* causal theories' (1977: 233). Either way, the question 'Why did you prefer/choose/do that?' is answered by means of a theory-mediated inference. If you have a false belief about why you chose as you chose then you are, to this extent, self-ignorant, and your self-ignorance is, as inferentialism predicts, the result of a faulty inference.

How does this apply to explanations of one's own standing attitudes? Let's start with explanations of one's own desires. Suppose you are a lapsed smoker and that you suddenly and unexpectedly find yourself with the desire for a cigarette. It's a long time since you last wanted to smoke and you ask yourself why you want to smoke now. You have been under quite a bit of stress recently—you are writing a book on self-knowledge, perhaps—and you convince yourself that that's why you want to smoke. In fact, that has nothing to do with it; you actually want to smoke because you have just watched a film in which the sympathetic lead character smokes a lot. You have a theory about why you want to smoke but your theory is no good; the true explanation of your desire is much more prosaic than you realize. In other cases, the true explanation might be less prosaic. For example,

Nietzsche speculates that our desires are explained by the presence of certain drives, such as the drive to sociality, to knowledge, to fight, to sex, and to avoid boredom.[8] Be that as it may, discovering the true explanation of a desire doesn't necessarily 'undermine' the desire. The realization that you only want to smoke because you have just seen a particular movie doesn't extinguish your desire for a cigarette or make it any less intense.

Beliefs are different. If Oliver were ever to be persuaded that he only believes that Q because of intellectual character defects then that will presumably loosen the grip of his belief. However, I have envisaged Oliver as insisting that he believes that Q because he believes that P, and that P shows that Q. My question was, 'Who are we to say he is wrong about this?' It doesn't matter whether P does show that Q; what matters is whether Oliver *thinks* that P shows that Q and that that's why he believes that Q. We can now see how to respond to this: the first thing to say is that beliefs are like other attitudes in respect of our knowledge of why we have them. Just as we are sometimes wrong about why we want the things we want, or do the things we do, there is no guarantee that our beliefs about why we believe what we believe are correct. Having said that, it's also plausible that Oliver's reasoning 'P, so Q' is part of the explanation for his believing that Q. The issue is whether it is the entire explanation or the deepest explanation, since one and the same belief can be explained in different ways and at different levels. Oliver wouldn't believe Q if he didn't believe P but it's also true that he would believe neither P nor Q if he weren't biased to believe conspiracy theories.

Let's agree, then, that there is one explanation of Oliver's belief that Q in terms of his reasoning and another explanation in terms of his intellectual character. Both explanations have something going for them, but in what sense is the latter a "deeper" explanation? The thought is that it is deeper in the sense that it places Oliver's reasoning in this instance in the context of his reasoning about other related matters. The explanation in terms of his intellectual character gives us an insight into the person that Oliver is, whereas merely talking about his inferential transitions in isolation doesn't do that; it doesn't explain why a particular claim or transition which in reality has little going for it is appealing to Oliver. What he has is a world view, and that is what the non-epistemic explanation enables us to understand. You can argue about whether talk of one explanation being 'deeper' than another is defensible, but the point about self-ignorance doesn't turn on the use of that terminology. The crux of the matter is that non-epistemic factors seem to be playing an important role in Oliver's thinking, and their role is unacknowledged by Oliver. His self-ignorance is curable but at a price: in principle he could

---

[8] See Katsafanas 2012.

infer that non-epistemic factors are playing an important role in his thinking, but accepting that this is so would require him to rethink his beliefs about 9/11.

The pessimism I've been defending on the basis of OLIVER is a moderate rather than an extreme Nietzschean pessimism. Nietzsche argues that ignorance of our own attitudes in the 'knowing why' sense is incurable. My pessimist allows that you *can* sometimes infer why your attitudes are as they are, but insists on the possibility of self-ignorance even where your reasoning is as simple as 'P, so Q'. Nietzsche seems to think that non-epistemic factors are *always* what explain your attitudes but this isn't something moderate pessimism needs to say. Imagine you are a master logician who reasons 'P, so Q' without being influenced by anything other than the fact that P genuinely entails Q. In such cases of 'pure' or 'pristine' deliberation, non-epistemic factors might indeed be playing no role, and Boyle might be right that what puts you in a position to know why you believe Q is your successful deliberation. Even so, the assumption that non-epistemic factors are playing no role is justified, to the extent that it is, by an implicit theory of *you*, an implicit theory of the kind of consideration that is or is not likely to be influencing your thinking in the case at hand.

It's worth adding that the purity of the master logician's thinking is rarely replicated in real life. For most of us, most of the time, reasoning is a messy business; it's a matter of drawing less than certain conclusions from less than perfect evidence. The range of factors which can influence 'impure' reasoning or attitude-formation is bewilderingly large, which is why there is always at least the possibility that one's thinking is being influenced by factors that are beyond one's ken. The conclusions we come to are a reflection of the weight we attach to one kind of evidence over another, one theory over another. It would be nice to think that our weightings are appropriately grounded, and no doubt they sometimes are. But when there is a bias to believe, there is a corresponding bias to attach undue weight to some kinds of evidence and to discount others. The self-ignorance that pessimism describes is ultimately a reflection of how bad we are at detecting such contortions and distortions. If you don't know that you are selectively privileging certain kinds of evidence then you don't know why you believe the things you believe on the basis of that evidence.

Not knowing why your attitudes are as they are is one respect in which you might lack substantial self-knowledge. Corresponding to other varieties of substantial self-knowledge are other varieties of self-ignorance: ignorance of your character, values, and emotions. Ignorance of one's character is easy to explain, and some of it may well be motivated. We all like to think well of ourselves, and this can lead us to be self-deceived about our character traits. Aside from motivated self-deception there is also the possibility that you are ignorant of aspects of your own character because you lack the necessary conceptual resources or fail to grasp the relevance of certain kinds of evidence for the purposes of assessing your character: for example, you have evidence that you are fastidious but fail to infer you are fastidious.

Ignorance of your own values sounds more mysterious. How can you value equality without realizing it? If valuing equality is a matter of desiring to desire equality then there is no mystery: you can desire to desire something without realizing it because such desires are not self-intimating. It might come out in your treatment of others and your political and other preferences that you value equality, but you might not be sufficiently self-aware to grasp that an underlying concern with equality is what organizes your thinking across a wide range of social and political issues. Knowing your own values is, as I argued in Chapter 13, a matter of interpreting your patterns of desire and thought on the basis of an understanding of what is, and what is not relevant to having certain values rather than others. As long as knowledge of one's values is viewed as a substantial cognitive achievement, as a form of self-insight, it has to be allowed that it is a form of self-insight that it is possible for a person to lack.

Ignorance of your own emotions is straightforwardly possible in the case of complex emotions like love. Marcel infers he loves Albertine from his suffering on hearing she has left but suppose that Albertine had decided to stick around, or that Marcel didn't hear news of her departure. In either case, he would still have loved her but not known that he loved her. When it comes to what might be regarded as less complex emotions, such as fear, it might seem harder to conceive of the possibility of self-ignorance. If self-knowledge of simple emotions is non-inferential, then self-ignorance in these cases can't be the result of flawed inferences. The inferentialist's reply is to argue that even knowledge of supposedly simple emotions like fear is inferential, or at least has a significant inferential component, and that self-ignorance in these cases *can* therefore be explained along inferentialist lines: you can be afraid without realizing it because you haven't reflected, or you infer that what you are feeling is something other than fear. Since the dividing line between different emotions isn't always sharp, there is always the possibility self-ignorance due to the subject misidentifying one kind of emotion for another.

The idea that knowledge of simple emotions is inferential might seem far-fetched but has empirical support. There is a famous study by Valins and Ray which describes how subjects infer their level of fear of snakes from false information about changes in their heart rate.[9] The snake-phobic subjects in

---

[9] Valins and Ray 1967.

the experiment were played recordings of what they believed falsely were their own heart beats. Then they were shown various slides, including slides of snakes. The snake slides weren't accompanied by any change in their apparent heart rate, from which the phobic subjects apparently inferred that they weren't as afraid of live snakes as they had previously thought. As a result, they were more willing to approach live snakes. This case is interesting because not only is the level of fear inferred, but the inference changes the actual level of fear. It is also suggestive that the inference is an inference from *bodily* data: given the connection between simple emotions and bodily changes (flushing, blushing, changes in heart rate and temperature), it comes as no surprise that such changes are often the basis on which a person interprets, and thereby knows, his own emotions.

In this chapter I set out to answer these three questions about self-ignorance:

1. How prevalent is it?
2. What are its sources?
3. To what extent can it be overcome?

I've concentrated on 2, on the idea that self-ignorance sometimes results from motivational factors, and sometimes from other factors, such as insufficient evidence, misinterpretation of the evidence, failure to perform the necessary inferences, and so on. To the extent that I have identified some sources of self-ignorance I have explained how self-ignorance is possible, but explaining how something is possible is different from demonstrating that it's prevalent, or even actual. So the question remains: how prevalent is self-ignorance? For all that I've said optimism is still an option: couldn't you think that self-ignorance is possible and explicable along inferentialist lines, but that in reality humans aren't actually self-ignorant?

You could think this but it wouldn't be a very sensible thing to think. Suppose you are convinced that self-ignorance is caused by a mixture of motivational and non-motivational factors. In that case, the more common these factors are the more prevalent one would expect the resulting self-ignorance to be. The prevalence among humans of the factors that cause us to be self-ignorant is, at least to some extent, an empirical matter. It's an empirical question how prone we are to misinterpreting the behavioural and psychological evidence for our own attitudes, or to what extent we are capable of avoiding various kinds of bias in thinking about our own characters. No doubt there are psychological studies that bear on these questions, but you don't have to have read these studies to realize that the cognitive vices which lead to self-ignorance are far from rare or unusual; reading great novels and talking to your friends would do just as well. Optimists who question whether self-ignorance is prevalent must either deny that the cognitive vices I have been describing in this chapter are prevalent or deny that these vices result in self-ignorance. Neither denial is remotely plausible.[10]

Having said that, it must also be admitted that there is something odd about discussing the prevalence of self-ignorance among humans, as if all humans are the same in this respect. We aren't equally reflective or sophisticated. Some of us reason better than others and engage in self-inquiry more than others. There are character traits you can only know you have if you have certain concepts which not all humans have. You might learn about yourself by reading great literature but we don't all have the time, energy, or inclination to read Proust. The point of saying this isn't to suggest that only the clever or educated can avoid self-ignorance. The truth is that no human can avoid being self-ignorant to some degree because the factors which lead to self-ignorance are so powerful and pervasive. All the same, individual differences *do* affect the degree as well as the type of self-ignorance individuals suffer from. We aren't all the same.

To what extent, and by what means, can self-ignorance be overcome? One way of approaching this is, at least initially, as a practical question: assuming you are as self-ignorant as the next man or woman, what can you do to overcome your self-ignorance? Once we have a list of practical steps we can assess their chances of success and thereby estimate the extent to which it might be possible for us to overcome the self-ignorance to which all humans are liable. This practical approach is in keeping with the suggestion in Chapter 5 that an account of self-knowledge for humans might be expected to provide guidance to those of us who seek self-knowledge. I described this as 'self-knowledge for human in the guidance sense', and it's reasonable to think that guidance to those who seek self-knowledge should include guidance as to the most effective ways overcoming of self-ignorance.

Sometimes overcoming self-ignorance requires no special measures because there is no obstacle that needs to be overcome. Before she has thought about it Katherine didn't know she wanted another child. When she wonders whether she wants another child it might be obvious to her that she does, and there need be nothing that blocks this realization. There is a smooth transition in this case from self-ignorance to self-knowledge but no 'overcoming' of self-ignorance except in

---

[10] Although the true extent of human self-ignorance can't be settled a priori I like this passage from a recent discussion: 'of our morally most important attitudes, of our real values and our moral character, of our intelligence, and of what really makes us happy and unhappy ... about such matters I doubt we have much knowledge at all. We live in cocoons of ignorance, especially where our self-conception is at stake. The philosophical focus on how impressive our self-knowledge is gets the most important things backwards' (Schwitzgebel 2012: 197). However, I would qualify this in one respect: we aren't all the same.

the sense that Katherine comes to know something about herself she didn't previously know. It's more natural to talk about a person 'overcoming' self-ignorance when there is an obstacle to self-knowledge or when special cognitive effort is required. This suggests that we should be concentrating on substantial self-knowledge and on practical steps for overcoming self-ignorance with regard to one's own character, emotions, and so on.

Suppose that the obstacles which prevent you from acquiring substantial self-knowledge are inattention, poor reasoning, or misinterpretation of the evidence. In that case, it might seem that the way to overcome self-ignorance is to pay attention, reason better, and be careful not to misinterpret the evidence. These are all improvements you might achieve by thinking 'slow' rather than 'fast'. The suggestion is that careful, patient, and slow self-inquiry is the key to overcoming self-ignorance, and that the more careful and patient you are the more likely you are to avoid self-ignorance. If, on the other hand, the source of your self-ignorance is motivational, then the key is to recognize that this is so. You need to be open to the idea that there may be truths about yourself you have difficulty seeing because they are unpalatable or anxiety-provoking. Acquiring self-know-ledge in such cases is a matter of steeling yourself, and making sure that your self-inquiry is as honest as possible, with as little wishful thinking as possible.

There is something to this, but less than meets the eye. Focusing your attention on your own character and emotions might end up distorting the very psycho-logical facts you are trying to uncover. Self-inquiry can be self-defeating, espe-cially if it turns into self-obsession, and the vision of someone spending a lot of time and energy in pursuit of self-knowledge is in any case not especially an attractive one. Slow thinking in the context of self-inquiry might help you to avoid certain types of illusion about yourself, but if your self-ignorance results from false assumptions or a poor background theory then thinking slowly on the basis of such assumptions or such a theory isn't necessarily going to help. However hard you try, you might find it impossible not to self-attribute to feelings and attitudes you don't have.

Other practical measures for overcoming self-ignorance are no less problem-atic. What about seeing ourselves through the eyes of others? This is less solipsistic than the project of overcoming self-ignorance through isolated self-inquiry but Wilson and Dunn point out that we aren't good at detecting how other people view us when their views are different from our own: 'rather than taking an objective look at how other people view them and noticing the fact that this view might differ from their own, people often assume that other people see them the way they see themselves' (2004: 508). As for observing your own behaviour and tackling one's self-ignorance on that basis there is always the danger of this resulting in ever more sophisticated fabrications rather than self-revelation.

This adds up to a pessimistic view of the prospects for overcoming self-ignorance. It's not that there is nothing you can do to tackle the most challenging forms of self-ignorance; no doubt the practical steps I have described are helpful to some extent but it's important not to exaggerate their prospects of success. The worst form of self-ignorance is ignorance of one's own self-ignorance, and overcoming such second-order self-ignorance isn't so much a matter of engaging in prolonged self-inquiry as approaching questions about the extent which self-ignorance can be overcome in a spirit of humility: the unknown unknowns about the self need to become known unknowns. There is just no getting away from the fact that substantial self-knowledge is often hard to get, and that we have less of it than many of us we like to think in our more optimistic moments. We need to be realistic, and that means acknowledging the full extent to which human beings can be, and frequently are, as opaque to themselves as they are to each other.

Should we care about the pervasiveness and intractability of self-ignorance? To the extent it's possible to overcome some of our self-ignorance by therapy, self-inquiry, or some other effortful means is it worth the effort? That depends on the value of self-knowledge. It's easy to see why some forms of self-knowledge, such as knowledge of your own abilities, has practical value but what about knowledge of your own attitudes or character? What possible use is that? If most self-knowledge is of little value—practical or otherwise—then pessimism about the prospects of overcoming self-ignorance is something we can happily live with. Yet both philosophers and non-philosophers tend to assume that self-knowledge is valuable, and that more is better than less. The next question is whether they right about this.

15

The Value of Self-Knowledge

What's so good about self-knowledge and bad about self-ignorance? Suppose I'm right that self-ignorance of various kinds is inevitable and normal for human beings, and that we are all, at least to some extent, 'strangers to ourselves'. Should we be upset? If by making an effort it's possible to overcome some of our self-ignorance is it worth making the effort? Obviously the answers to these questions depend on the answers to many other questions: just how self-ignorant are we? What kinds of self-ignorance do we suffer from? How much effort would be required to overcome our self-ignorance? However, underlying these questions is a more basic question: what is the value of self-knowledge? Humans are prone to thinking that self-knowledge matters, and some pay therapists large amounts of money in pursuit of it. Are we right to think that self-knowledge is worth having and even paying for?

The natural assumption that self-knowledge is valuable is the assumption that various forms of what I've been calling 'substantial' self-knowledge are valuable. If you are thinking of joining the army it's probably good to know if you are a coward. In this context, 'good to know' means 'useful to know'; you will save yourself a lot of trouble and distress if you realize before signing up that you aren't cut out for life in the military. It's less obvious what good it does you to know that you believe you are wearing socks. It's hard to imagine a more seemingly worthless form of self-knowledge, and yet the little that philosophers have written about the value of self-knowledge has focused on just this kind of case. It is not hard to work out why: the value of substantial self-knowledge is supposedly obvious, and so isn't worthy of philosophical attention. In sharp contrast, the value of knowing your own standing beliefs and other attitudes is far from obvious. That's why philosophers who think that this form of self-knowledge is valuable feel the need to explain how and why, usually by linking it with rationality.

As we will see, the idea that intentional self-knowledge is a precondition of rationality doesn't have much going for it. Another idea that doesn't have much going for it is that the value of substantial self-knowledge is too obvious to need explaining. You could think that substantial self-knowledge is intrinsically valuable or that its value is instrumental. It doesn't look like substantial self-knowledge has intrinsic value. Something is intrinsically valuable just if it is valuable or desirable for its own sake rather than because it promotes some other good. If X is valuable only because it leads to Y, then X is extrinsically valuable as long as Y is valuable. If Y is valuable but it is impossible or inappropriate to attempt to explain what makes it valuable in more basic terms, then Y has intrinsic value. So, for example, you might think that well-being is an example of something intrinsically valuable because its value can't be further explained. Well-being, for present purposes, includes happiness and success: it is what makes your life go better.[1] In contrast, it's reasonable to ask why self-knowledge is valuable; it's not like asking why well-being is valuable. Indeed, it seems likely that many people who think that self-knowledge is valuable think this because they think, perhaps mistakenly, that having it increases your well-being: crudely, your life is likely to go better with it than without it.

The idea that substantial self-knowledge is valuable because it promotes well-being isn't the only way of making sense of the notion that its value is extrinsic. You can imagine a high-minded philosopher who believes that the true value of self-knowledge derives from its links with "higher" ideals like authenticity and unity. To be authentic is to be true to yourself, and the suggestion might be that you can't be *true* to yourself unless you *know* yourself.[2] On this account, substantial self-knowledge is necessary for authenticity. You can argue about the value of authenticity, but if authenticity is valuable then so is self-knowledge. In the same way, you might think that a unified life, that is, one whose various elements fit together in a rationally and morally coherent way, must be underpinned by self-knowledge.

These are examples of what might be called *high road* arguments for the value of self-knowledge. They are 'high road' in two senses: they explain the value of self-knowledge by reference to abstract, high-sounding ideals, and they regard self-knowledge as necessary for the achievement of these ideals. The point of high road arguments is not to deny that self-knowledge can promote well-being or, as Carruthers puts it, 'make all the difference to the overall success of one's life' (2011: xi). The worry is that such explanations of the value of self-knowledge are too prosaic, and that its value goes deeper than that. One of my questions apart

---

[1] Scanlon 1998: 141.

[2] Feldman and Hazlett argue in their 2013 paper that the value of authenticity doesn't explain the value of self-knowledge. There is more on this below. Joshua Knobe points out that ordinary ethical thinking attaches a lot of importance to 'being yourself' or being true to yourself. See Knobe 2005.

from whether high road arguments are any good, is whether they are well-motivated, that is, whether it's right to think of self-knowledge as having a value that is deeper and more fundamental than its supposed role in promoting well-being.

I want to suggest that we should be sceptical about this and other aspects of high road arguments, even though it can't be denied that some such arguments have something going for them. The alternative to a high road account of the value of self-knowledge is a *low road* account. Low road accounts are content to explain the value of self-knowledge in pragmatic or practical terms, by reference to its contribution human well-being. Explaining the value of self-knowledge in this way doesn't means that you demean or devalue it. There isn't much doubt that self-knowledge *can* and often *does* promote well-being, and this is about as 'deep' an explanation of its value as one could reasonably wish for. As far as low road explanations are concerned there is no reason to think that there has to be more to it than that: there doesn't have to be, and there isn't. One attractive feature of low road explanations is that they offer some protection against scepticism about the value of self-knowledge. They do this because they don't see its value as depending on links with supposedly higher ideals whose own value is open to question. They are refreshingly straightforward and concrete. They keep things simple, and don't offer grandiose explanation of the value of self-knowledge.

Leaving aside questions about what motivates them, are high road explanations any good in their own terms? One line of attack questions the value of ideals like authenticity and unity. A different line of attack targets the thesis that substantial self-knowledge is *necessary* for authenticity and unity. The suggestion is that it's possible to live an authentic and unified life without substantial self-knowledge. If this is right, but you are still reluctant to abandon high road arguments altogether, then you can always retreat to a fallback position which says that self-knowledge matters not because it is strictly necessary for authenticity and unity but because it makes it easier to be authentic and unified. On this account, self-knowledge facilitates the achievement of high ideals, but even this is open to question. Radical sceptics about high road arguments can see no connection between self-knowledge and the high ideals which supposedly account for its value. Some even suggest that self-knowledge can obstruct the achievement of such ideals.

The plan for this chapter is as follows: first, I will criticize arguments for the view that intentional self-knowledge—knowledge of one's own thoughts, beliefs, desires, and other such 'intentional' mental states—is indispensable for rationality. Then I will move on to other substantial self-knowledge and consider various high road arguments for its indispensability. This will involve getting clearer about notions like authenticity and unity. Lastly, I will look at some low road arguments for the value of self-knowledge. I want to suggest that high road arguments face some formidable challenges, which can only be dealt with, to the extent that they can be dealt with, by retreating to their 'fallback' versions. Even then, there are questions about the value of authenticity and unity, though I won't be focusing on these questions here. Although high road accounts aren't totally useless, it's better to take the low road. High road accounts offer us 'depth', but the depth they offer is largely illusory. Low road accounts demystify self-knowledge and give us everything we need. However, they do raise questions about how much philosophy can contribute to our understanding of the value of self-knowledge.

Why would anyone think that intentional self-knowledge is essential for rationality? In Chapter 4, I talked about Burge's idea that self-knowledge is necessary for so-called critical reasoning. You need intentional self-knowledge to be a Burgean critical reasoner because such reasoning requires thinking about one's thoughts, and also that that thinking 'be normally knowledgeable' (Burge 1998: 248). So if critical reasoning is essential for rationality then so is intentional self-knowledge. But the problem with arguing this way is that the more you build into the notion of critical reasoning the harder it is to maintain that it is essential for rationality. A simple way of bringing this out is to go back to Peacocke's idea of 'second-tier' thinking.[3] First-tier thought is thought about the world, without consideration of relations of support, evidence, or consequence between thought contents. Consideration of such relations is built into second-tier thinking. Bearing this in mind, we can now argue like this: second-tier thinking is sufficient for rationality but doesn't require self-knowledge. From which it follows that rationality doesn't require self-knowledge.

In Peacocke's neat example of second-tier thinking you infer from the fact that no car is parked in your driveway that your spouse is not home yet. Then you remember that the car might have been taken to have its faulty brakes repaired, and suspend your original belief that your spouse is not home yet; you realize that the absence of the car is not necessarily good evidence that she isn't home. As Peacocke comments, there is nothing in this little fragment of thought which involves the self-ascription of belief. Yet there is thinking about relations of evidence and support, leading to the suspension of one's initial belief. If you can get as far as thinking in the manner Peacocke describes then it's hard to believe that you aren't rational or, even in the non-technical sense, a 'critical

---

[3] Peacocke 1998: 277.

reasoner'. And yet your thoughts are all about the world rather than about your own thoughts. The fact that you lack intentional self-knowledge might mean that you aren't a *Burgean* critical reasoner but that has little to do with whether you are rational being, thinking rationally.

Clearly, the notion of 'rationality' is fairly elastic but this should make you doubly suspicious of attempts to establish the value of intentional self-knowledge on the basis that it is indispensable for rationality. It's hard to avoid thinking that philosophers who argue in this way are merely extracting from the notion of rationality what they themselves put into it. This is basically the problem that afflicts Shoemaker's many arguments for the thesis that 'given certain conceptual capacities, rationality necessarily goes with self-knowledge' (2003: 128). One of Shoemaker's ideas is that 'it is a condition of being a rational subject that one's belief system will regularly be revised with the aim of achieving and preserving consistency and internal coherence, and that such revision requires awareness on the part of the subject of what the contents of the system are' (2009: 39). Shoemaker agrees that the updating of one's belief system can be largely auto-matic and sub-personal but insists that in an important class of cases the revision and updating does require beliefs about one's beliefs:

These are cases in which the revision of the belief system requires an investigation on the part of the subject, one that involves conducting experiments, collecting data relevant to certain issues, or initiating reasoning aimed at answering certain questions. Such an investigation will be an intentional activity on the part of the subject, and one motivated in part by beliefs about the current contents of the belief system ... Having full human rationality requires being such that one's revisions and updating of one's belief system can involve such investigations, and this requires awareness of, and so beliefs about, the contents of the system. (2009: 39)

There isn't much here about the importance of self-*knowledge*, as distinct from beliefs about one's own beliefs, but let that pass: the basic idea is that 'full human rationality' requires the capacity to form beliefs about one's beliefs, and we can grant for present purposes that such second-order beliefs must be normally knowledgeable. The crux of the matter is whether 'fully rational' belief revision requires second-order belief.

It's hard to see why. In Peacocke's example, you aren't conducting experiments but you are collecting data relevant to certain issues, in this case the issue of whether your spouse is home, and you have initiated reasoning aimed at answer-ing the question whether she is at home. Your investigation of this question is an intentional activity but beliefs about your beliefs don't come into it. You revise your belief that she is at home because you realize that your evidence isn't necessarily good evidence that she is at home. *That she is at home* is the content of your initial belief but you don't have to think of it as *what you believe* in order to understand the limitations of your evidence and take the necessary steps to modify your belief system. Your intentional activity can be partly motivated by beliefs about what are *in fact* the contents of your belief system without your having to think of them *as* what you believe. All your attention is focused on the world, on what is the case, and not on what you believe to be the case.

It might be objected that this doesn't really do justice to what Shoemaker has in mind when he talks about the intentional activity of belief revision. You aren't revising your beliefs intentionally if you don't know that this is what you are doing, and that means knowing what you believe. But then it's not clear why being able to revise your beliefs in this sense is in any sense a condition of being a rational subject. Belief revision, as Shoemaker conceives of it, is a reflective and self-conscious process, and it might be true that intentional self-knowledge is built into this particular form of belief revision. But then the question is: why do you have to be able to engage in reflective, self-conscious belief revision in order to qualify as a rational being? It's helpful to think again about second-tier thinking: if you can engage in second-tier thinking then you are, to that extent, a rational being, but 'a thinker can engage in second-tier thought without conceptualizing the process as one of belief-assessment and revision' (Peacocke 1998: 277).

If you are a Kant aficionado you might be tempted to say at this point that if you can't self-ascribe your own thoughts then they can't be conscious thoughts. That is the point of Kant's insistence that it must be possible for what he calls the 'I think' to accompany all my representations if they are to mean anything to me. It's not clear that Kant is right about this, since non-human animals presumably have conscious representations without being able to attach an 'I think' to them. It's also unclear what any of this has to do with rationality: even if consciousness requires self-consciousness, does rationality require consciousness? David Rosenthal points out that rational thinking is not always conscious and that rational solutions to problems often come to us as a result of thinking that isn't conscious. Indeed, there is some evidence that 'complex decisions are more rational when the thinking that led to them was not conscious' (2008: 832). Maybe you can be rational without being conscious, and you can also be conscious without being self-conscious. If this is right then you aren't going to get very far in trying to explain the value of intentional self-knowledge in Kantian terms.

None of this is to say that intentional self-knowledge is redundant or plays no part in our cognitive lives. Whether or not you think that intentional self-knowledge is essential to rationality per se, there is no denying that the reflective reasoning which philosophers like Burge and Shoemaker have in mind represents a significant and perhaps distinctively human cognitive achievement. Intentional self-knowledge makes it possible for us to think about our own beliefs and desires in ways that go beyond mere second-tier thinking. To the extent that reflective reasoning is valuable to us, so is the intentional self-knowledge which facilitates it. The interesting question is not, 'Does reflective, critical reasoning require self-knowledge?', but rather, 'What's so great about reflective, critical reasoning?' The answer to this question might seem obvious but isn't. Being too reflective and critical can slow you down and lead to poorer decision-making than fast or unconscious thinking. This suggests that the value of intentional self-knowledge is highly context-dependent, as is the value of the kind of thinking it makes possible. It can be good to be reflective, but sometimes it's counter-productive.

Bearing these complications in mind, perhaps it's worth trying a different approach to explaining the value of intentional self-knowledge. Instead of focusing on rationality maybe it's better to focus on examples of substantial self-knowledge such as knowledge of your own character. To know your own character you have to know your own beliefs, desires, and other attitudes. So if substantial self-knowledge is valuable then so is intentional self-knowledge, substantial or otherwise. What makes it valuable, on this view, is its essential contribution to *substantial* self-knowledge. You need to know your attitudes in order to know yourself, and this brings us neatly to the next item on the agenda: what exactly is the value of substantial self-knowledge? In particular, how good are the prospects for a 'high road' explanation of the value of substantial self-knowledge? If the prospects are good then we can remain reasonably optimistic about the value of the intentional self-knowledge which substantial self-knowledge presupposes. Unfortunately, however, matters aren't quite so straightforward.

The first 'high road' explanation of the value of substantial self-knowledge appeals to the notion of authenticity. Let's assume that to be authentic is to be 'true to yourself'. You might wonder whether authenticity, as such, has any value. Perhaps Stalin was being true to himself in ordering the summary trial and execution of thousands of former comrades but that doesn't go on the plus side of a cosmic ledger whose minus side is infinitely long. Being true to yourself is not much good if the self to which you are being true happens to be a monster. Scepticism about the value of authenticity per se is a serious possibility but let's not worry about that here. The issue is whether, *on the assumption* that it's good to be authentic, what makes substantial self-knowledge valuable is that it is indispensable for authenticity.

What would it be to be 'true to yourself'? Suppose we say that to be true to yourself is to be true to your own character, values, and emotions. If you are by nature generous then you are being true to yourself when you behave generously. If for some reason you fail to behave generously on a particular occasion then your behaviour is 'out of character', and you aren't being 'true to yourself'. Similarly, being true to your values and emotions means thinking and behaving in ways that reflect your values and emotions. When you are being true to yourself your actions and thoughts reflect the way you are because they are appropriately influenced by the way you are. If you are a generous person but only give generously at a charity event in order to impress your date then you aren't really being true to yourself because it isn't your usually generous nature that is motivating you to act on this occasion.

On this view of authenticity, why would you think it requires self-knowledge? A high road explanation of the value of self-knowledge would have to assume that you can't be true to your character, values, and emotions unless you know your character, values, and emotions. It's hard to see why. Why would you have to *know* you are generous in order to *be* generous, or to behave generously because you are generous? If you are generous, your generosity might be enough to explain your generous behaviour, and self-knowledge needn't come into it. The same goes for other character traits. In a previous chapter, I gave the example of fastidious Woody. Now imagine teenage Woody. Teenage Woody is as fastidious as grown up Woody but in order to fit in with his teenage friends he talks and behaves as if he couldn't care less about neatness and order. When he goes to the cinema he litters the floor with popcorn, just like his friends, even though doing so makes him inwardly cringe. In aping the behaviour of his friends Woody isn't being true to himself, and the reason he isn't being true to himself is that he is pretending to be other than he is. To be authentic he would need to stop pretending, but that has nothing to do with him knowing that he is fastidious. He doesn't need to know or believe that he is fastidious in order for him not to pretend to be like his friends. In order to be authentic his actions would need to reflect his true character, and his actions can do that without being mediated by *knowledge* of his true character, or any other substantial self-knowledge.

Being true to one's values and emotions is no different from this. You don't need to know your values in order for them to be reflected by your thoughts and behaviour, any more than you need to know your emotions in order for you to be true to them. Indeed, when it is a question of being true to your emotions you might think that self-knowledge can actually be an obstacle to authenticity. This is what Simon Feldman and Allan Hazlett argue. They distinguish several different conceptions or aspects of authenticity. On one conception, what it is to be authentic is to avoid pretence, and Feldman and Hazlett confine themselves to arguing that authenticity in this sense doesn't require self-knowledge. This is the point I have just been making. There is, however, also the option of understanding authenticity as spontaneity. On this account you aren't being true to yourself when you aren't being 'spontaneous'. Feldman and Hazlett argue that, far from *requiring* self-knowledge, authenticity on this conception is *incompatible* with it.

They give the example of self-conscious Sam, a philosopher from Boringtown, Connecticut, who had an affair with visiting speaker Grace and is now wondering whether to join her at her seaside Mediterranean villa. After much self-investigation self-conscious Sam concludes 'I am in love with Grace, therefore I shall go on a tryst.' Compare unselfconscious Sam. His story is the same, with the same resulting action, but minus the self-investigation and self-knowledge. He also decides to visit Grace but makes his decision spontaneously, not knowing whether it is the right thing to do. Unselfconscious Sam takes a romantic risk, and this leads Feldman and Hazlett to comment:

[U]nselfconscious Sam enjoys a species of intuitively appealing authenticity, which self-conscious Sam lacks. The difference comes down (at least in part) to self-knowledge: unselfconscious Sam lacks self-knowledge, while self-conscious Sam has self-knowledge and acts on that basis . . . Self-conscious Sam's action is motivated by the knowledge that he loves Grace; unselfconscious Sam's action is motivated (only) by his love of Grace . . . In the case of self-conscious Sam, self-knowledge interferes with a proper focus of his attention on Grace. His action seems less motivated by genuine romantic love, and more by his self-directed concern. (2013: 177)

Borrowing Bernard Williams' terminology, Feldman and Hazlett suspect self-conscious Sam of having 'one thought too many', a thought about himself and his own feelings. When Sam wonders how he feels about Grace his thinking is unappealingly self-focused, and that is why his decision to visit her lacks the authenticity of unselfconscious Sam's decision to visit. If authenticity is spontaneity then what it requires in such cases is not self-knowledge but self-ignorance.

This example raises tough questions about our understanding of authenticity, as well as the relationship between self-knowledge and spontaneity. Suppose that unselfconscious Sam is normally an unspontaneous and careful person who hardly ever makes important life decisions without thinking through the pros and cons. However, on this occasion he is smitten and rushes off to see Grace without asking himself any of the questions he would normally be asking himself in these circumstances about his feelings for Grace or the wisdom of going to visit her. His behaviour has an uncharacteristic wantonness. On the assumption that being true to one's own character is at least necessary for being authentic, Sam's behaviour on this occasion is *in*authentic. He might have acted 'spontaneously' in deciding to visit Grace, but that doesn't alter the fact that he wasn't being true to himself. Spontaneity isn't authentic when it is out of character, and it's not clear in any case that Sam's wantonness is a form of spontaneity, as distinct from a manifestation of a loss of his characteristic self-control.

It's worth adding that romantic love is a special case. Suppose that Sam's question is not whether he should visit Grace in Greece but whether he should switch from philosophy to investment banking. It would be bizarre to suppose that a spontaneous, spur-of-the-moment decision to switch to banking is more 'authentic' than a properly thought through decision. In arriving at his decision, self-conscious Sam might ask himself 'What do I want to do with my life?' or 'Will I be any happier as a banker?' Although these questions are self-focused, that doesn't make the resulting choice any less authentic. In this case, authenticity is compatible with self-knowledge, but still doesn't require it. Even if Sam is by nature a reflective person who rarely leaps before he looks, being true to his reflective nature only requires him to *think about* what would be best for him before decides. He doesn't need to *know* what would be best for him.

This isn't quite the end of the road for the 'authenticity account' of the value of self-knowledge. Substantial self-knowledge might not be necessary for authenticity, but there is still the fallback position that you are more likely to be true to your own character, emotions, and values if you know what they are. There is something to this. After all, most humans are buffeted by external events over which they have little control, and can easily be led by such events to operate in ways that are out of character, at odds with their values, or in some other way inauthentic. The fallback position maintains that the likelihood of this happening can be reduced by reflecting in an admittedly self-focused way on one's values and character. For example, imagine being tempted to do something that doesn't feel right, and thinking 'I don't do that sort thing'. This can be read as a statement about your values, your character, or both. Recognizing that you don't do that sort of thing can help you not to do that sort of thing on this occasion, whatever the pressures or temptations. This claim has some plausibility, and is probably the best that can be done for a high road explanation of the value of self-knowledge by reference to authenticity. Having given up on the notion that self-knowledge is necessary for authenticity, those who still want to take the high road should concentrate on the different ways in which substantial self-knowledge can *promote* or *facilitate* authenticity. Thinking self-consciously about who you are—about what kind of person you are and would like to be—can make a difference to what you do by anchoring your thoughts about what to do in who you really are.

The next high road argument for the value of substantial self-knowledge claims you need this kind of self-knowledge in order to live a properly *unified* life. What is that? Imagine your life as constituted by your standing attitudes, actions, decisions, relationships, projects, and so on. Sometimes it's very easy to see how all the various elements that constitute a life fit together. For example, your decisions make sense in the light of your values, your personal relationships and life projects are mutually supportive, and so on. Coherence in this sense is about intelligibility rather than mere consistency, though consistency certainly comes into it. A disunified life is one whose various elements do not fit together in a way that is rationally or morally intelligible, and the question is whether it's possible to live a unified life without substantial self-knowledge.

This issue can be approached via the following semi-rhetorical question: how are you supposed to make it the case that the different elements of your life fit together if you don't know what the different elements are? But if you know the different elements of your life and how they fit together then what you have is substantial self-knowledge. Your self-knowledge can regulate your life and maintain its coherence and unity by making it clear to you when a proposed course of action doesn't mesh with your values, projects, or other elements of your life. For example, suppose you are doing your tax return and you think of a barely legal tax avoidance scheme which would substantially reduce your tax liability. This is another case in which you might think 'I don't do that sort of thing'. This is now not just a statement about your character and values but also about how you live your life. The realization that cheating on your taxes is inconsistent with a life like yours may deter you from cheating on your taxes. If it does, then the unity of your life is preserved by your deciding not to cheat on your taxes, and you decide not to cheat on your taxes because you know you don't do that sort of thing.

One question about this argument is whether, in order for the various elements of your life to be unified, you need to *make it the case* that they are unified. Imagine deciding not to cheat on your taxes, but not because you are thinking about the unity of your life. You decide not to cheat because you think it's wrong to cheat. By deciding to pay your taxes you are 'making it the case' that your life remains consistent in this respect but self-knowledge does not come into it because you aren't paying taxes *with a view* to preserving the unity of your life: you don't refrain from cheating because you know or believe that you don't do that sort of thing. Self-knowledge would only be needed if 'making it the case' that your life is unified is something you do intentionally and self-consciously. Perhaps you can't intentionally and self-consciously 'make it the case' that your life is unified if you don't know its different elements and how they fit together but you can live a unified life without setting out to live in a unified way, just as you can live authentically without setting out to live authentically.

One way of putting this would be to say that the unity of a life can be a spontaneous or 'given' unity rather than a reflective or 'imposed' unity. A reflective unity is the product of self-focused thinking: your life is unified because you think in a first-personal way about what to do and how to live. That's what you are doing when you are thinking thoughts such as 'I don't do that sort of thing'. A given unity is one that doesn't arise as a result of this kind of thinking. The objection to the unity account of the value of self-knowledge is that the unity of your life can be a given unity, and so not depend on self-knowledge. It's worth adding that the fact that the unity of your life is not anchored in self-knowledge doesn't make its unity accidental. Just because the thought 'I don't do that sort of thing' played no part in your decision not to cheat on your taxes, that doesn't make it an accident that you declared all of your income. You declared your income because you *are* the kind of person who declares his income, and not because you *know* that you are that kind of person.

So much for the idea that self-knowledge is valuable because you can't live a unified life without it. You could argue in response that a *reflectively* unified life has more going for it than a spontaneously unified life, but this still won't explain the value of self-knowledge. If a reflectively unified life has any added value that is because of the value we attach to self-knowledge, yet the value of self-knowledge is what we were supposed to be explaining. The best explanation of the value of self-knowledge is a fallback explanation: the point about substantial self-knowledge is not that your life can't be unified without it but that your life is more likely to be unified, or be better unified, if you have self-knowledge. Why is that? There is no knockdown argument available, just a piece of common-sense psychology: you are more likely to live consistently and coherently if you reflect on how you live your life and on what fits your existing commitments, values, relationships, and so on. You are more likely to be led astray if you don't do this kind of thinking and just go with the flow.

It's not clear how much weight to attach to this common-sense argument. One issue is whether it's actually true that self-focused thinking is a more reliable route to unified living than thinking that isn't self-focused. If you are basically honest and law-abiding, are you any less likely to cheat on your taxes if you think about whether it's like you to cheat than if you think in impersonal terms about the acceptability or otherwise of cheating? It's certainly possibly to imagine self-focused thinking as a highly effective tool for regulating your life, but it's just as easy to imagine such thinking as inefficient, disruptive, and unreliable. It may not be quite clear to you what meshes with the rest of your life, and you might be more likely to be true to yourself if you just concentrate on the rights and wrongs of tax avoidance than if you try to calculate what would uphold the coherence of your life. The reason too much navel gazing can easily lead you astray is that it's hard to think clearly and honestly about your own life. The necessary perceptiveness and self-honesty may be in short supply for any number of reasons, including fatigue, self-deception, and confusion.

There is also the question why unity matters anyway. There is no doubt that 'I don't do that sort of thing' can give expression to a disagreeable self-importance and conservatism that limits the possibilities of change and destroys any element of spontaneity in one's life. Too much consistency can be deadening, and doing what you don't always do can be more fulfilling and meaningful than sticking to the well-trodden and familiar pathways of your life. However, there is also a point beyond which a lack of consistency or coherence can threaten your well-being. Most of us need to find our lives rationally and morally intelligible, and self-knowledge facilitates a degree of unity, consistency, and coherence in our lives. This explains the value of self-knowledge in line with the fallback position: to the extent that unity matters, and that self-knowledge facilitates unity, self-knowledge also matters. Unity matters to some extent, and self-knowledge facilitates the unity of life to some extent. To that extent, self-knowledge matters.

This is about as far as we need to go in assessing the merits of high road explanations of the value of substantial self-knowledge. Two things are striking about such explanations: the abstractness of the ideals by reference to which they explain the value of self-knowledge and their insistence on the indispensability of self-knowledge. The fallback approach targets the second of these features and does so very effectively. Once you have the fallback position clearly in view it becomes hard to see why anyone would care deeply about indispensability. Why does it matter whether self-knowledge is strictly indispensable for, say, unity if it can be shown that self-knowledge promotes unity? Searching for necessary conditions is a bad habit you can pick up by reading too much Kant. When Kant tries to bring out the importance of a certain kind of knowledge, or a certain kind of thinking, he often does so by talking about how indispensable it is for something else we do or value. His arguments break down because it is extraordinarily difficult to establish non-trivial indispensability claims. You think that X is necessary for Y but then someone else thinks up a way in which you can have Y without X. That's how it is with high road arguments for the value of self-knowledge. In every case in which it looks as though self-knowledge might be necessary for the achievement of some high ideal it turns out not to be. However, the right reaction to this is not disappointment but reflection on why it ever seemed a good idea to defend claims of this form. Self-knowledge is still valuable if it leads to other goods, even if those other goods could be achieved without it.

Necessary conditions aren't necessary, however neat it would be if they could be established.

Although the fallback view doesn't explicitly target the other dimension of high road arguments, their emphasis on high ideals like authenticity, unity, and self-improvement, there is certainly room for debate about whether it's right to explain the value of self-knowledge in such abstract terms. We have seen that unity and authenticity can be overrated, in the former case because it can be deadening, and in the latter case because it's not clear what is so great about being true to yourself. We clearly don't want people like Stalin and Hitler to be true to themselves but authenticity can be a mixed blessing even in less extreme cases. Do we want garden-variety prigs and bores to be true to themselves, or over-ambitious politicians who would sell their own grandmothers in return for high office? In the case of the thrusting politician who metaphorically does just that, do we view them any more favourably when someone points out, 'Well, at least he was being true to himself'? No doubt there are limits to how far scepticism about authenticity can be pushed, but it's hard not to think that the effectiveness of high road explanations of the value of self-knowledge is diminished by such scepticism.

In that case, why not take the low road? The most straightforward low road account of the value of self-knowledge says that having more of it rather than less of it makes a positive difference to one's overall happiness or well-being. There are several reasons why, at least from a philosophical perspective, you might be reluctant to take the low road. Here are three:

1. You think that it devalues self-knowledge to explain its value in these terms.
2. You aren't convinced that having self-knowledge does make a positive difference to your well-being.
3. You don't see what philosophy has to contribute to our understanding of the value of self-knowledge if we take the low road.

Taking these in turn, 1 can be dismissed fairly quickly. Why does it devalue self-knowledge to explain its value by reference to well-being? There might be something to this if you think that its value is intrinsic rather than extrinsic, but that is not a defensible view. It's really just a form of obscurantism to say that self-knowledge is intrinsically valuable, and the possibility of explaining its value in pragmatic terms shows why: to say that self-knowledge is valuable because it increases our well-being *is* to explain its value in more basic terms, by reference to another good. You might wonder whether this account satisfies our longing for a deeper explanation of the value of self-knowledge. Perhaps not, but the appropriate reaction to this is to question the longing. Talk of the connection between self-knowledge and 'higher' ideals has a nice ring to it but low road explanations see the depth on offer in high road explanations as largely bogus. The downgrading of well-being as the main source of its value is a form of puritanism about self-knowledge which there is no very compelling reason to endorse. There remains the nagging thought that there must surely be more to it than that, but *why* must there be? On any sane view, what the low road explanation offers us should be good enough, even if high road explanations offer tantalizing glimpses of what more can be said.

There are three kinds of worry that might underpin 2:

(a) Having more rather than less self-knowledge doesn't always make a positive difference to one's overall well-being. You can have too much self-knowledge for your own good, and less can be better than more.

(b) In cases in which self-knowledge seems to be making a positive difference what is making the difference isn't your knowledge but your beliefs about yourself. These beliefs don't have to be true, or qualify as knowledge, in order to be beneficial.

(c) Even if self-knowledge is good for you that doesn't mean that seeking out self-knowledge is good for you. There are costs in terms of time, effort, and energy to the pursuit of self-knowledge, and these might outweigh the value of self-knowledge.

With regard to (a), it's undoubtedly true that self-knowledge can be a mixed blessing. There may be painful truths about yourself you would be better off not knowing, and there is no question that mild self-ignorance can increase levels of well-being. For example, having a more positive self-image than is warranted by the facts might be beneficial. Depending on the kind of person you are, self-illusions can motivate self-improvement, and thereby make your life go better. However, there is also plenty of evidence that only moderate self-illusions are beneficial, and that extreme self-illusions can easily undermine well-being.[4] By and large, the positive effects of self-knowledge outweigh the mild benefits of self-ignorance. Self-illusions can promote self-improvement but so can self-knowledge. Suppose that you are chronically unassertive and that your lack of assertiveness is causing problems in your personal and professional life. You are unhappy because you have the impression that people don't take you seriously but it's a mystery to you why they don't take you seriously. Eventually you figure it out and sign up for assertiveness training. As a result you become more assertive and your life goes better. In this example, it is knowing that you aren't

---

[4] See Wilson and Dunn 2004: 511–12.

assertive—a piece of painful and perhaps hard-won self-knowledge—which prompts you to do things which boost your well-being. In this case, as in many others, the link between self-knowledge and well-being is indirect. It isn't realizing you are unassertive that increases your well-being but the things you do as a result of realizing that you are unassertive. Obviously, you could figure out that you have a problem and still do nothing about it. Self-knowledge without the motivation to improve gets you nowhere, but it's part and parcel of what gets you to improve when you are motivated.

A way of putting this would be to say that self-knowledge serves as a guide. Knowing what you are like, good at, what makes you happy, what is important to you, or how you feel can improve your choices and thinking in ways that objectively make your life go better. But does it matter that you *know* these things, and don't just have the corresponding beliefs? This is the question (b) raises. In the last example, knowing that you are chronically unassertive might prompt you to try to be more assertive, but merely believing you are unassertive would presumably have the same effect. The belief doesn't even have to be *true*, and so doesn't even have to amount to self-*knowledge*: the belief that you are unassertive might encourage you to be more assertive even if you are already assertive.

There are two things to say in response to this. First, it *does* sometimes matter that your beliefs are true. In the case of the coward who is saved from a life of misery in the army by his recognition that he is a coward, he is better off for not having joined the army because it's *true* that he is a coward. In the last example, being more assertive makes your life go well because you *are* chronically unassertive. Being more assertive when you are already assertive enough might diminish your well-being. Second, depending on your theory of knowledge, the difference between merely having the true belief that you are unassertive and knowing you are unassertive might be the difference between your true belief having an unreliable source and its having a reliable source, or the difference between having a true belief about yourself on inadequate grounds and having the same belief on adequate grounds. There is no denying that having a true belief on inadequate grounds can lead to increases in well-being, but it's important not to exaggerate the significance of this. Your life will go better on the whole, and your well-being maximized, if your self-assessments are reliable and well-grounded than if they are not. What matters is not just that you have true beliefs about your character, values, talents, and so on, but that your self-assessments are reliably true, that you can trust them and act on their basis. This kind of trustworthiness is what you get when your self-assessments are not just true but knowledgeably true: self-knowledge is better than mere true belief because when you have self-knowledge your self-assessments are guided by the facts.[5]

As for (c), there is no question time spent seeking self-knowledge isn't always time well spent. Self-knowledge can result from self-inquiry, and self-inquiry takes time and energy. When the costs of self-inquiry outweigh the benefits of self-knowledge, the net value of self-knowledge is diminished. The principle here is that 'the disvalue of inquiry about whether P might trump the value of knowing whether P, as when acquiring knowledge about some question is not worth the cost of inquiry about that question' (Feldman and Hazlett 2013: 160). Aside from considerations of cost, there is also something deeply unattractive about the vision of the sadhu or mystic who dedicates himself to the search for self-knowledge. The self-indulgence and self-importance of such characters is hard to stomach. Still, to the extent that self-knowledge is worth having, it must sometimes be worth the effort of acquiring it. Anyway, the effort required isn't always that great. Sometimes you only have to listen to what other people are saying; the acquisition of substantial self-knowledge can be passive as well as active.

That leaves 3, the worry that philosophy has little to contribute to an understanding of the value of self-knowledge if we take the low road. This isn't exactly an objection to taking the low road since you might be happy to accept that philosophy doesn't have a great deal to contribute on this topic. After all, you don't need philosophy to tell you that self-knowledge has something to do with well-being, and if you want to understand how the two are connected you would probably do better to read the work of empirical psychologists or novelists like Proust or Henry James. Does philosophy really have anything to add? Maybe not as much as its practitioners would like to think, but not nothing. Philosophy has things to say about the nature and sources of self-knowledge, as it does about the nature and sources of well-being. It is for philosophy to explore and, if necessary, debunk claims about the links between self-knowledge and other ideals, and comment on whether the value of self-knowledge is intrinsic or extrinsic. Clearly, there are limits to what philosophy can say about the means by which self-knowledge enhances well-being or the extent to which it does so. These are empirical matters, and indeed many of the most pressing questions about self-knowledge are empirical. It's no insult to philosophy to say that these are questions it isn't really equipped to answer. Philosophy, biology, psychology, and literature all contribute to our understanding of the value of self-knowledge, and taking the low road enables you to do justice to that obvious fact.

---

[5] My argument here draws on Hyman 2006.

The last question is this: suppose it's true that the value of substantial self-knowledge has something to do with human well-being, or even ideals like authenticity or unity. Where does that leave the value of intentional self-knowledge that isn't substantial? Having rejected the suggestion that intentional self-knowledge is strictly necessary for rationality, it started to look as though its value might be related to the value of substantial self-knowledge: you can't have substantial self-knowledge unless you know your beliefs, desires, and other attitudes. In that case, can it not be said that intentional self-knowledge derives its value in part from the value of substantial self-knowledge? This wouldn't be wrong but there is more to it than that. There is now also the possibility of giving a more direct low road explanation of the value of intentional self-knowledge: having it makes it possible for us to think and reason in ways that not only make us what we are but enable us to live better than would otherwise be the case. These are the types of thinking and reasoning people like Burge and Shoemaker are interested in, and I'm suggesting that their value is also partly practical. Explanations of the value of intentional self-knowledge by reference to what is necessary for rationality are high road explanations but in this domain, as in others, the low road is more straightforward. Once again, the lesson is: when you are trying to explain the value of self-knowledge, don't be shy about stating the obvious: self-knowledge derives whatever value it has from the value of what it makes possible, and what it ultimately makes possible is for us to live well.

Bibliography

Aaronovitch, D. (2009), *Voodoo Histories: How Conspiracy Theory Has Shaped Modern History* (London: Jonathan Cape).

Alston, W. (1986), 'Does God Have Beliefs?', *Religious Studies*, 22: 287–306.

Ariely, D. (2009), *Predictably Irrational* (London: Harper).

Ariely, D. (2011), *The Upside of Irrationality* (London: Harper).

Armstrong, D. M. (1993), *A Materialist Theory of the Mind*, revised edition (London: Routledge).

Austin, J. L. (1962), *Sense and Sensibilia*, ed. G. J. Warnock (Oxford: Oxford University Press).

Ayers, M. R. (1991), *Locke, Volume 1: Epistemology* (London: Routledge).

Bar-On, D. (2004), *Speaking My Mind: Expression and Self-Knowledge* (Oxford: Oxford University Press).

Bem, D. (1972), 'Self-Perception Theory', in L. Berkowitz (ed.), *Advances in Experimental Social Psychology* (New York and London: Academic Press): 1–62.

Benn, T. (1994), *Years of Hope: Diaries, Papers and Letters 1940–62*, ed. Ruth Winstone (London: Hutchinson).

Boghossian, P. (1998), 'Content and Self-Knowledge', in P. Ludlow and N. Martin (eds.), *Externalism and Self-Knowledge* (Stanford: CSLI Publications): 149–73.

BonJour, L. (2001), 'Externalist Theories of Empirical Knowledge', in H. Kornblith (ed.), *Epistemology: Internalism and Externalism* (Oxford: Blackwell): 10–35.

Boyle, M. (2009), 'Two Kinds of Self-Knowledge', *Philosophy and Phenomenological Research*, 78: 133–63.

Boyle, M. (2011a), '"Making Up Your Mind" and the Activity of Reason', *Philosophers' Imprint*, 11: 1–24.

Boyle, M. (2011b), 'Transparent Self-Knowledge', *Aristotelian Society*, supp. vol. 85: 223–41.

Boyle, M. (2012), 'Essentially Rational Animals', in J. Conant and G. Abel (eds.), *Rethinking Epistemology*, volume 2 (Berlin and Boston: De Gruyter): 395–427.

Burge, T. (1994), 'Individualism and Self-Knowledge', in Q. Cassam (ed.), *Self-Knowledge* (Oxford: Oxford University Press): 65–79.

Burge, T. (1998), 'Our Entitlement to Self-Knowledge', in P. Ludlow and N. Martin (eds.), *Externalism and Self-Knowledge* (Stanford: CSLI Publications): 239–64.

Byrne, A. (2011), 'Knowing That I Am Thinking', in A. Hatzimoysis (ed.), *Self-Knowledge* (Oxford: Oxford University Press): 105–24.

Byrne, A. (2012), 'Review of Peter Carruthers *The Opacity of Mind: An Integrative Theory of Self-Knowledge*', *Notre Dame Philosophical Reviews* (2012.05.11), <http://ndpr.nd.edu/news/30799-the-opacity-of-mind-an-integrative-theory-of-self-knowledge/>.

Camerer, C., and Loewenstein, R. (2004), 'Behavioural Economics: Past, Present, Future', in C. Camerer, G. Loewenstein, and M. Rabin (eds.), *Advances in Behavioural Economics* (Princeton: Princeton University Press): 3–52.

Carruthers, P. (1996), 'Simulation and Self-Knowledge: A Defence of Theory-Theory', in P. Carruthers and P. K. Smith (eds.), *Theories of Theories of Mind* (Cambridge: Cambridge University Press): 22–38.

Carruthers, P. (2009), 'How We Know Our Own Minds: The Relationship between Mindreading and Metacognition', *Behavioral and Brain Sciences*, 32: 1–18.

Carruthers, P. (2011), *The Opacity of Mind: An Integrative Theory of Self-Knowledge* (Oxford: Oxford University Press).

Cassam, Q. (2007), *The Possibility of Knowledge* (Oxford: Oxford University Press).

Cassam, Q. (2010), 'Judging, Believing and Thinking', *Philosophical Issues*, 20: 80–95.

Child, W. (1994), *Causality, Interpretation, and the Mind* (Oxford: Clarendon Press).

Church, J. (2002), 'Taking It To Heart: What Choice Do We Have?', *The Monist*, 85: 361–80.

Conee, E., and Feldman, R. (2001), 'Internalism Defended', in H. Kornblith (ed.), *Epistemology: Internalism and Externalism* (Oxford: Blackwell): 231–60.

Cottingham, J., Stoothoff, R., and Murdoch, D. (1985), *The Philosophical Writings of Descartes*, vol. 1 (Cambridge: Cambridge University Press).

Craig, E. (1987), *The Mind of God and the Works of Man* (Oxford: Oxford University Press).

Davidson, D. (1980), 'Mental Events', in *Essays on Actions and Events* (Oxford: Clarendon Press): 207–25.

Davidson, D. (1998), 'Knowing Your Own Mind', in P. Ludlow and N. Martin (eds.), *Externalism and Self-Knowledge* (Stanford: CSLI Publications): 87–110.

Davidson, D. (2001), 'First-Person Authority', in *Subjective, Intersubjective, Objective* (Oxford: Clarendon Press): 3–14.

Dennett, D. (1987), 'Three Kinds of Intentional Psychology', in *The Intentional Stance* (Cambridge, MA: MIT Press): 43–68.

Doris, J. (2002), *Lack of Character: Personality and Moral Behaviour* (Cambridge: Cambridge University Press).

Dummett, M. (1993), 'What Do I Know When I Know a Language?', in *The Seas of Language* (Oxford: Oxford University Press): 94–105.

Edgley, R. (1969), *Reason in Theory and Practice* (London: Hutchinson University Library).

Evans, G. (1982), *The Varieties of Reference*, ed. J. McDowell (Oxford: Oxford University Press).

Fazio, R., Zanna, M., and Cooper, J. (1977), 'Dissonance and Self-Perception: An Integrative View of Each Theory's Proper Domain of Application', *Journal of Experimental Social Psychology*, 13: 464–79.

Feldman, S., and Hazlett, A. (2013), 'Authenticity and Self-Knowledge', *Dialectica*, 67: 157–81.

Fernández, J. (2013), *Transparent Minds: A Study of Self-Knowledge* (Oxford: Oxford University Press).

Festinger, L., and Carlsmith, J. M. (1959), 'Cognitive Consequences of Forced Compliance', *Journal of Abnormal and Social Psychology*, 58: 203–10.

Finkelstein, D. H. (2003), *Expression and the Inner* (Cambridge, MA: Harvard University Press).

Finkelstein, D. H. (2012), 'From Transparency to Expressivism', in J. Conant and G. Abel (eds.), *Rethinking Epistemology*, volume 2 (Berlin and Boston: De Gruyter): 101–18.

Frankfurt, H. (1998), 'The Importance of What We Care About', in *The Importance of What We Care About: Philosophical Essays* (Cambridge: Cambridge University Press): 80–94.

Frankfurt, H. (2002), 'Reply to Richard Moran', in S. Buss and L. Overton (eds.), *Contours of Agency: Essays on Themes from Harry Frankfurt* (Cambridge, MA: MIT Press): 218–25.

Frederick, S. (2005), 'Cognitive Reflection and Decision Making', *Journal of Economic Perspectives*, 19: 25–42.

Gaukroger, S. (1986), 'Vico and the Maker's Knowledge Principle', *History of Philosophy Quarterly*, 3: 29–44.

Gendler, T. (2008), 'Alief in Action (and Reaction)', *Mind and Language*, 23: 552–85.

Gertler, B. (2008), 'Self-Knowledge', *Stanford Encyclopedia of Philosophy*, <http://plato.stanford.edu/entries/self-knowledge/>.

Gertler, B. (2011a), *Self-Knowledge* (London: Routledge).

Gertler, B. (2011b), 'Self-Knowledge and the Transparency of Belief', in A. Hatzimoysis (ed.), *Self-Knowledge* (Oxford: Oxford University Press): 125–54.

Gigerenzer, G. (1996), 'On Narrow Norms and Vague Heuristics: A Reply to Kahneman and Tversky (1996)', *Psychological Review*, 103: 592–6.

Gilbert, D. (1991), 'How Mental Systems Believe', *American Psychologist*, 46: 107–19.

Goldman, A. (1978), 'Epistemics: The Regulative Theory of Cognition', *Journal of Philosophy*, 75: 509–23.

Goldman, A. (2006), *Simulating Minds: The Philosophy, Psychology, and Neuroscience of Mindreading* (Oxford: Oxford University Press).

Gopnik, A. (1993), 'How We Know Our Minds: The Illusion of First-Person Knowledge of Intentionality', *Behavioral and Brain Sciences*, 16: 1–14.

Griswold, C. L. (1986), *Self-Knowledge in Plato's Phaedrus* (New Haven: Yale University Press).

Hampshire, S. (1979), 'Some Difficulties in Knowing', in T. Honderich and M. Burnyeat (eds.), *Philosophy As It Is* (Harmondsworth: Penguin): 281–308.

Harman, G. (1973), *Thought* (Princeton: Princeton University Press).

Harman, G. (1986), *Change in View: Principles of Reasoning* (Cambridge, MA: Bradford Books).

Harman, G. (1999), 'Moral Philosophy Meets Social Psychology: Virtue Ethics and the Fundamental Attribution Error', *Proceedings of the Aristotelian Society*, 99: 315–31.

Harman, G. (2000), 'The Nonexistence of Character Traits', *Proceedings of the Aristotelian Society*, 100: 223–326.

Hetherington, S. (2007), *Self-Knowledge: Beginning Philosophy Right Here and Now* (Peterborough, ON: Broadview Press).

Hintikka, J. (1974), 'Practical vs. Theoretical Reason: An Ambiguous Legacy', in S. Körner (ed.), *Practical Reason* (Oxford: Blackwell): 83–102.

Hunt, T. (2009), *The Frock-Coated Communist: The Revolutionary Life of Friedrich Engels* (London: Allen Lane).

Hyman, J. (2006), 'Knowledge and Evidence', *Mind*, 115: 891–916.

Jones, W. E. (2002), 'Explaining Our Own Beliefs: Non-Epistemic Believing and Doxastic Instability', *Philosophical Studies*, 111: 217–49.

Kahneman, D. (2011), *Thinking, Fast and Slow* (London: Allen Lane).

Kahneman, D., and Tversky, A. (1996), 'On the Reality of Cognitive Illusions', *Psychological Review*, 103: 582–91.

Katsafanas, P. (2012), 'Nietzsche on Agency and Self-Ignorance', *Journal of Nietzsche Studies*, 43: 5–17.

Kean, T. H., and Hamilton, L. (2012), *The 9/11 Commission Report: Final Report of the National Commission on Terrorist Attacks Upon the United States* (United States: Pacific Publishing Studio).

Knobe, J. (2005), 'Ordinary Ethical Reasoning and the Ideal of "Being Yourself"', *Philosophical Psychology*, 18: 327–40.

Langton, R. (2006), 'Kant's Phenomena: Extrinsic or Relational Properties? A Reply to Allais', *Philosophy and Phenomenological Research*, 73: 170–85.

Lawlor, K. (2009), 'Knowing What One Wants', *Philosophy and Phenomenological Research*, 79: 47–75.

Levitt, S., and List, J. (2008), 'Homo Economicus Evolves', *Science*, 319: 909–10.

Lew, H. S., Bukowski, R., and Carino, N. (2005), *Design, Construction, and Maintenance of Structural and Life Safety Systems. Federal Building and Fire Safety Investigation of the World Trade Center Disaster* (Washington, DC: NIST NCSTAR 1-1).

Lewis, D. (1989), 'Dispositional Theories of Value', *Aristotelian Society*, supp. vol. 63: 113–37.

McDowell, J. (1998), 'Functionalism and Anomalous Monism', in *Mind, Value, and Reality* (Cambridge, MA: Harvard University Press): 325–40.

Mackie, J. L. (1974), 'Comment on Hintikka's Paper', in S. Körner (ed.), *Practical Reason* (Oxford: Blackwell): 103–12.

McKinsey, M. (1991), 'Anti-Individualism and Privileged Access', *Analysis* 51: 9–16.

Moran, R. (2001), *Authority and Estrangement* (Princeton: Princeton University Press).

Moran, R. (2003), 'Responses to O'Brien and Shoemaker', *European Journal of Philosophy*, 11: 402–19.

Moran, R. (2004), 'Replies to Heal, Reginster, Wilson, and Lear', *Philosophy and Phenomenological Research*, 69: 455–72.

Moran, R. (2012), 'Self-Knowledge, "Transparency", and the Forms of Activity', in D. Smithies and D. Stoljar (eds.), *Introspection and Consciousness* (Oxford: Oxford University Press): 211–36.

Nietzsche, F. (1997), *On the Genealogy of Morality*, trans. C. Diethe, ed. K. Ansell-Pearson (Cambridge: Cambridge University Press).

Nisbett, R., and Ross, L. (1980), *Human Inference: Strategies and Shortcomings of Social Judgment* (Engelwood Cliffs, New Jersey: Prentice-Hall).

Nisbett, R., and Wilson, T. (1977), 'Telling More Than We Know: Verbal Reports on Mental Processes', *Psychological Review*, 84: 231–59.

Nussbaum, M. (1990), 'Love's Knowledge', in *Love's Knowledge: Essays on Philosophy and Literature* (Oxford: Oxford University Press): 261–85.

O'Brien, L. (2003), 'Moran on Agency and Self-Knowledge', *European Journal of Philosophy*, 11: 375–90.

Parfit, D. (2011), *On What Matters*, vol. 1 (Oxford: Oxford University Press).

Peacocke, C. (1998), 'Our Entitlement to Self-Knowledge: Entitlement, Self-Knowledge and Conceptual Redeployment', in P. Ludlow and N. Martin (eds.), *Externalism and Self-Knowledge* (Stanford: CSLI Publications): 265–303.

Peacocke, C. (2000), 'Conscious Attitudes, Attention, and Self-Knowledge', in C. Wright, B. Smith, and C. Macdonald (eds.), *Knowing Our Own Minds* (Oxford: Oxford University Press): 63–98.

Pollock, J. L., and Cruz, J. (1999), *Contemporary Theories of Knowledge* (Lanham: Rowman & Littlefield Publishers).

Proust, M. (1982), *Remembrance of Things Past*, trans. C. K. Scott Moncrieff and Terence Kilmartin (London: Chatto & Windus).

Pryor, J. (2005), 'There is Immediate Justification', in M. Steup and E. Sosa (eds.), *Contemporary Debates in Epistemology* (Oxford: Blackwell): 181–202.

Reed, B. (2010), 'Self-Knowledge and Rationality', *Philosophy and Phenomenological Research*, 80: 164–81.

Rödl, S. (2007), *Self-Consciousness* (Cambridge, MA: Harvard University Press).

Rosenthal, D. (2008), 'Consciousness and its Function', *Neurophysiologia*, 46: 829–40.

Ross, L., Lepper, M. R., and Hubbard, M. (1975), 'Perseverance in Self-perception and Social Perception: Biased Attributional Processes in the Debriefing Paradigm', *Journal of Personality and Social Psychology*, 32: 880–92.

Ross, L., and Nisbett, R. (2011), *The Person and the Situation: Perspectives of Social Psychology* (London: Pinter & Martin).

Ryle, G. (1949), *The Concept of Mind* (London: Hutchinson).

Scanlon, T. (1998), *What We Owe to Each Other* (Cambridge, MA: Harvard University Press).

Schwitzgebel, E. (2002), 'A Phenomenal Dispositional Account of Belief', *Noûs*, 36: 249–75.

Schwitzgebel, E. (2010), 'Acting Contrary to our Professed Beliefs or the Gulf Between Occurrent Judgment and Dispositional Belief', *Pacific Philosophical Quarterly*, 91: 531–53.

Schwitzgebel, E. (2011), 'Knowing Your Own Beliefs', *Canadian Journal of Philosophy*, supp. vol. 35: 41–62.

Schwitzgebel, E. (2012), 'Self-Ignorance', in J. Liu and J. Perry (eds.), *Consciousness and the Self: New Essays* (Cambridge: Cambridge University Press): 184–97.

Shah, N., and Velleman, J. (2005), 'Doxastic Deliberation', *Philosophical Review*, 114: 497–534.

Shermer, M. (2007), *Why People Believe Weird Things* (London: Souvenir Press).

Shermer, M. (2011), *The Believing Brain* (London: Robinson).

Shoemaker, S. (1996), 'The Royce Lectures: Self-Knowledge and "Inner Sense"', in *The First-Person Perspective and Other Essays* (Cambridge: Cambridge University Press): 201–68.

Shoemaker, S. (2003), 'On Knowing One's Own Mind', in B. Gertler (ed.), *Privileged Access: Philosophical Accounts of Self-Knowledge* (Aldershot: Ashgate): 111–29.

Shoemaker, S. (2009), 'Self-Intimation and Second Order Belief', *Erkenntnis*, 71: 35–51.

Stich, S. (1985), 'Could Man be an Irrational Animal?', *Synthese*, 64: 115–35.

Stroud, B. (2000), 'Understanding Human Knowledge in General', in *Understanding Human Knowledge in General* (Oxford: Oxford University Press): 99–121.

Sturm, T. (2012), 'The "Rationality Wars" in Psychology: Where They Are and Where They Could Go', *Inquiry*, 55: 66–81.

Taylor, C. (1985), 'Self-Interpreting Animals', in *Human Agency and Language: Philosophical Papers 1* (Cambridge: Cambridge University Press): 45–76.

Thaler, R., and Sunstein, C. (2008), *Nudge: Improving Decisions about Health, Wealth and Happiness* (London: Penguin).

Thompson, M. (1998), 'The Representation of Life', in R. Hursthouse, G. Lawrence, and W. Quinn (eds.), *Virtues and Reasons: Philippa Foot and Moral Theory* (Oxford: Oxford University Press): 247–96.

Thompson, M. (2004), 'Apprehending Human Form', in A. O'Hear (ed.), *Modern Moral Philosophy* (Cambridge: Cambridge University Press): 47–74.

Valins, S., and Ray, A. (1967), 'Effects of Cognitive Desensitization on Avoidance Behavior', *Journal of Personality and Social Psychology*, 7: 345–50.

Velleman, J. D. (2007), *Practical Reflection* (Stanford: CSLI Publications).

Way, J. (2007), 'Self-Knowledge and the Limits of Transparency', *Analysis*, 67: 223–30.

Williamson, T. (2000), *Knowledge and its Limits* (Oxford: Oxford University Press).

Wilson, T. D. (2002), *Strangers to Ourselves: Discovering the Adaptive Unconscious* (Cambridge, MA: Harvard University Press).

Wilson, T. D., and Dunn, E. (2004), 'Self-Knowledge: Its Limits, Value, and Potential for Improvement', *Annual Review of Psychology*, 55: 493–518.

Wodehouse, P. G. (2008), *Ring for Jeeves* (London: Arrow Books).

Zagzebski, L. (1996), *Virtues of the Mind: An Inquiry into the Nature of Virtue and the Ethical Foundations of Knowledge* (Cambridge: Cambridge University Press).

Zimmerman, A. (2006), 'Basic Self-Knowledge: Answering Peacocke's Criticisms of Constitutivism', *Philosophical Studies*, 128: 337–79.

Zimmerman, A. (2008), 'Self-Knowledge: Rationalism vs. Empiricism', *Philosophy Compass*, 3: 325–52.

Index